IN THE NAME OF ALLAH,
THE MERCIFUL,
THE MERCY-GIVING

ISLAM
Its Meaning and Message

Edited by
KHURSHID AHMAD
Director General
The Islamic Foundation

Foreword by
SALEM AZZAM
Secretary General
Islamic Council of Europe

The Islamic Foundation

First Edition 1975
Second Edition 1976
Reprinted 1980, 1983, 1988 and 1992
Third Edition 1999

ISBN 0 86037 287 1 (Paperback)

Published by
The Islamic Foundation
Markfield Dawah Centre
Ratby Lane, Markfield
Leicester LE67 9SY
United Kingdom
Tel: 01530 244944/5, Fax: 01530 244946
E-Mail: i.foundation@islamic-foundation.org.uk
http: //www.islamic-foundation.org.uk/islamfound

Quran House
PO Box 30611
Nairobi, Kenya

PMB 3193
Kano, Nigeria

Printed and bound in Great Britain by
The Cromwell Press,Trowbridge,Wiltsire

CONTENTS

Part I

THE ISLAMIC OUTLOOK ON LIFE

Part II

THE PROPHET AND THE QUR'ĀN

Part III

THE ISLAMIC SYSTEM

Part IV

ISLAM AND THE WORLD

Foreword

ISLAM today is the second largest religion in Europe. There are between seven and eight million Muslims in Western Europe and over 25
million in the whole of Europe, including European Russia. There are
Mosques, Islamic Centres, institutions for the education of Muslim
youth and other organizations engaged in a multitude of Islamic
activities. The realization of an Islamic presence in Europe is increasing; so also is the need on the one hand, to have greater co-operation
and co-ordination between the activities of Islamic organizations and
centres and on the other hand, to develop a better understanding of
Islam as a religion and culture amongst all the people of Europe,
Muslim and non-Muslim alike.

Islam literally means commitment and obedience — as a religion, it
stands for belief in one God and in all the prophets of God, the last of
whom was Muḥammad (peace be upon him), and for complete submission to the Divine Will as revealed through His prophets. A Muslim
believes in the prophethood of Abraham, Moses and Jesus, holding
that all of them conveyed to mankind the same message from God. The
final revelation came through Prophet Muḥammad (peace be upon
him) and is known as Islam — the religion of all prophets, not
'Mohammadenism'. This revelation is preserved in the Qur'ān, in the
form in which it was revealed to the Prophet Muḥammad (peace be
upon him).

Islam is a complete way of life. It integrates man with God, awakens
in him a new moral consciousness and invites him to deal with all the
problems of life — individual and social, economic and political,
national and international — in accord with his commitment to God.

Islam does not divide life into domains of the spiritual and the secular. It spiritualizes the entire existence of man and produces a social movement to reconstruct human life in the light of principles revealed by God. Prayer and worship in Islam are means to prepare man to fulfil this mission. Islam aims at changing life and producing a new man and a new society, both committed to God and to the welfare of mankind. That is why Islam is not a religion in the limited sense of the word; rather it is a complete code of life and a culture-producing factor. Muslim culture profits from all available sources, local and international, but its unique characteristic is that it grows from the foundations of the Qur'ān and *Sunnah*. Hence the distinctiveness of Muslim culture and life in Europe and elsewhere.

The need for a better and more sympathetic understanding of Islam in the West was never as great as it is today. The presence of significant Muslim populations in every country of Europe, in almost every city and region, has made it necessary for the local communities to understand the beliefs and life-patterns of their Muslim neighbours. The western world is coming into close contact economically, politically and culturally with the world of Islam. As the world shrinks under the impact of technology, the interdependence of nations, cultures and economies is increasing. This development demands greater mutual understanding of ideas, values and life-styles of the different peoples of the world. The Muslims in the West are not only in need of obtaining a better understanding of the values, ideals and practices of Western culture but also of refreshing their understanding of their own religion and culture so that they may continue to strengthen their roots in the Islamic tradition. In view of all these considerations, the Islamic Council of Europe proposes to produce, in English and other European languages, a number of books on different aspects of Islam. First in the series is the present book, *Islam: Its Meaning and Message,* edited by Professor Khurshid Ahmad, Director General, The Islamic Foundation, England. This book has been specially compiled to serve the needs we have mentioned above and is drawn from the writings of leading Islamic scholars of our age. It not only provides a comprehensive introduction to Islamic religion and ideology, it also captures the essential spirit of Muslim thought in the second half of the twentieth century. For many a reader, this book will act as a window on the contemporary Muslim mind.

Now a word about the Islamic Council of Europe.

The Islamic Council of Europe was founded in May, 1973, by the Conference of Islamic Cultural Centres and Organizations of Europe, held in London at the initiative of the Islamic Secretariat, Jeddah, in response to the resolutions adopted by the Conferences of the Ministers of Foreign Affairs of the Muslim States held at Jeddah and Benghazi. It is an independent organization and acts as a co-ordinating body for the promotion of Islamic activities in Europe. The Council tries to work in co-operation with leading International Islamic organizations like the Islamic Secretariat, the Rābita al-'Ālam al-Islāmī and others, and the governments of all the Muslim states for serving the cause of da'wah al-Islāmiyyah. It has its headquarters in London and constituents in almost every country of Europe. The Council sponsors a number of religious, educational and cultural activities directly and through its constituents. Although the Council is still in its early phases of development, it has successfully evolved an infrastructure for the co-ordination and promotion of Islamic activities in Europe. This it has been able to achieve with the co-operation and assistance of a large number of Islamic Centres and Organizations of Europe, and of the leaders of the Muslim community. The encouragement it has received from His Majesty King Faisal bin 'Abdul 'Aziz, the Khādim al-Ḥaramayn needs special mention and I would like to take this opportunity to sincerely and warmly thank His Majesty for taking a keen interest in the problems of Islamic Da'wah in Europe and for graciously extending moral and material support and encouragement to the Islamic Council of Europe in all its activities.

The Council is devoted to developing a better understanding of Islam and Muslim culture in the West. It is in pursuance of this objective that we are sponsoring the publication of the present book. We hope this will be read with interest by Muslims and non-Muslims alike and will be helpful in projecting the image of Islam in its true perspective.

Before I conclude, I would like to thank Professor Khurshid Ahmad for compiling this book for us, and Dr. Muhammad Manazir Ahsan and Mr. Ashraf Abu Turab of the Islamic Foundation for assisting the editor. I am also grateful to His Excellency Mahmood Suleiman Maghribi, the Libyan Ambassador to the Court of St. James, whose encouragement and financial co-operation have enabled us to overcome some of the difficulties in the publication of this book. We are also thankful to all the authors who have kindly permitted us to include their writings in this book. The Islamic Council of Europe records its deep gratitude to all these brothers-in-faith for their unstinted co-operation in the pursuit of a noble cause.

Salem Azzam

London
1st Ramadan 1394
18th September 1974

Preface to the Second Edition

MAN has conquered the seas and the skies; man has harnessed the forces of nature to his service; man has created vast and complex institutions and organizations to administer his affairs: man seems to have reached the pinnacle of material progress!

Man also claims to have deeply reflected upon his position in the universe. He has begun to interpret reality with the sole use of his reason and the knowledge yielded by his senses. With a new-found confidence in his own reasoning power and in the powers of science and technology, he has jettisoned his link with tradition, with revealed truth, indeed with every form of guidance from beyond himself.

From this elevated position he seeks to mould the world according to his whims and fancies. But the 'Brave New World' he has created drives an ordinary human being into profound disillusionment. In spite of unprecedented technological advancement and overall material development the condition of man remains highly unsettled. He sees the powerful subjugating the weak, the rich dominating the poor, the 'have-nots' arrayed against the 'haves'; he sees the injustice and exploitation at national and international levels; he sees disintegration of the family, alienation of individual from society and its institutions, even from himself; and he sees the abuse of trust and authority in all spheres. Although he has shown his ability to fly in the air like the birds, and to swim in the oceans like the fishes, he has failed to show his ability to live on the earth as a good human being. His failure here brings into doubt his capability to conduct his affairs in society without clear-cut guidelines for human action.

Man finds himself caught in a dilemma. He believes that he has reached the apex of civilization. But on reaching the apex he faces a new and greater void. He finds himself and the civilization he has built threatened with forces of his own creation. He frantically searches for remedies to rid his life of those portents of destruction which threaten to deprive him of his cherished dream of ultimate bliss. He finds that his world-view lacks definitive criteria to help him judge between right and wrong; he finds that his learning and expertise fail to give him universal criteria to distinguish between good and bad; he finds that change and the pace of change have swept him off his feet—nothing tangible and lasting remains. Increasingly man becomes dubious about the direction he is heading for. Inability to conceive a way out of this dilemma leads him to despair and gloom. Man becomes increasingly selfish and unmindful of humanity's collective needs. Man becomes aware of a choice – either he relinquishes all pretences to be anything other than an animal and sadly pronounce himself as the 'naked ape' or strive further to regain and retain his sanity.

His search leads him to the awareness that the fruits of his reason are not in themselves sufficient for comprehending the reality around him. He turns to meditation, to mysticism, to occult practices, to pseudo-spiritualism for gaining further insight and inspiration. His thirst remains unquenched; he fails to find a comprehensive doctrine based on reality and capable of universal application.

At this stage, man needs to discover the Word of God. It informs him of his Creator, informs him of the purpose of his creation, informs him of his place as the 'best of creation', provides him with guidance to lead a fulfilling and rewarding life, tells him of the hereafter, teaches him the value of his fellow beings, makes everything else subservient to the criterion of truth – in short, enables him to be at peace with himself, with the whole of creation and with the Creator.

The religion of Islam embodies the final and most complete Word of God. It is the embodiment of the code of life which God, the Creator and the Lord of the Universe, has revealed for the guidance of mankind. Islam intergrates man with God and His Creation in such a way that man moves in co-operation with all that exists. Neglect of this dimension has impoverished human life and has made most of man's material conquests meaningless. Over-secularization has deprived human life of its spiritual significance. But spiritual greatness cannot be achieved by a simple swing of the pendulum to the other extreme. Harmony and equilibrium can be attained only by the intergration of the material with the spiritual. This is the approach that Islam brings to bear: it makes the whole of the domain of existence spiritual and religious. It stands for the harmonization of the human will with the Divine Will – this is how peace is achieved in human life. It is through peace with God that man attains peace in the human order as also peace with nature, outside as well as within him.

This is the essential message of Islam. But an average reader in the West finds it difficult to reach the true spirit of Islam. Whatever be the contributions of western scholarship in different fields of Islamic studies, the fact remains that very little is available that presents with precision and authenticity the meaning and message of Islam as the Muslims understand it. No effort worth the name would seem to have been made to understand Islam in the way Muslims believe and practise it. Our endeavour is to make a humble contribution in this neglected area.

Islam: Its Meaning and Message is primarily a book of readings on Islam. But it is a new book in the sense that all the material it contains was scattered and buried in a number of journals and books, some of them not easily accessible to a Western reader. Moreover, the scope and variety of topics covered in depth in the present collection is unusually broad. We have tried to select some of the best writings of contemporary Muslim scholars and have compiled them into a systematic study of Islam as an ideology and way of life. We hope the reader will find a freshness in the book's content and approach.

The book is divided into four parts, each focusing attention on an important aspect of Islam. There are three readings in the first part, elucidating the Islamic outlook on life. The second part is devoted to a study of the two sources of Islam: The Qur'ān and the Prophet Muhammad (peace be upon him), the guidance and the guide, the revelation and the man to whom the book was revealed and who practised it in such a way as to create a living model of the Islamic personality and of the Islamic social order. In part three there are six readings which throw light on different aspects of the Islamic system of life, social, cultural, spiritual, political and economic. The last part deals with the impact of Islam on human history and culture and with some of the problems that confront present-day Muslims as an ideological community. In all, there are fourteen selections in this book, nine of which were originally written in English, four in Arabic and one in Urdu. We are giving English translations of articles written in Arabic and Urdu. Among the authors, five originally come from Pakistan, one from India, four from Egypt, and one each from Syria, Iran, Austria and Canada. The editor has also added a short annotated Bibliography on Islam. Those who want to pursue further studies on the themes covered in this book will, we hope, find it useful. In view of the constraints of space and the demands of the scheme of the book, the editor had to abridge certain portions of the original essays. I am very grateful to the authors for consenting to unavoidable excerpting of their writings. Some modifications had to be made in language, particularly in the articles that are translations from Urdu and Arabic. An effort has been made to introduce some degree of uniformity in the translation of different verses of the Qur'ān. Similarly differences in the method and style of referencing have also been reduced to a minimum. This, we hope, will impart a certain degree of uniformity to the book.

I am grateful to Mr. Salem Azzam for inviting me to compile this book. He has also kindly contributed a foreword to it. My grateful thanks are due to my colleagues in The Islamic Foundation, Dr. M. M. Ahsan and Mr. Ashraf Abu Turab for assisting me in editing the book, to Mrs. K. Hollingworth for typing the manuscript, to Mr. Youssef Omar for reading the proofs and to Mr. Ajmal Ahmad for preparing the index.

In this second edition, we have tried to improve the quality of this book by trying to correct some of the mistakes which had inadvertently crept into the earlier edition. We are also grateful to King Abdul Aziz University, Jeddah, for helping us in producing the present edition. And finally to my wife Azra and my brother Anis, who silently and cheerfully bore with the strain of the work and willingly allowed me to neglect many of their rights and demands, I would like to whisper my realization that a burden shared is affection deepened.

Khurshid Ahmad

The Islamic Foundation
Leicester

10 Rabī' al-Thānī, 1396
9 April, 1976

Preface to the Third Edition

Islam: Its Meaning and Message, has, *alhamdulillāh* been acknowledged all over the English-speaking world as an authentic and popular book of readings on Islam – both for the general reader as well as university students and scholars. Several reprints of the second edition have appeared during the last two decades. Reprints have also appeared from Pakistan, India and Malaysia. The book has been translated in half a dozen languages of the world. It is being used as recommended reading for degree courses on Islam at over twenty universities of Europe, U.S.A. and Asia, and also for Superior Services' courses in Pakistan. It has achieved the status of an essential reading on Islam. We thank Allah, *subḥānhū wa ta'ālā* for opening up all these avenues of mind and heart for one of the earliest publications of the Islamic Foundation.

The chief merit of the book has been its direct approach to present Islam as it is, as the Muslims believe it, and not as the academic spin-doctors of orientalism tried to project it. Clarity of thought and felicity of style have made this book of readings distinct. It represents an effort to present the essential teachings of Islam with lucidity and conviction, without getting embroiled in polemics or apologetics. The focus has been on the central meaning and message of Islam and not on fringe controversies. It covers a vast canvas – beliefs, worldview, value-framework, socio-economic principles and institutions, role in history and contemporary challenges and prospects. While preparing the present edition (third), for publication, necessary revisions and additions have been made in the Bibliography to include new material that has appeared since the publication of the first edition in 1975. Biographical notes have also been updated. Five of the contributors have met their Lord since the publication of the book. May Allah bless their souls and give them the best of rewards for all they did. Their writings will *Inshā' Allāh* continue to serve mankind as *Ṣādaqah Jāriyah*. The rest of the book remains essentially unchanged as re-reading the material the editor found it as fresh and relevant in 1999 as it was when first published in the form of this compilation.

Khurshid Ahmad

Leicester
23rd March 1999
5 Dhu'l-Ḥijjah 1419

Acknowledgments

The editor records his grateful acknowledgement to the following publishers for permitting him to include material in this book: Arafat Publications, Lahore (*The Spirit of Islam*); Islamic Publications, Lahore (*Islam: Basic Principles and Characteristics* and *Political Theory of Islam*), The Devin-Adair Company, New York (*The Life of the Prophet Muhammad*); Impact International, London (*Islam and Social Responsibility*); Criterion, Karachi (*Islamic Approach to Social Justice* and *What Islam Gave to Humanity*); MSA, Gary, U.S.A. (*Woman in Islam*); Bureau of Publications, University of Karachi (*Objectives of the Islamic Economic Order*); *The Islamic Quarterly*, London (*The Western World and its Challenge to Islam*); and Dārul Bayān, Kuwait (*Islam and the Crisis of the Modern World*).

K. A.

CONTRIBUTORS

KHURSHID AHMAD (U.K.)

Chairman, Islamic Foundation, U.K. and Institute of Policy Studies, Islamabad, Pakistan. Holds Masters in Economics and Islamic Studies, first degree in Law, and Hon. Ph.D. in Education from the University of Malaysia. Taught at the University of Karachi (1980-94) and International Institute of Islamic Economics, International Islamic University, Islamabad (1983-87). Served as Federal Minister for Planning and Deputy Chairman, Planning Commission, Pakistan (1978-79), as a member of the Senate of Pakistan (1985-97) and Chairman, Senate Standing Committee on Finance and Economy (1992-97). Prof. Khurshid received the prestigious King Faisal Award for Service to Islam, 1990, the Islamic Development Bank Award for his contribution to Islamic Economics, 1989, and the Islamic Finance Award sponsored by the Islamic Finance House, U.S.A., 1998. Published work: *Islamic Ideology* (Urdu), University of Karachi, 1973; *Socialism or Islam* (Urdu), Karachi, 1969; *Islam and the West*, Lahore, 1970; *Studies in the Family Law of Islam*, Karachi, 1960; *Principles of Islamic Education*, Lahore, 1970; *Economic Development in an Islamic Framework*, Leicester, 1979; *Elimination of Riba from the Economy*, Islamabad, 1995; *Islamic Resurgence*, Tampa, Florida, 1993, and Islamabad, 1995.

MUHAMMAD ASAD (Morocco) (1900-92)

An Austrian convert to Islam and a scholar of international repute. Published work: *Islam at the Crossroads*, Lahore, 1969; *Saḥīḥ Bukhārī*, English Translation and Commentary (incomplete), Srinagar and Lahore, 1938, Gibraltar, 1980; *The Road to Mecca*, London and New York, 1954, Gibraltar, 1980; *The Message of the Qur'ān*, Gibraltar, Dar al-Andalus, 1980, reprinted 1987.

'ABD AL-RAHMĀN 'AZZĀM (Egypt)

Scholar and statesman, 'Abd al-Rahmān 'Azzām was the first Secretary-General of the Arab League (1945-52). Published work: *The Eternal Message of Muhammad*, New York: Mentor Books, 1964.

ALLAHBUKHSH K. BROHI (Pakistan) (d. 1987)

A leading scholar, lawyer and statesman and a former Minister of Law, Government of Pakistan. Published work: *Adventures in Self-Expression*, Karachi, 1953; *Fundamental Law of Pakistan*, Karachi, 1958; *Islam and the Modern World*, Karachi, 1968.

T. B. IRVING (U.S.A.)

A Canadian convert to Islam and a leading authority in Spanish language and history. Holds Ph.D. from Princeton and has served as Professor of Romance Languages and Islamic Studies at the University of Tennessee, Knoxville. Published work: *Falcon of Spain*, Lahore, 1958; *The Noble Reading*, Cedar Rapids, Iowa, 1971; *The Noble Quran. First American Version*, Amana Books, Brattleboro, Vermont, 1985.

MUSTAFĀ AHMAD AL-ZARQĀ (Jordan)

A leading authority on Islamic Law. Holds Ph.D. in Islamic Law and has served as Professor of Islamic Law in the University of Jordan. A former Minister of Justice, Government of Syria. Published work: over one dozen books in Arabic on Islamic law.

SYED QUTB (Egypt) (1906-66)

One of the greatest Islamic scholars of the twentieth century and a martyr to the Islamic cause. A former educational adviser to the Government of Egypt and a leader of the Muslim Brotherhood. Syed Qutb Shahīd served a long sentence in prison for his Islamic and political opinions and was sentenced to death in Nasser's Egypt in 1966. Published work: *Social Justice in Islam*, Washington, 1953; *This Religion of Islam*, Beirut, 1970; and over two dozen books in Arabic on Islam. His greatest work is an eight-volume *Tafsīr* (Exegesis) of the Qur'ān, *Fī Zilāl al-Qur'ān*. The 30th *Juz'* (London: MWH, 1979 and Vol.1 (containing *sūrahs al-Fātiḥah* and *al-Baqarah*), Leicester: The Islamic Foundation, 1999, are available in English entitled *In the Shade of the Qur'ān*.

GAMĀL A. BADAWĪ (Canada)

A Ph.D. in Business Management, Dr. Badawī is Associate Professor in the School of Management, Halifax, Canada. He has contributed a number of articles to different journals and spoken at International Conferences and Seminars on Islam, some of which are available on video/audio cassette.

ABŪ'L A'LĀ MAWDŪDĪ (Pakistan) (1903-79)

One of the greatest thinkers of the contemporary Muslim world. Editor, *Tarjumān al-Qur'ān*, Lahore, and founder of the Jamā'at-i-Islāmī, Pakistan. Mawdūdī was a member of the Foundation Committee of the Muslim World League, a member of its Islamic Law Academy and a member of the Governing Body of the Islamic University, Madinah. Mawlana Mawdūdī was the first Muslim scholar to receive the prestigious King Faisal Award for service to Islam, 1979/1400 Hijrah. He wrote over two hundred books and pamphlets on Islam. Most important of his works being a six-volume *Tafsīr* (Exegesis) of the Qur'ān – *Tafhīm al-Qur'ān*. He wrote in Urdu but his works have been translated into English, Arabic, Turkish, Persian, French, German, Swahili, Hindi and a number of other languages of the world. Selected published work in English: *Towards Understanding Islam*, Karachi, Beirut, Nairobi, 1973; *Islamic Law and Constitution*, Lahore, 1968; *Islamic Way of Life*, Lahore, 1970; *Birth Control*, Lahore, 1968; *Ethical Viewpoint of Islam*, Lahore, 1967; *Towards Understanding the Qur'ān* (Vols. I-VI) Leicester, 1989-98).

MUHAMMAD UMAR CHAPRA (Saudi Arabia)

Ph.D. in Economics from Minnesota, Dr. Umar Chapra is Senior Economic Adviser to the Saudi Monetary Agency. He has also served as Assistant Professor in an American University, as Senior Economist, Pakistan Institute of Development Economics and as Associate Professor, Institute of Islamic Research, Pakistan. Published work: *Economic System of Islam*, London and Karachi, 1970; *Towards a Just Monetary System*, Leicester, 1985; *Islam and the Economic Challenge*, Leicester, 1992. Dr. Chapra received the prestigious King Faisal Award for his contribution to Islamic Economics, 1990. He also received the Islamic Development Bank prize for his book, *Towards a Just Monetary System*.

ABDUL HAMID SIDDIQUI (Pakistan) (1923-78)

Fellow, Islamic Research Academy, Karachi, and Associate Editor, *Tarjumān al-Qur'ān*, Lahore. Mr. Siddiqui had a Masters degree in Economics and served as Professor of Economics at Islamic College, Gujranwalah. Published work: *The Life of Muhammad*, Lahore, 1969; *Sahih Muslim* (English translation), Lahore, 1974; *Philosophical Interpretations of History*, Lahore, 1969; *Prayers of the Prophet*, Lahore, 1968; *Prophethood in Islam*, Lahore, 1968.

SEYYED HOSSEIN NASR (Iran)

Former Chancellor, Arya-Mehr University of Technology, Tehran, Prof. Nasr, a Ph.D. from Harvard, is a specialist in Physics, History of Science and Islamic Philosophy. During 1964-65, he was the first holder of the Aga Khan Chair of Islamic Studies at the American University of Beirut. Presently Prof. Nasr is Professor of Comparative Religion, Temple University, Philadelphia. Published work: *Ideals and Realities of Islam*, London, 1966; *Three Muslim Sages: Avicenna, Suhrawardy, Ibn 'Arabī*, Cambridge, Mass., 1964; *The Encounter of Man and Nature: The Spiritual Crisis of Modern Man*, London, 1971; *Sufi Essays*, London, 1972; *Science and Civilization in Islam*, 1980; *A Young Muslim's Guide to the Modern World*, Cambridge, 1993.

MUHAMMAD QUTB (Saudi Arabia)

Professor of Islamic Studies, King Abdul Aziz University, Makkah, a renowned Islamic scholar and a leader of the Muslim Brotherhood, Egypt. Prof. Qutb is the author of over one dozen books on Islam, some of which have been translated into a number of languages, including English, French, German, Urdu and Persian. One of his well-known books is *Islam: The Misunderstood Religion*, Kuwait, 1969.

PART I

The Islamic Outlook On Life

1

Islam: The Essentials*

'ISLAM' is an Arabic word. It means the act of resignation to God. The root word is *SLM,* pronounced *'salm'* which means peace from which comes the word *'aslama'* which means he submitted, he resigned himself. Al-Islam or Islam is the religion which brings peace to mankind when man commits himself to God and submits himself to His will. According to the Holy Book revealed to Muḥammad (peace and blessings of God be on him), this is the only true religion professed by all Prophets from Adam to Muḥammed, the Last Prophet. A 'Muslim' is one who resigns himself to God and thereby professes the faith of al-Islam. A Muslim therefore believes in all the Prophets and makes no distinction between one and the other. He also believes that God has sent His prophets to all corners of the earth to preach the same religion, that His message stopped coming after the last revelations received by the last Prophet Muḥammad (peace and blessings of God be on him), and that the message received by the last Prophet is the most comprehensive and the final form of God's message to Man.

FAITH, ACTION AND REALIZATION

In order to be a true 'Muslim' three things are necessary: Faith, Action according to that faith and the realization of one's relation to God as a result of action and obedience.

Faith which is described in the Qur'ān, the Holy Book of Islam, as *Īmān* consists in believing that Allah (God) alone is worthy of worship

* This introductory statement on the Essentials of Islam has been prepared under the auspices of the Islamic Foundation, England.

and that Muḥammad (peace be on him) is the Messenger of Allah, and in bearing witness to the above statement. This implies:

(1) True existence is that of Allah alone; Man and the entire creation exist only because Allah wills them to exist.

(2) As there cannot be two sources of creation, as Allah alone is the creator, everything comes from Him and goes back to Him; hence the entire creation including Man is the manifestation of Allah's power and glory and hence of His qualities or attributes.

(3) The relation between Man and Allah is that of a servant and the Master. As Man owes his very existence to Allah, to worship anything else is to commit the gravest of sins.

(4) The above three aspects of Faith in Allah are realized by Man only when he responds to the Message of Allah and this is possible when Man believes in Muḥammad (peace be on him) as the messenger of Allah.

(5) As a messenger he is the last and the greatest, about whom all the early messengers have predicted and who thus completes the process of revelation.

(6) He is therefore the Perfect Ideal for Mankind, the perfect servant of Allah and hence the most complete and the ideally balanced manifestation of the attributes of Allah.

(7) To believe in him is to believe in all the other prophets of Allah.

(8) To believe in him is also to believe that the Qur'ān contains all the revelations sent to mankind through him, that these revelations provide guidance to us and that we should worship Allah by following these revelations according to the method prescribed for us by Muḥammad (peace be on him) and hence in accordance with his sayings and practice, known as *Ḥadīth* or *Sunnah*.

(9) To believe in him is also to believe in the carriers of this message, the angels, who are described in the Qur'ān as functionaries.

Action, described in Arabic by the word *'amal*, is the manifestation in actuality how far we are true servants of God. As action needs rules and regulations according to which we organise our individual and social behaviour, the revelations and the actual physical embodiment of these revelations in the action of the Prophet (peace be on him) provide both the basis and the structure of the Law of human conduct, known as *Sharī'ah*. Besides *Īmān* (faith) which provides the central pillar that sustains the whole structure, the four other pillars in the four corners are: *Prayer (ṣalāt); Fasting (ṣawm); Charity (zakāt); Pilgrimage (Ḥajj).*

A Muslim has to pray five times a day, before sunrise, between mid-day and afternoon, in the afternoon, immediately after sunset and between the time when the twilight is over and just before dawn. It means he cannot be forgetful of his dependence of Allah and derives sustenance and new initiatives and strength through this remembrance.

He fasts for one lunar month in a year, every day from dawn till sunset, the month of Ramadān. Physically he does not eat, drink or smoke or have sexual intercourse. Spiritually he abstains from all evil thoughts, actions and sayings. In other words he tries to realize his true self by striving to realize within himself some aspects of the divine character.

Charity (*Zakāt*) implies that everything that he seems to possess belongs to Allah and therefore anyone in need has a share in it and he should willingly and gladly help individuals and society when they are in need. As mankind has never been free from some kind of need, an annual amount is prescribed out of one's income and savings.

Pilgrimage to Makka implies Man's temporary suspension of all worldly activities and his realization of himself as a naked soul in front of Allah alone. This also symbolises the unity of the Muslim *Ummah* and the oneness of Mankind.

All these four are intimately tied up with all other aspects of man's individual and social behaviour. By following them and thereby living a life of complete dedication to the Will of Allah, a man becomes a true Muslim.

A Muslim is one whose outlook on life is permeated with this consciousness. He is committed to the values of life given by the Qur'ān and the *Sunnah*. He tries to live according to the guidance given by God and His Prophet and he strives to promote the message of Islam through his word and actions. This striving is known as *Jihād* which means a striving and a struggle in the path of God. It consists in exerting one's self to the utmost in order to personally follow the teachings of Islam and to work for their establishment in society. *Jihād* has been described in the Qur'ān and the *Sunnah* as the natural corollary of these pillars of faith. Commitment to God involves commitment to sacrifice one's time, energy and wealth to promote the right cause. It may be necessary at times to give one's life in order to preserve Truth. *Jihād* implies readiness to give whatever one has, including his life, for the sake of Allah.

This striving in the path of Allah with *Īmān* (faith) as the guiding light and the scheme of *'amal* (action) as the system and structure has the following implications:

(1) Man is accountable to Allah for all that he does. Allah will judge him on the Last Day of Judgement and send him either to Heaven, a stage of existence which leads to further blessings, or to Hell, a stage of suffering and punishment.

(2) This implies that Man's life does not end with his death in this world. He has life after death.

(3) Therefore all human action should be organised in such a manner that he may not suffer in life after death.

(4) This organization of action in this world implies the organization of all facets of human existence, individual and collective, hence educational, economic, political and social. *Sharī'ah* provides the guidelines, the rules of external conduct.

(5) This means Man is free in his will, choice and action.

Realization of man's relation to Allah is a spiritual aspect known in Arabic as *'iḥsān'*, which Prophet Muḥammad (peace be on him) explained in the following way: 'You should worship Allah as if you are seeing Him, for He sees you though you do not see him' (Bukhārī and Muslim). It means that all action should be performed with Allah in your vision. If that is not possible always you must realize that Allah is seeing you. This realization is regarded as the basis of true devotion. It signifies that man has identified his will with the Will of God and has brought it, at least as far as he is concerned, completely in tune with the Divine Will. Consequently, he begins to like what is liked by his Lord and to abhor what is disapproved by Him. Man, then, not only avoids evils which God does not like to be spread on the earth, but uses all his energy to wipe them off the surface of the earth. Similarly he is not content merely with adorning himself with the virtues which God likes, but also engages himself in an unceasing struggle to propagate and establish them in the world. Man comes nearest to God by excelling in this process of identification of man's will with the Divine Will. This enables him to develop the divine spark within him and to illuminate his entire being with that. The most complete example of the realization is that of the Prophet (peace be on him). Through constant remembrance of Allah, through Man's Love of God and the Prophet, through obedience to the commandments of Allah and His Prophet (peace be on him), and through constant struggle to promote good and forbid evil Man may attain nearness to Allah. Contact with and guidance from those who attain this nearness help the rest of mankind to attain this nearness or to be alive in spirit and hence to perform individual and collective action not mechanically but with whole-hearted devotion and for the sake of Allah alone. This realization is the basis of *piety*. This piety is the source of *righteousness* which is regarded by Islam as the core of *just* action. Persons who, through *Īmān*, *'amal* and *iḥsān* become living symbols of truth represent the reform movement established by the Prophet (peace be upon him) to reconstruct human life and bring it in accord with Divine Guidance. Such persons constantly remind the rest of Mankind of the true significance of Man's submission to the Will of Allah. And a society which realises these values in its collective life would be the ideal society which Islam wants to establish for the ultimate welfare (*Falāḥ*) of Man.

MAN AS THE REPRESENTATIVE OF GOD ON EARTH

According to Islam, when faith, action and realization are in perfect harmony, Man manifests the fact that he is the vicegerent of God on Earth. Though Man derives everything from Allah, he is the most complete manifestation of the attributes of Allah and as such he is Allah's representative on Earth. The entire creation is potentially under his dominion. Therefore Islam does not set any limit to Man's knowledge, authority and power except the fundamental limit that they are all derived and hence Man is not self-sufficient. Allah may take away his power whenever He wishes. Islam, therefore, teaches the sanctity of human personality, confers equal rights on all without any distinction of colour, sex or language and subjects the highest and the humblest, the richest and the poorest, the king and the commoner to the sovereignty of Allah and at the same time gives Man the highest imaginable initiative to proceed in the path of self-realization, hence the wielding of God's authority on the Creation.

GOD, PROPHETHOOD, THE QUR'ĀN AND THE SUNNAH

Islam therefore enjoins Man to:

(1) believe that God is One, Omniscient and Omnipresent; He begetteth not, nor is He begotten;
(2) believe further that Man is the vicegerent of God on Earth and has freedom of choice;
(3) believe also that as he has freedom of choice he may go astray and therefore needs guidance from time to time so that he may

know how to realize his own true greatness and that is why God sent His messengers from Adam to Muḥammad (peace be on them) and completed this process during the life of Muḥammad (peace be on him);

(4) act on this message which is preserved in purity without any adulteration in the Qur'ān which asks Man to follow the Prophet (peace be on him) as his supreme ideal;

(5) know and act upon that ideal preserved in collection of sayings of the Prophet (peace be on him) and the reports of his actions — the *Sunnah* or the traditions of the Prophet.

ISLAM AND OTHER RELIGIONS

Islam does not deny Truth to other religions but says that later followers adulterated that Truth by their own inventions and that was why God sent Prophet Muḥammad (peace be on him) to purify God's religion. Each religion manifests some aspect of the same Truth, but the emphasis may differ according to the need of Man of that period or age or race. Islam is the religion for all and as it is the most comprehensive manifestation of that Truth, it provides a complete way and a perfect equilibrium.

The second fact about this relationship with other religions is the chronology stated in the Qur'ān. Islam is in the line of all religions whose Prophets belonged to the family of Abraham. The Judaic tradition that started with Abraham's son Isḥāq (Isaac) came to an end with Jesus who was the last Prophet in that family tree. Muhammad (peace be on him) was the descendant of the other son of Ibrāhīm (Abraham), Ismā'īl (Ishmael). Prophets in other lines among the descendants of Adam have been hinted at but not referred to except Nūḥ (Noah) as examples in the Qur'ān. But, as the Qur'ān clearly states that there is not a single human habitation on the face of this earth where a Prophet has not emerged and where God has not sent His messenger to guide people, a Muslim cannot deny Truth to religions not belonging to this tradition. All that he can point out is the adulteration of that Truth, the mixing up of the Word of God and the word of man, its non-preservation in its original form.

2

Islam: Basic Principles and Characteristics*

Khurshid Ahmad

ISLAM is the religion of truth. It is the embodiment of the code of life which God, the Creator and the Lord of the universe, has revealed for the guidance of mankind.

For the proper development of human life man needs two kinds of things, viz.: (a) resources to maintain life and fulfil the material needs of the individual and society, and (b) knowledge of the principles of individual and social behaviour to enable man to have self-fulfilment and to maintain justice and tranquility in human life. The Lord of the universe has provided for both of these in full measure. To cater for the material needs of man He has provided nature with all kinds of resources, which lie at the disposal of man. To provide for his spiritual, social and cultural needs He raised His prophets from among men and revealed to them the code of life which can guide man's steps to the Right Path. This code of life is known as Islam, the religion preached by all the prophets of God.[1]

Allah said: 'Say, we believe in God, and in the revelation given to us, and to Abraham, Ishmael, Isaac, Jacob and the Tribes. We believe in the revelation that was sent to Moses, Jesus and all other Prophets from their Lord. We make no distinction between them, and unto Him we surrender.' (al-Qur'ān, 3: 83. See also 2: 136).

* This is a revised version of an earlier pamphlet published by the Islamic Publications Ltd., Lahore, Pakistan.
1. The Qur'ān says: 'He has ordained for you (O Muhammad) that faith which He commended to Noah, and that which We commended to Abraham, Moses and Jesus, saying: "Establish the Faith, and be not divided therein." ' (al-Qur'ān, 42: 13).

Also: 'He has revealed to you (O Muḥammad) the scripture with truth, confirming that which was revealed before it even as He revealed the Torah and the Gospel, before as a guide to mankind and has revealed the Criterion (of judging between right and wrong). (al-Qur'ān, 3: 3-4).

All of the prophets called humanity to the way of the Lord, the way of submission to Allah. All of them gave the same message; all of them stood for the same cause, Islam.

THE MEANING OF ISLAM

Islam is an Arabic word and denotes submission, surrender and obedience. As a religion, Islam stands for complete submission and obedience to Allāh — that is why it is called *Islām*. The other literal meaning of the word Islam is 'peace' and this signifies that one can achieve real peace of body and of mind only through submission and obedience to Allah.[2] Such a life of obedience brings peace of the heart and establishes real peace in society at large.

> 'Those who believe and whose hearts find rest in the remembrance of Allah — indeed it is in the thought of Allah alone that the heart of man really finds rest — those who believe and act righteously, joy is for them, and a blissful home to return to.' (al-Qur'ān, 13: 28-29).

This message was preached by all the prophets of God, who guided man to the right path. But man not only veered away from the right path again and again, but also lost or distorted the code of guidance which the prophets had bequeathed. That was why other prophets were sent to re-state the original message and guide man to the right path. The last of these prophets was Muḥammad (peace be upon him),

2. The word Islam is from the root SLM (pronounced *silm*) which means (a) to surrender, to submit, to yield, to give one's self over, thus *aslama amrahū ilā Allāh*, means 'he committed his cause to God' or 'he resigned himself to the will of God'. *Aslama* alone would be 'he committed himself to the will of God', or 'he became a Muslim'. The other major shade of meaning in the root is (b) 'to become reconciled with one another', 'to make peace'. *Salm* means peace. So does *silm*, which also means 'the religion of Islam'. See Hans Wehr, *A Dictionary of Modern Written Arabic*, Wiesbaden: Otto Harrassowitz, 1971, p. 424-425. Imām Rāghib says in *al-Mufridāt fī Gharīb al Qur'ān:* 'Islam in law is of two kinds; one is a simple confession with the tongue . . . the other that along with confession, there is belief in the heart and a fulfilment in practice, and resignation to God in whatever He brings to pass or decree'. Rāghib further says: 'Islam means entering into *salm*, amd *salm* and *silm* both signify peace.'

who presented God's guidance in its final form and arranged to preserve it for all time. It is this guidance which is now known as *al-Islām*
and is enshrined in the Qur'ān and the life-example of the Prophet.

The basic Islamic concept is that the entire universe was created by
God, whom Islam calls Allah and who is the Lord and the Sovereign of
the Universe. He is the Lord of the universe which He alone sustains.
He created man and appointed for each human being a fixed period of
life which he is to spend upon the earth. Allah has prescribed a certain
code of life as the correct one for him, but has at the same time conferred on man freedom of choice as to whether or not he adopts this code
as the actual basis of his life. One who chooses to follow the code revealed by God becomes a *Muslim* (believer) and one who refuses to
follow it becomes a *Kāfir* (non-believer).

A man joins the fold of Islam by honestly believing in and professing
faith in the unity of God and the Prophethood of Muhammad (peace
be upon him). Both these beliefs are epitomised in the *Kalima*:

　　Lā ilāha illallāhu Muhammad ur-Rasūlullāh.

('There is no God except Allah; Muhammad is His Prophet'.)

The first part of this *Kalima* presents the concept of *Tawhīd* (unity of
God) and its second part affirms the Prophethood of Muhammad
(peace be upon him).

TAWHĪD — THE BED-ROCK OF ISLAM

Tawhīd is a revolutionary concept and constitutes the essence of the
teachings of Islam. It means that there is only One Supreme Lord of
the universe. He is Omnipotent, Omnipresent and the Sustainer of the
world and of mankind.

How can one observe the inexhaustible creativity of nature, its
purposefulness, its preservation of that which is morally useful and
destruction of that which is socially injurious, and yet fail to draw the
conclusion that behind nature there is an All-Pervading Mind of
whose incessant creative activity the processes of nature are but an
outward manifestation? The stars scattered through the almost
infinite space, the vast panorama of nature with its charm and beauty,
the planned waxing and waning of the moon, the astonishing harmony of the seasons — all point towards one fact: there is a God, the
Creator, the Governor. We witness a superb, flawless plan in the universe — can it be without a Planner? We see great enchanting beauty
and harmony in its working — can they be without a Creator? We

observe wonderful design in nature — can it be without a Designer?
We feel a lofty purpose in physical and human existence — can it be
without a Will working behind it? We find that the universe is like a
superbly written fascinating novel — can it be without an Author?
Truly, Allah said:

> O, Mankind: worship your Lord, who created you and those
> before you, so that you may ward off evil. Who has appointed the
> earth a resting place for you, the sky a canopy? and who causes
> water to pour down from the heavens, thereby producing fruits as
> food for you? So, do not set up rivals to Allah, when you know
> better.' (al-Qur'ān, 2: 21-22).

This is the basic tenet to which Muḥammad (peace be upon him)
asked humanity to adhere.

It is an important metaphysical concept and answers the riddles of
the universe. It points to the supremacy of the law in the cosmos, the all
pervading unity behind the manifest diversity.

It presents a unified view of the world and offers the vision of an
integrated universe. It is a mighty contrast to the piecemeal views of
the scientists and the philosophers and unveils the truth before the
human eye. After centuries of groping in the dark, man is now coming
to realise the truth of this concept and modern scientific thought is
moving in this direction.[3]

But it is not merely a metaphysical concept. It is a dynamic belief
and a revolutionary doctrine. It means that all men are the creatures of
one God — they are all equal. Discrimination based on colour, class,
race or territory is unfounded and illusory. It is a remnant of the days of
ignorance which chained men down to servitude. Humanity is one
single family of God and there can be no sanction for those barriers.
Men are one — and not bourgeois or proletarian, white or black,
Aryan or non-Aryan, Westerner or Easterner. Islam gives a revolutionary concept of the unity of mankind. The Prophet came to unite
humanity on the word of God and make the dead live again. Allah
says:

> 'Hold tight to the rope of God, altogether and never let go again.
> Remember God's gifts and blessings unto you all, when you were
> enemies; remember how He forged your hearts together in love, and
> by His grace, you became brethren.' (al-Qur'ān, 3: 103).

3. See Francis Mason (Ed.) *The Great Design,* London: Duckworth.

This concept also defines the true position of man in the universe. It says that God is the Creator, the Sovereign; and that man is His vicegerent on the earth.[4] This exalts man to the noble and dignified position of being God's deputy on earth and endows his life with a lofty purpose; to fulfil the Will of God on earth. This will solve all the perplexing problems of human society and establish a new order wherein equity and justice and peace and prosperity will reign supreme.

The starting point of Islam is this belief in the Unity of God (*Tawḥīd*).

PROPHETHOOD AND LIFE AFTER DEATH

The second part of the *Kalima,* on the other hand, signifies that God has not left man without any guidance for the conduct of his life. He has revealed His Guidance through His prophets and Muḥammad (peace be upon him) was the last Prophet. And to believe in a prophet means to believe in his message, to accept the Law which he gave and to follow the Code of Conduct which he taught.

Thus the second basic postulate of Islam is to believe in the Prophethood of Muḥammad (peace be upon him), to accept the religion which he presented and to follow his commands.

Every prophet of God, according to the Qur'ān, strove to build man's relationship with God on the principle of God's sovereignty and the acknowledgement of the authority of the prophet as source of divine guidance. Every one of them said: 'I am to you God's apostle, worthy of all trust. So be committed to God, fear Him, and obey me.'[5]

The Guidance is revealed through the prophets. It is a part of their mission to translate that into practice, in their own lives and in the society they try to reform. All the prophets are representatives of God, but they are human beings and their lives are models for mankind. Muḥammad (peace be upon him) is the last prophet and as such the final model for mankind. To·believe in him means to accept his authority as representative of the Supreme Ruler and to follow his example in thought and behaviour. The code of behaviour, the law which is to decide the rightness or otherwise (*ḥalāl* and *ḥarām*) of things, is given by God through the prophet and is known as the *Sharī'ah.* Belief in the prophet involves acceptance of the *Sharī'ah,* the Path, he has

4. al-Qur'ān, 2: 30-39.

5. al-Qur'ān, 26: 107-108; 110; 125-126; 131; 143-144; 150; 162-163; 178-179.

conveyed and to implement that in all walks of life. This is how the Will of God is fulfilled on the earth.[6] The Qur'ān said:

'Every Messenger who was sent by Us was sent for the purpose that he should be obeyed under the sanction of Allah.' (al-Qur'ān, 4: 69).

And about the last prophet it is explicitly stated that:

'Nay, O Muḥammad: by your Lord, they will not be believers until they accept you as the final arbiter in all their disputes and submit to your decision whole-heartedly without any heartache.' (al-Qur'ān, 4: 65).

The test of acceptance of God and His prophet lies in conducting all human affairs in accord with the Law revealed by them.

'And those who do not make their decisions in accordance with that revealed by Allah, they (in fact) are the disbelievers.' (al-Qur'ān, 5: 44).

Thus, belief in God and His prophet means commitment to obey them and to fashion individual and collective life in the light of the Law and Guidance provided by them.

This automatically raises the question: Would those who follow the law and those who refuse to accept it or abide by it be at the same level of existence? Are they going to be treated in the same way or differently? What would be the consequences of differing attitudes and behaviours?

This brings us to the third basic postulate of Islam: belief in the hereafter.

The world, according to Islam, is a place of trial and man is being judged in it. He will have to give account of all that he does herein. Life on the earth will, one day, come to an end, and after that a new world will be resurrected. It will be in this Life-after-death that man will be rewarded or punished for his deeds and misdeeds. Those who live in the present world a life of obedience to the Lord will enjoy eternal bliss in the hereafter and those who disobey His commands will have to garner the bitter fruits of their disobedience. According to the Qur'ān:

'And every man's deeds have We fastened around his neck, and

6. Jesus, like other prophets, presented the same message. This is what he aims at when he says: 'Thy Kingdom come. Thy Will be done in earth, *as it is* in heaven.' *New Testament*, St. Matthew, 6: 10.

on the day of Resurrection will We bring forth a book which shall be proffered to him wide open: "Read your record: This day there need be none but yourself to make out an account against you." ' (al-Qur'ān, 17: 13-14).

'Whosoever will come with a good deed, for him there shall be the like of it tenfold, while whosoever will come with an ill-deed, he shall be requited with only one like it, and they shall not be treated unjustly.' (al-Qur'ān, 6: 160).

Thus the basic articles of Islamic faith are three, viz.:

(a) Belief in the Unity of God;
(b) Belief in the Prophethood of Muḥammad (peace be upon him) and in the guidance which he bequeathed; and
(c) Belief in the Life-after-death and in man's accountability before God on the Day of Judgement.

Whoever professes these beliefs is a Muslim. And all these concepts are epitomised in the *Kalima*: 'There is no God but Allah; Muḥammad is His Prophet.'

III

Some Basic Characteristics of Islamic Ideology

George Bernard Shaw is reported to have said:

'I have always held the religion of Muḥammad in high estimation because of its wonderful vitality. It is the only religion which appears to me to possess that assimilating capacity to the changing phase of existence which can make itself appeal to every age. I have studied him — the wonderful man — and in my opinion far from being an anti-Christ, he must be called the Saviour of Humanity. I believe that if a man like him were to assume the dictatorship of the modern world, he would succeed in solving its problems in a way that would bring it the much needed peace and happiness: I have prophesied about the faith of Muḥammad that it would be acceptable to the Europe of tomorrow as it is beginning to be acceptable to the Europe of today.'[7]

The question is what are those characteristics of Islam which have

7. G. B. Shaw, *The Genuine Islam*, Singapore, Vol. I, No. 8, 1936.

won millions of followers to the faith in the past and which make it so appealing to the modern age? Some of the major characteristics of Islam are given in the following pages.

1. Simplicity, Rationalism and Practicalism

Islam is a religion without any mythology. Its teachings are simple and intelligible. It is free from superstitions and irrational beliefs. The unity of God, the prophethood of Muḥammad (peace be upon him) and the concept of life-after-death are the basic articles of its faith. They are based on reason and sound logic. All the teachings of Islam follow from those basic beliefs and are simple and straightforward. There is no hierarchy of priests, no far-fetched abstractions, no complicated rites and rituals. Everybody may approach the Book of God directly and translate its dictates into practice.

Islam awakens in man the faculty of reason and exhorts him to use his intellect. It enjoins him to see things in the light of reality. The Qur'ān advised man to pray: 'O, my Lord! Advance me in knowledge' (20: 114). It asserts that those who have no knowledge are not equal to those who have (39: 9); that those who do not observe and understand are worse than cattle (7:P179); that the meanings of revelation become manifest to those 'who have knowledge' (6: 97) and 'who have understanding' (6: 98); that 'whosoever has been given knowledge indeed has been given an abundant good' (2: 269); that basic qualifications for leadership are, among other things, knowledge and physical strength (2: 247) and that of all things it is by virtue of knowledge that man is superior to angels and has been made vicegerent of God on earth (2: 30). The Prophet of Islam said:

'He who leaves his home in search of knowledge walks in the path of God.'
'To seek knowledge is obligatory for every Muslim.'
'Acquire knowledge, because he who acquires it in the way of the Lord performs an act of piety; he who disseminates it bestows alms and he who imparts it to others performs an act of devotion to Allah.'

This is how Islam brings man out of the world of superstition and darkness and initiates him into that of knowledge and light.

Then, Islam is a practical religion and does not indulge in empty and futile theorisings. It says that faith is not a mere profession of beliefs; it is the very mainspring of life. Righteous conduct must follow belief in Allah. Religion is something to be lived, and not an object of mere lip-service. The Qur'ān says:

'Those who believe and act righteously, joy is for them, and a blissful home to return to.' (al Qur'ān, 13: 29).

And the Prophet Muḥammad (peace be upon him) said:

'God does not accept belief, if it is not expressed in deeds, and does not accept deeds, if they do not conform to belief.'

Thus, Islam is a simple, rational and practical religion.

2. Unity of Matter and Spirit

A unique feature of Islam is that it does not divide life into water-tight compartments of matter and spirit. It stands not for life-denial, but for life-fulfilment. Islam does not believe in asceticism. It does not ask man to avoid things material. It holds that spiritual elevation is to be achieved by living piously in the rough and tumble of life and not by renouncing the world. The Qur'ān advises us to pray as follows:

'Our Lord! Give us the good in this world and the good in the hereafter.' (al-Qur'ān, 2: 201).

Allah strongly censures those who refuse to benefit from His blessings. The Qur'ān says:

'Say (to them): By whose order have you denied yourself those amenities which God has created for His people and those good things to eat and use (which He has made for you)?' (al-Qur'ān, 7: 32).

Islam's injunction is: 'Eat and drink, but do not exceed (the limits of moderation and decency)' (al-Qur'ān, 7: 31).

The Holy Prophet said:

'A Muslim who lives in the midst of society and bears with patience the afflictions that come to him is better than the one who shuns society and cannot bear any wrong done to him.'

He said:

'Keep fast and break it (at the proper time) and stand in prayer and devotion (in the night) and have sleep — for your body has its rights over you, and your eyes rights over you, and your wife has a claim upon you, and the person who pays a visit to you has a claim upon you.'

On another occasion he said:

'These three things also are enjoined upon the faithful:
(a)   to help others, even when one is economically hard-pressed;
(b)   to pray ardently for the peace of all mankind; and
(c)   to administer justice to one's own self.'

Thus Islam does not admit any separation between 'material' and 'moral', 'mundane' and 'spiritual' life and enjoins man to devote all his energies to the reconstruction of life on healthy moral foundations. It teaches him that moral and material powers must be welded together and spiritual salvation can be achieved by using material resources for the good of man in the service of just ends, and not by living a life of asceticism or by running away from the challenges of life.

The world has suffered at the hands of the 'brilliant' one-sidedness of many a religion and ideology. Some have laid emphasis on the spiritual side of life but have ignored its material and mundane aspects. They have looked upon the world as an illusion, a deception and a trap.

On the other hand materialistic ideologies have totally ignored the spiritual and moral side of life and have dismissed it as fictitious and imaginary. Both these attitudes have spelt disaster. They have robbed mankind of peace, contentment and tranquility. Even today the imbalance is manifest in one or the other direction. Dr. De Brogbi, a French scientist, rightly says:

'The danger inherent in too intense a material civilization is to that civilization itself; it is the disequilibrium which would result if a parallel development of the spiritual life were to fail to provide the needed balance.'

Christianity erred on one extreme; the Modern Western Civilization, in both of its variants of secular capitalistic democracy and Marxist socialism, has erred on the other. According to Lord Snell:

'We have built a nobly proportioned outer structure, but we have neglected the essential requirement of an inner order; we have carefully designed, decorated and made clean the outside of the cup; but the inside was full of extortion and excess; we used our increased knowledge and power to administer to the comforts of the body, but we left the spirit impoverished.'[8]

Islam aims at establishing an equilibrium between these two aspects of life — the material and the spiritual. It says that everything in the

8. Lord Snell, *The New World,* London: Watts & Co., 1947, p. 11.

world is for man — but man himself is for the service of a higher purpose: the establishment of a moral and just order so as to fulfil the Will
of God. Its teachings cater for the spiritual as well as the temporal
needs of man. Islam enjoins man to purify his soul and also to reform
his daily life — both individual and collective — and to establish the
supremacy of right over might and of virtue over vice. Thus Islam
stands for the middle path and the goal of producing a moral man in
the service of a just society.

3. A Complete Way of Life

Islam is not a religion in the common, distorted meaning of the
word, confining its scope to the private life of man. It is a complete way
of life, catering for all the fields of human existence. Islam provides
guidance for all walks of life — individual and social, material and
moral, economic and political, legal and cultural, national and international. The Qur'ān enjoins man to enter the fold of Islam without
any reservation and to follow God's guidance in all fields of life. [9]

In fact it was an unfortunate day when the scope of religion was
confined to the private life of man and its social and cultural role was
reduced to naught. No other factor has, perhaps, been more important
in causing the decline of religion in the modern age than its retreat into
the realm of the private life. In the words of a modern philosopher:

> 'Religion asks us to separate things of God from those of Caesar.
> Such a judicial separation between the two means the degrading of
> both the secular and the sacred . . . That religion is worth little, if the
> conscience of its followers is not disturbed when war clouds are
> hanging over us all and industrial conflicts are threatening social
> peace. Religion has weakened man's social conscience and moral
> sensitivity by separating the things of God from those of Caesar.'

Islam totally denounces this concept of religion and clearly states
that its objectives are purification of the soul and the reform and the
reconstruction of the society. Says the Qur'ān:

> 'We verily sent Our messengers with clear proofs and revealed
> with them the Scripture and the Balance (i.e. the authority to esta-
> blish justice), that mankind may observe justice and the right
> measure; and He revealed iron (i.e. coercive power) wherein is
> mighty power and many uses for mankind and that Allah may see

9. al-Qur'ān, 2: 208.

who helps Him and His Messenger through unseen.' (al-Qur'ān, 57: 25).

'The command is for none but Allah; He has commanded that you obey none but Him; that is the right path.' (al-Qur'ān, 12: 40).

'(Muslims are) those who if We give them power in the land, establish (the system of) *Ṣalāt* (prayers and worship) and *Zakāt* (poor due) and enjoin virtue and forbid vice and evil.' (al-Qur'ān, 22: 41).

The Holy Prophet said:

'Everyone of you is a keeper or a shepherd and will be questioned about the well-being of his fold. So, the Head of the State will be questioned about the well-being of the people of the State. Every man is a shepherd to his family and will be answerable about every member of it. Every woman is a shepherd to the family of her husband and will be accountable for every member of it. And every servant is a shepherd to his master and will be questioned about the property of his master.'

Thus even a cursory study of the teachings of Islam shows that it is an all-embracing way of life and does not leave out any field of human existence to become a playground for satanic forces.[10]

4. Balance between the Individual and Society

Another unique feature of Islam is that it establishes a balance between individualism and collectivism. It believes in the individual personality of man and holds everyone personally accountable to God. It guarantees the fundamental rights of the individual and does not permit any one to tamper with them. It makes the proper development of the personality of man one of the prime objectives of its educational policy. It does not subscribe to the view that man must lose his individuality in society or in the state.

According to the Qur'ān:

'Man shall have nothing but what he strives for.' (al-Qur'ān, 53: 39).

10. For a more thorough study of different aspects of the Islamic way of life see: Mawdudi, Abul A'la, *Islamic Law and Constitution* (Lahore: Islamic Publications Ltd., 1960); Mawdudi, *Islamic Way of Life,* Lahore, 1967; Khurshid Ahmad (editor), *Studies in the Family Law of Islam,* Karachi, 1960; Khurshid Ahmad, *Family Life in Islam,* Leicester: Islamic Foundation, 1974; Siddiqui, M. N., *Some Aspects of the Islamic Economy,* Lahore, 1970; Chapra, M. U., *Economic System of Islam,* Karachi: University of Karachi, 1971.

'And whatever suffering ye suffer, it is what your hands have wrought.' (al-Qur'ān, 42: 30).

'God does not change the condition of a people unless they first change that which is in their hearts.' (al-Qur'ān, 13: 11).

'For each is that which he has earned and against each is only that which he has deserved.' (al-Qur'ān, 2: 286).

'For us are our deeds and for you are yours.' (al-Qur'ān, 28: 55).

On the other hand, it also awakens a sense of social responsibility in man, organises human beings in a society and a state and enjoins the individual to subscribe to the social good. Prayer, in Islam, is offered in congregation which inculcates social discipline among the Muslims. Every one is enjoined to pay *Zakāt* and it has been laid down in the Qur'ān that: 'The alm-seeker and the destitute have their due rights in their wealth.' (al-Qur'ān, 51: 19).

Jihād has been made obligatory, which means that the individual should, when the occasion arises, offer even his life for the defence and protection of Islam and the Islamic state. The Holy Prophet said:

'All mankind is a fold every member of which shall be a keeper or shepherd unto every other, and he accountable for the entire fold.'

'Live together, do not turn against each other, make things easy for others and do not put obstacles in each other's way.'

'He is not a believer who takes his fill while his neighbour starves.'

'The believer in God is he who is not a danger to the life and property of any other.'

In short, Islam neither neglects the individual nor society — it establishes a harmony and a balance between the two and assigns to each its proper due.[11]

11. It might be worthwhile to recall here what the late Professor H. A. R. Gibb said some time ago:

'Within the Western world Islam still maintains the balance between exaggerated opposites. Opposed equally to the anarchy of European nationalism and the regimentation of Russian communism, it has not yet succumbed to that obsession with the economic side of life which is characteristic of present-day Europe and present-day Russia alike. Its social ethic has been admirably summed up by Professor Massignon: "Islam has the merit of standing for a very equalitarian conception of the contribution of each citizen by the tithe to the resources of the community; it is hostile to unrestricted exchange, to banking capital, to state loans, to indirect taxes on objects of prime necessity, but it holds to the rights of the father and the husband, to private property, and to commercial capital. Here again it occupies an inter-

5. Universality and Humanism

The message of Islam is for the entire human race. God, in Islam, is the God of all the world (al-Qur'ān, 1: 1) and the Prophet is a Messenger for the whole of mankind. In the words of the Qur'ān:

> 'O people! I am the Messenger of God to you all.' (al-Qur'ān, 7: 158).
>
> 'One who comes as a warning to all the nations.' (al-Qur'ān, 25: 1) and 'We have not sent thee but as a (source of) mercy for all the nations' (al-Qur'ān, 21: 107).

In Islam all men are equal, whatever be their colour, language, race or nationality. Islam addresses itself to the conscience of humanity and banishes all false barriers of race, status and wealth. There can be no denying the fact that such barriers have always existed, and do exist even today in this so-called enlightened age. Islam removes all these impediments and proclaims the idea of the whole of humanity being one family of God.

The Holy Prophet said:

> 'All creatures of God form the family of God and he is the best loved of God who loveth best His creatures.'
>
> 'O Lord! Lord of my life and of everything in the universe! I affirm that all human beings are brothers to one another.'
>
> 'Respect God and be affectionate to the family of God.'

Islam is international in its outlook and approach and does not admit barriers and distinctions based on colour, clan, blood or terri-

---

mediate position between the doctrines of bourgeois capitalism and Bolshevist communism."

'But Islam has a still further service to render to the cause of humanity. It stands after all nearer to the real East than Europe does, and it possesses a magnificent tradition of inter-racial understanding and co-operation. No other society has such a record of success in uniting in an equality of status, of opportunity, and of endeavour so many and so various races of mankind . . . Islam has still the power to reconcile apparently irreconcilable elements of race and tradition. If ever the opposition of the great societies of East and West is to be replaced by co-operation, the mediation of Islam is an indispensable condition. In its hands lies very largely the solution of the problem with which Europe is faced in its relation with the East. If they unite, the hope of a peaceful issue is immeasurably enhanced. But if Europe, by rejecting the co-operation of Islam, throws it into the arms of its rivals, the issue can only be disastrous for both." ' H. A. R. Gibb, *Whither Islam*, London, 1932, p. 379.

tory such as were prevalent before the advent of Muḥammad (peace be upon him) and which are rampant in different forms even in this modern age. It wants to unite the entire human race under one banner. To a world torn by national rivalries and feuds, it presents a message of life and hope and of a glorious future.

Historian Toynbee has some interesting observations to make in this respect. In *Civilization on Trial* he writes:

'Two conspicuous sources of danger — one psychological and the other material — in the present relations of this cosmopolitan proletariat (i.e. westernised humanity) with the dominant element in our modern Western society are race consciousness and alcohol; and in the struggle with each of these evils the Islamic spirit has a service to render which might prove, if it were accepted, to be of high moral and social value.

'The extinction of race consciousness as between Muslims is one of the outstanding moral achievements of Islam, and in the contemporary world there is, as it happens, a crying need for the propagation of this Islamic virtue . . . It is conceivable that the spirit of Islam might be the timely reinforcement which would decide this issue in favour of tolerance and peace.

'As for the evil of alcohol, it is at its worst among primitive populations in tropical regions which have been "opened up" by Western enterprise . . . the fact remains that even the most statesmanlike preventive measures imposed by external authority are incapable of liberating a community from a social vice unless a desire for liberation and a will to carry this desire into voluntary action on its own part are awakened in the hearts of the people concerned. Now Western administrators, at any rate those of "Anglo-Saxon" origin, are spiritually isolated from their "native" wards by the physical "colour bar" which their race-consciousness sets up; the conversion of the natives' souls is a task to which their competence can hardly be expected to extend; and it is at this point that Islam may have a part to play.

'In these recently and rapidly "opened up" tropical territories, the Western civilization has produced an economic and political plenum and, in the same breath, a social and spiritual void . . .

'Here, then in the foreground of the future, we can remark two valuable influences which Islam may exert upon the cosmopolitan proletariat of a Western society that has cast its net around the world and embraced the whole of mankind; while in the more distant future we may speculate on the possible contributions of Islam to some new manifestation of religion.'[12]

6. Permanence and Change

The elements of permanence and change co-exist in human society and culture and are bound to remain so. Different ideologies and cultural systems have erred in leaning heavily towards any one of these ends of the equation. Too much emphasis on permanence makes the system rigid and robs it of flexibility and progress; while lack of permanent values and unchanging elements generate moral relativism, shapelessness and anarchy. What is needed is a balance between the two — a system that could simultaneously cater for the demands of permanence and change. An American judge Mr. Justice Cardozo rightly says: 'that the greatest need of our time is a philosophy that will mediate between conflicting claims of stability and progress and supply a principle of growth.'[13] Islam presents an ideology which satisfies the demands of stability as well as of change.

Deeper reflection reveals that life has within it elements of permanence and change — neither is it so rigid and inflexible that it cannot admit of any change even in matters of detail nor is it so flexible and fluid that even its distinctive traits have no permanent character of their own. This becomes clear from observing the process of physiological change in the human body: every tissue of the body changes a number of times in one's life-time, but the person remains the same. Leaves, flowers, and fruits of a tree change, but the character of the tree remains unchanged. It is a law of life that elements of permanence and change must co-exist in a harmonious equation. Only that system of life can cater for all the cravings of human nature and all the needs of society which can provide for both these elements. The basic problems of life remain the same in all ages and climes, but the ways and means to solve them and the techniques of handling the phenomenon undergo change with the passage of time. Islam brings to focus a new perspective on this problem and tries to solve it in a realistic way.

The Qur'ān and the *Sunnah* contain the eternal guidance given by the Lord of the universe. This guidance comes from God Who is free from the limitations of 'space' and 'time' and as such the principles of

12. Arnold J. Toynbee, *Civilization on Trial*, London, 1957, pp. 205-299 (See also pp. 87-88).

13. Justice Cardozo, 37, *Harvard Law Review*, p. 279.

individual and social behaviour revealed by Him are based on reality and are eternal. But God has revealed only broad principles and has endowed man with the freedom to apply them in every age in the way suited to the spirit and conditions of that age. It is through the *Ijtihād* that people of every age try to implement and apply divine guidance to the problems of their times. Thus the basic guidance is of a permanent nature, while the method of its application can change in accordance with the peculiar needs of every age. That is why Islam always remains as fresh and modern as tomorrow's morn.

7. Complete Record of Teachings Preserved

Last, but not least, is the fact that the teachings of Islam have been preserved in their original form and God's Guidance is available without adulteration of any kind. The Qur'ān is the revealed book of God which has been in existence for the last fourteen hundred years and the Word of God is available in its original form. Detailed accounts of the life of the Prophet of Islam and his teachings are available in their pristine purity. There has not been an iota of change in this unique historic record. The sayings and the entire record of the life of the Holy Prophet have been handed down to us with unprecedented precision and authenticity in works of the *Hadīth* and the *Sīrah*. Even a number of non-Muslim critics admit this eloquent fact. Professor Reynold A. Nicholson in his *Literary History of the Arabs* says:

> 'The Koran is an exceedingly human document, reflecting every phase of Muhammad's relationship to the outward events of his life; so that there we have materials of unique and incontestable authority for tracing the origin and early development of Islam such materials as do not exist in the case of Buddhism or Christianity or any other ancient religion.'[14]

These are some of the unique features of Islam and establish its credentials as the religion of man — the religion of today and the religion of tomorrow. These aspects have appealed to hundreds of thousands of people in the past and the present and have made them affirm that Islam is the religion of truth and the right path for mankind; and this will continue to appeal to them in the future. Men with pure hearts and sincere longing for truth will always continue to say:

.14. Nicholson, R. A., *Literary History of the Arabs*, Cambridge, p. 143.

'I affirm that there is none worthy of worship except Allah, that He is One, sharing His authority with no one; and I affirm that Muḥammad is His servant and His Prophet.'

3

*The Spirit of Islam**

Muhammad Asad

ONE of the slogans most characteristic of the present age is 'the conquest of space.' Means of communication have been developed which are far beyond the dreams of former generations; and these new means have set in motion a far more rapid and extensive transfer of goods than ever before within the history of mankind. The result of this development is an economic inter-dependence of nations. No single nation or group can today afford to remain aloof from the rest of the world. Economic development has ceased to be local. Its character has become world-wide. It ignores, at least in its tendency, political boundaries and geographical distances. It carries with itself — and possibly this is even more important than the purely material side of the problem — the ever-increasing necessity of a transfer not only of merchandise but also of thoughts and cultural values. But while those two forces, the economic and the cultural, often go hand in hand, there is a difference in their dynamic rules. The elementary laws of economics require that the exchange of goods between nations be mutual; this means that no nation can act as buyer only while another nation is always seller in the long run, each of them must play both parts simultaneously, giving to, and taking from, each other, be it directly or through the medium of other actors in the play of economic forces. But in the cultural field this iron rule of exchange is not a necessity, at least not always a visible one, that is to say, the transfer of ideas and cultural influences is not necessarily based on the principle of give and take. It

* This chapter is taken from Muhammad Asad's *Islam at the Crossroads*, Lahore: Arafat Publications, 1969, pp. 7-31.

lies in human nature that nations and civilizations, which are politically and economically more virile, exert a strong fascination on the weaker or less active communities and influence them in the intellectual and social spheres without being influenced themselves.

Such is the situation today with regard to the relations between the Western and the Muslim worlds.

From the viewpoint of the historical observer the strong, one-sided influence which Western civilization at present exerts on the Muslim world is not at all surprising, because it is the outcome of a long historic process for which there are several analogies elsewhere. But while the historian may be satisfied, for us the problem remains unsettled. For us who are not mere interested spectators, but very real actors in this drama; for us who regard ourselves as the followers of Prophet Muḥammad (peace and blessings be upon him) the problem in reality begins here. We believe that Islam, unlike other religions, is not only a spiritual attitude of mind, adjustable to different cultural settings, but a self-sufficing orbit of culture and a social system of clearly defined features. When, as is the case today, a foreign civilization extends its radiations into our midst and causes certain changes in our own cultural organism, we are bound to make it clear to ourselves whether that foreign influence runs in the direction of our own cultural possibilities or against them; whether it acts as an invigorating serum in the body of Islamic culture, or as a poison.

An answer to this question can be found through analysis only. We have to discover the motive forces of both civilizations — the Islamic and that of the modern West — and then to investigate how far a co-operation is possible between them. And as Islamic civilization is essentially a religious one, we must, first of all, try to define the general role of religion in human life.

Religion and Human Life

What we call the 'religious attitude' is the natural outcome of man's intellectual and biological constitution. Man is unable to explain to himself the mystery of life, the mystery of birth and death, the mystery of infinity and eternity. His reasoning stops before impregnable walls. He can, therefore, do two things only. The one is, to give up all attempts at understanding life as a totality. In this case, man will rely upon the evidence of external experiences alone and will limit his conclusions to their sphere. Thus he will be able to understand single fragments of life, which may increase in number and clarity as rapidly or as slowly as human knowledge of Nature increases, but will, none-theless, always remain only fragments — the grasp of the totality itself remaining beyond the methodical equipment of human reason. This is the way the natural sciences go. The other possibility — which may well exist side by side with the scientific one — is the way of religion. It leads man, by means of an inner, mostly intuitive, experience, to the acceptance of a unitary explanation of life, generally on the as-sumption that there exists a supreme Creative Power which governs the Universe according to some pre-conceived plan above and beyond human understanding. As has just been said, this conception does not necessarily preclude man from an investigation of such facts and fragments of life as offer themselves for external observation; there is no inherent antagonism between the external (scientific) and internal (religious) perception. But the latter is, in fact, the only speculative possibility to conceive all life as a unity of essence and motive power; in short, as a well-balanced, harmonious totality. The term 'harmo-nious', though so terribly misused, is very important in this connec-tion, because it implies a corresponding attitude in man himself. The religious man knows that whatever happens to him and within him can never be the result of a blind play of forces without consciousness and purpose; he believes it to be the outcome of God's conscious will alone, and, therefore, organically integrated with a universal plan. In this way man is enabled to solve the bitter antagonism between the human Self and the objective world of facts and appearances which is called Nature. The human being, with all the intricate mechanism of his soul, with all his desires and fears, his feelings and his speculative uncertainties, sees himself faced by a Nature in which bounty and cruelty, danger and security are mixed in a wondrous, inexplicable way and apparently work on lines entirely different from the methods and the structure of the human mind. Never has purely intellectual philosophy or experimental science been able to solve this conflict. This exactly is the point where religion steps in.

In the light of religious perception and experience, the human, self-conscious Self and the mute, seemingly irresponsible Nature are brought into a relation of spiritual harmony; because both, the indi-vidual consciousness of man and the Nature that surrounds him and is within him, are nothing but co-ordinate, if different, manifestations of one and the same Creative Will. The immense benefit which religion thus confers upon man is the realisation that he is, and never can cease to be, a well-planned unit in the eternal movement of Creation: a definite part in the infinite organism of universal destiny. The psychological consequence of this conception is a deep feeling of spiritual security — that balance between hopes and fears which distinguishes the positively religious man, whatever his religion, from the irreligious.

The Islamic Approach

This fundamental position is common to all great religions, whatever their specific doctrines be; and equally common to all of them is the moral appeal to man to surrender himself to the manifest Will of God. But Islam, and Islam alone, goes beyond this theoretical explanation and exhortation. It not only teaches us that all life is essentially a unity — because it proceeds from the Divine Oneness — but it shows us also the practical way how everyone of us can reproduce, within the limits of his individual, earthly life, the unity of Idea and Action both in his existence and in his consciousness. To attain that supreme goal of life, man is, in Islam, not compelled to renounce the world; no austerities are required to open a secret door to spiritual purification; no pressure is exerted upon the mind to believe incomprehensible dogmas in order that salvation be secured. Such things are utterly foreign to Islam: for it is neither a mystical doctrine nor a philosophy. It is simply a programme of life according to the rules of Nature which God has decreed upon His creation; and its supreme achievement is the complete co-ordination of the spiritual and the material aspects of human life. In the teachings of Islam, both these aspects are not only 'reconciled' to each other in the sense of leaving no inherent conflict between the bodily and the moral existence of man, but the fact of their co-existence and actual inseparability is insisted upon as the natural basis of life.

This, I think, is the reason for the peculiar form of the Islamic prayer in which spiritual concentration and certain bodily movements are co-ordinated with each other. Inimical critics of Islam often select this way of praying as a proof of their allegation that Islam is a religion of formalism and outwardness. And, in fact, people of other religions, who are accustomed to neatly separate the 'spiritual' from the 'bodily' almost in the same way as the dairyman separates the cream from the milk, cannot easily understand that in the unskimmed milk of Islam both these ingredients, though distinct in their respective constitutions, harmoniously live and express themselves together. In other words, the Islamic prayer consists of mental concentration and bodily movements because human life itself is of such a composition, and because we are supposed to approach God through the sum-total of all the faculties He has bestowed upon us.

A further illustration of this attitude can be seen in the institution of the *ṭawāf,* the ceremony of walking round the *Ka'bah* in Makka.[1] As it is an indispensable obligation for everyone who enters the Holy City to go seven times round the *Ka'bah,* and as the observance of this injunction is one of the three most essential points of the pilgrimage, we have the right to ask ourselves: What is the meaning of this? Is it necessary to express devotion in such a formal way?

The answer is quite obvious. If we move in a circle around some object we thereby establish that object as the central point of our action. The *Ka'bah,* towards which every Muslim turns his face in prayer, symbolises the Oneness of God. The bodily movement of the pilgrims in the *ṭawāf* symbolises the activity of human life. Consequently, the *ṭawāf* implies that not only our devotional thoughts but also our practical life, our actions and endeavours, must have the idea of God and His Oneness for their centre — in accordance with the words of the Holy Qur'ān:

'I have not created Jinn and Man but that they should worship Me' (al-Qur'ān, 51: 56).

Thus, the conception of 'worship' in Islam is different from that in any other religion. Here it is not restricted to the purely devotional practices, for example, prayers or fasting, but extends over the whole of man's practical life as well. If the object of our life as a whole is to be the worship of God, we necessarily must regard this life, in the totality of all its aspects, as one complex moral responsibility. Thus, all our actions even the seemingly trivial ones, must be performed as acts of worship; that is, performed consciously as constituting a part of God's universal plan. Such a state of things is, for the man of average capability, a distant ideal; but is it not the purpose of religion to bring ideals into real existence?

The position of Islam in this respect is unmistakable. It teaches us, firstly, that the permanent worship of God in all the manifold actions of human life is the very meaning of this life; and, secondly, that the achievement of this purpose remains impossible so long as we divide our life into two parts, the spiritual and the material: they must be bound together, in our consciousness and our action, into one harmo-

1. Makka is usually written as Mecca. In this book, the word has been spelled uniformly as Makka.—Editor.

nious entity. Our notion of God's Oneness must be reflected in our own striving towards a co-ordination and unification of the various aspects of our life.

A logical consequence of this attitude is a further difference between Islam and all other known religious systems. It is to be found in the fact that Islam, as a teaching, undertakes to define not only the metaphysical relations between man and his Creator but also — and with scarcely less insistence — the earthly relations between the individual and his social surroundings. The worldly life is not regarded as a mere empty shell, as a meaningless shadow of the Hereafter that is to come, but as a self-contained, positive entity. God Himself is a Unity not only in essence but also in purpose; and therefore, His creation is a Unity, possibly in essence, but certainly in purpose.

Perfection: The Islamic Ideal

Worship of God in the wide sense just explained constitutes, according to Islam, the meaning of human life. And it is this conception alone that shows us the possibility of man's reaching perfection within his individual, earthly life. Of all religious systems, Islam alone declares that individual perfection is possible in our earthly existence. Islam does not postpone this fulfilment until after a suppression of the so-called 'bodily' desires, as the Christian teaching does; nor does Islam promise a continuous chain of rebirths on a progressively higher plane, as is the case with Hinduism; nor does Islam agree with Buddhism, according to which perfection and salvation can only be obtained through an annihilation of the individual Self and its emotional links with the world. NO: Islam is emphatic in the assertion that man can reach perfection in the earthly, individual life and by making full use of all the worldly possibilities of his life.

To avoid misunderstandings, the term 'perfection' will have to be defined in the sense it is used here. As long as we have to do with human, biologically limited beings, we cannot possibly consider the idea of 'absolute' perfection, because everything absolute belongs to the realm of Divine attributes alone. Human perfection, in its true psychological and moral sense, must necessarily have a relative and purely individual bearing. It does not imply the possession of all imaginable good qualities, nor even the progressive acquisition of new qualities from outside, but solely the development of the already existing, positive qualities of the individual in such a way as to rouse his innate but otherwise dormant powers. Owing to the natural variety of the life-phenomena, the inborn qualities of man differ in each individual case. It would be absurd, therefore, to suppose that all human beings should, or even could, strive towards one and the same 'type' of perfection — just as it would be absurd to expect a perfect race-horse and a perfect heavy draught horse to possess exactly the same qualities. Both may be individually perfect and satisfactory, but they will be different, because their original characters are different. With human beings the case is similar. If perfection were to be standardised in a certain 'type' — as Christianity does in the type of the ascetic saint — men would have to give up, or change, or suppress, their individual differentiation. But this would clearly violate the divine law of individual variety which dominates all life on this earth. Therefore Islam, which is not a religion of repression, allows to man a very wide margin in his personal and social existence, so that the various qualities, temperaments and psychological inclinations of different individuals should find their way to positive development according to their individual predisposition. Thus a man may be an ascetic, or he may enjoy the full measure of his sensual possibilities within the lawful limits; he may be a nomad roaming through the deserts, without food for tomorrow, or a rich merchant surrounded by his goods. As long as he sincerely and consciously submits to the laws decreed by God, he is free to shape his personal life to whatever form his nature directs him. His duty is to make the best of himself so that he might honour the life-gift which His Creator has bestowed upon him; and to help his fellow-beings, by means of his own development, in their spiritual, social and material endeavours. But the form of his individual life is in no way fixed by a standard. He is free to make his choice from among all the limitless lawful possibilities open to him.

The basis of this 'liberalism' in Islam, is to be found in the conception that man's original nature is essentially good. Contrary to the Christian idea that man is born sinful, or the teachings of Hinduism, that he is originally low and impure and must painfully stagger through a long chain of transmigrations towards the ultimate goal of Perfection, the Islamic teaching contends that man is born pure and — in the sense explained above — potentially perfect. It is said in the Holy Qur'ān:

'Surely We created man in the best structure.'

But in the same breath the verse continues:

> '. . . and afterwards We reduced him to the lowest of low: with the exception of those who have faith and do good works.' (al-Qur'ān, 95: 4, 5).

In this verse is expressed the doctrine that man is originally good and pure; and, furthermore, that disbelief in God and lack of good actions may destroy his original perfection. On the other hand, man may retain, or regain, that original, individual perfection if he consciously realises God's Oneness and submits to His laws. Thus, according to Islam, evil is never essential or even original; it is an acquisition of man's later life, and is due to a misuse of the innate, positive qualities with which God has endowed every human being. Those qualities are, as has been said before, different in every individual, but always potentially perfect in themselves; and their full development is possible within the period of man's individual life on earth. We take it for granted that the life after death, owing to its entirely changed conditions of feeling and perception, will confer upon us other, quite new, qualities and faculties which will make a still further progress of the human soul possible; but this concerns our future life alone. In this earthly life also, the Islamic teaching definitely asserts, we—every-one of us — can reach a full measure of perfection by developing the positive, already existing traits of which our individualities are composed.

Of all religions, Islam alone makes it possible for man to enjoy the full range of his earthly life without for a moment losing its spiritual orientation. How entirely different is this from the Christian conception! According to the Christian dogma, mankind stumbles under a hereditary sin committed by Adam and Eve, and consequently the whole life is looked upon — in dogmatic theory at least — as a gloomy vale of sorrows. It is the battlefield of two opposing forces: the evil, represented by Satan, and the good, represented by Jesus Christ. Satan tries, by means of bodily temptations, to bar the progress of the human soul towards the light eternal; the soul belongs to Christ, while the body is the playground of satanic influences. One could express it differently: the world of Matter is essentially satanic, while the world of Spirit is divine and good. Everything in human nature that is material, or 'carnal', as Christian theology prefers to call it, is a direct result of Adam's succumbing to the advice of the hellish Prince of Darkness and Matter. Therefore, to obtain salvation, man must turn his heart away from this world of the flesh towards the future, spiritual world, where the 'sin of mankind' is redeemed by the sacrifice of Christ on the cross.

Even if this dogma is not — and never was — obeyed in practice, the very existence of such a teaching tends to produce a permanent feeling of bad conscience in the religiously inclined man. He is tossed about between the peremptory call to neglect the world and the natural urge of his heart to live and to enjoy this life. The very idea of an unavoidable, because inherited, sin, and of its mystical — to the average intellect incomprehensible — redemption through the suffering of Jesus on the cross, erects a barrier between man's spiritual longing and his legitimate desire to live.

In Islam, we know nothing of Original Sin; we regard it as incongruent with the idea of God's justice; God does not make the child responsible for the doings of his father: and how could He have made all those numberless generations of mankind responsible for a sin of disobedience committed by a remote ancestor? It is no doubt possible to construct philosophical explanations of this strange assumption, but for the unsophisticated intellect it will always remain as artificial and as unsatisfactory as the conception of Trinity itself. And as there is no hereditary sin, there is also no universal redemption of mankind in the teachings of Islam. Redemption and damnation are individual. Every Muslim is his own redeemer; he bears all possibilities of spiritual success and failure within his heart. It is said in the Qur'ān of the human personality:

'In its favour is that which it has earned and against it is that which it has become guilty of.' (al-Qur'ān, 2: 286).

Another verse says:

'Nothing shall be reckoned to man but that which he has striven for.' (al-Qur'ān, 53: 39).

The Middle Way

But if Islam does not share the gloomy aspect of life as expressed in Christianity, it teaches us, nonetheless, not to attribute to earthly life that exaggerated value which modern Western civilisation attributes to it. While the Christian outlook implies that earthly life is a bad business, the modern West — as distinct from Christianity — adores life in exactly the same way as the glutton adores his food: he devours it, but has no respect for it. Islam on the other hand, looks upon earthly life with calm and respect. It does not worship it, but regards it as an organic stage on our way to a higher existence. But just because it is a stage and a necessary stage, too, man has no right to despise or even to underrate the value of his earthly life. Our travel through this world is a necessary positive part in God's plan. Human life, therefore, is of tremendous value; but we must never forget that it is a purely instrumental value. In Islam there is no room for the materialistic optimism of of the modern West which says: 'My Kingdom is of this world alone.' — nor for the life-contempt of the Christian saying: 'My Kingdom is not of this world.' Islam goes the middle way. The Qur'ān teaches us to pray:

> 'Our Lord, give us the good in this world and the good in the Hereafter.' (al-Qur'ān, 2: 201).

Thus, the full appreciation of this world and its goods is in no way a handicap for our spiritual endeavours. Material prosperity is desirable, though not a goal in itself. The goal of all our practical activities always ought to be the creation and the maintenance of such personal and social conditions as might be helpful for the development of moral stamina in men. In accordance with this principle, Islam leads man towards a consciousness of moral responsibility in everything he does, whether great or small. The well-known injunction of the Gospels: 'Give Caesar that which belongs to Caesar, and give God that which belongs to God' — has no room in the theological structure of Islam, because Islam does not admit the existence of a conflict between the moral and the socio-economic requirements of our existence. In everything there can be only one choice: the choice between Right and Wrong — and nothing in-between. Hence the intense insistence on action as an indispensable element of morality.

Every individual Muslim has to regard himself as personally responsible for all happenings around him, and to strive for the establishment of Right and the abolition of Wrong at every time and in every direction. A sanction for this attitude is to be found in the verse of the Qur'ān:

> 'You are the best community that has been sent forth to mankind: You enjoin the Right and forbid the Wrong; and you have faith in God.' (al-Qur'ān, 3: 110).

This is the moral justification of the healthy activism of Islam, a justification of the early Islamic conquests. It has meant, as it means today, the construction of a worldly frame for the best possible spiritual development of man. For, according to the teachings of Islam, moral knowledge automatically forces moral responsibility upon man. A mere Platonic discernment between Right and Wrong, without the urge to promote Right and to destroy Wrong, is a gross immorality in itself. In Islam, morality lives and dies with the human endeavour to establish its victory upon earth.

PART II

The Prophet and the Qur'ān

4

The Life of the Prophet Muhammad*

'Abd-al-Raḥmān 'Azzām

Lo! My worship and my prayers and my life and my death are for Allah, Lord of the worlds. He hath no partner. This I am commanded, and I am the first of the Muslims (those who surrender (unto Him)). (al-Qur'ān, 6: 163-164).

THE Muslims form a nation over thirteen centuries old, and comprise at present more than six hundred million human beings in all parts of the world. The Prophet Muhammad was the first citizen of this nation, its teacher and its guide. He lived and died in the full memory of history. The evolution of his personality, religion, and nation assumed the force of a human drama of the greatest magnitude, witnessed not only by his contemporaries but also by the rest of the world in subsequent times.

The hero of this drama did not die until his Message was delivered and a Muslim nation established in the Arabian peninsula. Says Bernard Lewis, 'In an essay on Muḥammad and the origin of Islam Ernest Renan remarks that, unlike other religions which were cradled in mystery, Islam was born in the full light of history. "Its roots are at surface level, the life of its founder is as well known to us as those of the Reformers of the sixteenth century" '[1]

* This chapter is reproduced from Abd-al-Rahman Azzam's book *The Eternal Message of Muhammad*, London: The New English Library, 1964. Translated from Arabic by Caesar E. Farah.

1. Bernard Lewis, *'The Arabs in History'* (2nd ed., reprinted; New York: Harper & Brothers, 1960), p. 36.

During the half-century following the death of the Prophet (in A.D. 632), his Message was carried forth by five of his Companions,[2] who adhered closely to the precedents which he had established for ruling his nation. Four of them[3] were intimate, reliable friends and students who had followed him from the earliest days of his call, through persecution and ultimate triumph. The fifth Caliph[4] was Mu'āwiyah, son of Abū-Sufyān, the formidable leader of the opposition to Muḥammad. Mu'āwiyah's career as Caliph was longer than that of his predecessors. He presided over the affairs of the Islamic community for forty years as governor of Syria, then caliph.

Yet in spite of the wealth of historical facts available to us, perhaps no prophet and religion are so little known or understood by the Western world as Muḥammad and Islam. The West, which has maintained now for several centuries a tradition of freedom of thought, a high grade of literacy, and boundless knowledge in all spheres of human learning, knows far less about Muḥammad — both as a prophet and as a leader of men who exercised a direct influence on the course of human events — than about Alexander or Caesar, whose influences have been less than those of Muḥammad and Islam.[5]

What is the cause of such indifference in a world so eager to learn and to understand? Two explanations merit consideration. The first is from the pen of a distinguished Swedish scholar, who writes:

The cause . . . may perhaps be best expressed by the proverb: Relatives understand each other least of all. A Christian sees much in Islam which reminds him of his own religion, but he sees it in an extremely distorted form. He finds ideas and statements of belief clearly related to those of his own religion, but which, nevertheless, turn off into strangely different paths. Islam is so familiar to us that we pass it by

2. The principal Companions of the Prophet, called the *Sahābah* (singular: *Sāhib*) might be compared to the apostles and disciples of Jesus.
3. Abū-Bakr, 'Umar, 'Uthmān and 'Alī — the 'Orthodox Caliphs' (A.D. 632-661). In the Arabic, the word orthodox in this phrase actually means mature, well-guided, correct; the usage in this book follows that of Western scholars, who have long written of the 'Orthodox Caliphs'. The reason these four Caliphs are considered thus by Muslims is that, having known the Prophet personally and lived so closely according to his principles, they are looked to as great authorities and their decisions are considered precedents.
4. From the Arabic *Khalīfah*, successor.
5. Indeed, it would seem that a conspiracy of silence has replaced the old enmity in the West concerning the Message, which is diametrically opposed to so many injustices perpetrated in the name of God and an enlightened progress.

with the careless indifference with which we ignore that which we know and know only too well. And yet it is not familiar enough to us to enable us really to understand its uniqueness, and the spirit by which it has won its own place in the sphere of religion, a place which is still rightly occupies by virtue of its very existence. We find it much easier to understand religions that are completely new and strange to us — as, for example, the religions of India and China. A greater degree of insight and of spiritual freedom is required of him who would under-stand the Arabian Prophet and his book.[6]

A second explanation is presented by another scholar:

History has been such that the West's relations with the Islamic world have from the first been radically different from those with any other civilization . . . Europe has known Islam thirteen centuries, mostly as an enemy and a threat. It is no wonder that Muḥammad more than any other of the world's religious leaders has had a 'poor press' in the West, and that Islam is the least appreciated there of any of the world's other faiths. Until Karl Marx and the rise of communism, the Prophet had organised and launched the only serious challenge to Western civilization that it has faced in the whole course of its history . . . The attack was direct, both military and ideological. And it was very powerful.[7]

The Prophet was born in Makka. The exact date of his birth is dis-puted, but it is agreed to be around A.D. 570. This uncertainty is usual in Arabia, 'the country of illiterate people,' as the Qur'ān called it. Even today it is difficult to establish the exact birthdates of other famous men; for instance, it is hard to date the birth of the famous 'Abd-al-'Azīz ibn-Su'ūd (or ibn-Sa'ūd), the conqueror and unifier of Arabia, a man who ruled for more than fifty years (he died in 1953), and whose personality, conduct and biography are known in great detail.

The undisputed source for Muḥammad's life is the Qur'ān; there are also many siyar (singular: sīrah) or biographical studies of the Prophet, written from the accounts of those who knew him personally or to whom his memory was quite vivid.

6. Tor Andrae, *Mohammed: The Man and His Faith,* tr. Theophil Menzel (Lon-don: George Allen Unwin Ltd., 1936), p. 11 (reprinted: New York: Barnes and Noble, 1957). It will surprise Western readers to learn that the Muslim world always has been far more familiar with Christianity and Judaism than the West with Islam. Muslims have always regarded Christian and Judaic tenets and beliefs with the greatest respect and interest.

7. Wilfred Cantwell Smith, *Islam in Modern History* (New York: The New American Library, 1957), p. 109.

Both his parents died young, his father, 'Abd-Allāh, first and his mother, Āminah, shortly after. It is said that he was about six years of age at the time of his mother's death. His grandfather 'Abd-al-Muttalib, a prominent leader in Makka, then took charge of him. It is related that 'Abd-al-Muttalib loved the boy dearly and often kept him close beside him, even in meetings where important affairs were discussed, usually in the shade of the Ka'bah.[8] When his uncles would try to remove the child, the grandfather would prevent them, saying, 'Let him be; my child will be leader of his people.'

Upon the death of his grandfather, Muhammad's guardianship passed to his uncle Abū-Tālib, a no less devoted patron, whose love for and protection of Muhammad persisted long after the Prophet proclaimed his mission and the new faith. Even though Abū-Tālib was never converted to the new religion, he continued to show love and protection for his nephew, despite extreme hardships and dangers, until his death, when Muhammad was fifty years old.

Makka was the traditional centre of Arabia in both religion and trade; it was the crossroad of commercial transit between east and west, north and south. Abū-Tālib's clan, the Banū 'Abd Manāf, the most influential in all Arabia, was a part of the great Quraysh tribe,[9] and formed an important element in the oligarchy that ruled Makka and its surrounding tribes. The Prophet's youth was that of the normal young Qurayshī — he fought the battles, joined the peace negotiations, and shared in the duties and rights of his society[10] — except

8. The Ka'bah is a simple cube-like structure towards which Muslims all over the world face in their prayers. It is the first place of worship man had built on the earth. The present building was erected by the Prophets Abraham and Ishmael.

9. Muhammad's immediate family on his father's side were the Banū-Hāshim or Hāshimites, so named for Muhammad's great-grandfather Hāshim. (Banū means son of, and is the plural of ibn.) One of Hāshim's brothers, al-Muttalib, gave his name to the Banū-Muttalibes, and the son, Umayyah, of another founded the Umayyads. These three families, which will figure prominently in this chapter, were in turn subgroups within the Quraysh of the clan Banū-'Abd-Manāf. To clarify relationships further, note that 'Abd-al-Muttalib was the son of Hāshim (and hence a Hashimite, not a Muttalibite) and the father of Abū-Tālib and of Muhammad's father, 'Abd-Allāh.

10. Of these obligations, one remained extremely dear to him, even after his prophetic call, when he severed all his ties with his tribe. This was his membership in the league called *Hilf al-Fudūl*, which originated to protect the defenceless and guarantee the safety of strangers in Makka. The league came about because a stranger from the Yemen sold goods in Makka to an influen-

that he manifested from early years a revulsion to the worship of idols. Once when he was besought to act in the name of the gods al-Lāt and al-Uzzā, he replied with the startling answer, 'Do not ask me anything for the sake of these idols. I have never hated anything more.'

But such strong expressions of disbelief in the gods or idols of his tribe did not alienate his kinsmen and friends from him or close him out from their friendly society, for he was loved by all for his noble character and great kindness and honesty. It was only at the age of forty, when his duty to the one God compelled him to preach against idol worship, that his people began to persecute him.

Muhammad, like the rest of the young men in Abū-Tālib's family, had to work and help preserve the dignity of a generation of Hāshimites who, though they were less prosperous than their predecessors, still remained proud and powerful. He acted as a shepherd, and later, while participating in business, his relations with his people gained him the name of al-Amīn (trustworthy).

At the age of twenty-five, he married a lady of forty, his first wife, Khadījah, a relative and a rich widow. They lived twenty-five years together in prosperity and happiness, and had four daughters and two sons, but of the daughters who lived and married, only Fātimah had descendants.[11] Muhammad was a devoted, loving father, and was kind to children in general. In his twenty-five years of life with Khadījah, he was the ideal husband. When she died, he remained several years without a wife, and even after he married — for a number of reasons — several wives, he always remembered Khadījah. 'When I was poor, she enriched me; when they called me a liar, she alone remained true.' It is an undisputed fact that Khadījah was the first to believe in Muhammad's mission.

11. Fātimah was the mother of Hasan and Husain. Her husband 'Alī was a cousin and the fourth Caliph.

---

tial member of a powerful local clan who subsequently refused either to pay the price or to return the goods, whereupon the aggrieved seller stood up in the vicinity of the Ka'bah and implored aid for himself as a stranger in the city. Several members of the Quraysh aristocracy rallied to his assistance and secured the return of his goods. Meeting next in the house of 'Abd-Allāh ibn-Jud'ān, they pledged henceforth to combat oppressive acts and uphold justice. Muhammad, then only twenty-five years old, was present at this gathering, and was so impressed with the merits of the pledge that when he commenced his mission, he legalised it in Islam. As the years went by, even after his mission had become a success, the Prophet continued to express both his high regard for the league and his willingness to abide by its provisions.

When he received his first revelation while on a retreat in the coun-
tryside, he returned home frightened and shivering. Khadījah received him with the comforting words, 'No, you have nothing to fear. God
will never let you down; you are kind to your relatives, you are astute
and patient, you give to the needy, you are generous to guests, and you
never fail to relieve people from distress.'[12]

So was Muḥammad described by the one who knew him best before
the call and the prophetic revelation. Let us now follow his role in the
great drama that was destined to transform his land, his people and the
world.

Muḥammad, at the age of forty, was inclined to worship in solitude
in a cave on Mount Hirā outside the city. It was while praying, during
the sacred month of his people, that he heard a voice command him,
'Read.' 'I cannot read,' he replied. But the voice again commanded
him, 'Read: in the name of the Lord Who creates . . . man from a clot.
Read: And your Lord is the Most Bounteous. Who teaches (writing)
by the pen, teaches man that which he knew not.'[13]

Trembling, Muḥammad rushed home to Khadījah and told her of
his experience. She comforted him and encouraged him. After a short
interlude, he again heard the voice calling to him: 'You are the messenger of God, and I am Gabriel.' Rushing back to Khadījah in a state
of complete exhaustion, he asked that she cover him with a cloak. Then
he heard the call: 'O you enveloped in your cloak, arise and warn! your
Lord magnify, your raiment purify, pollution shun! And show not
favour, seeking worldly gain! For the sake of the Lord, be patient!'[14]

It was then Muḥammad realised what his mission to his people was
to be, and that was how it began. It is this mission which forms the
subject of this book — this mission which conquered the hearts of men,
and continues to do so with soaring vitality over thirteen centuries
later.

Muḥammad's sincerity was never doubted by those who knew him
well — his wife, his attendant-secretary, and his young cousin 'Alī who
lived with him; these were his first converts. And though to his grief he
could not convert his uncle Abū-Ṭālib, the old man never ceased to
show faith in the sincerity of his nephew: when 'Alī, his son, converted,
he told him, 'Go, my son: he will never call you but to what is good.'

12. A. R. 'Azzām, *Baṭal al-Abṭāl Muhammad* (2nd ed. Cairo: The House of
Arabic Books, 1954), p. 16.
13. al-Qur'ān, 96: 1-5.
14. Ibid., 74: 1-7.

Was Muḥammad's inspiration genuine? Did he speak in entirely good faith? The Muslims, of course, had no doubt; but this was also the attitude of knowledgeable men and serious scholars. Such men were and still are convinced of Muḥammad's earnestness, faithfulness and sincerity.

Some thirty years ago, I asked Sir Denison Ross, then dean of the London School of Oriental Studies, if he believed that Muḥammad had been sincere and faithful. He answered, 'I am sure of that; he never lied or deceived; he was sincere and truthful.' I asked further, 'Do you believe that he was the Prophet of God?' To this he replied, 'That is another matter.' Modern scholars no longer question his truthfulness. According to Tor Andrae:

> Formerly, men thought that his character revealed a certain premeditation, a calculating cleverness . . .That Muḥammad acted in good faith can hardly be disputed by anyone who knows the psychology of inspiration. That the message which he proclaimed did not come from himself nor from his own ideas and opinion, is not only a tenet of his faith, but also an experience whose reality he never questioned. Possibly he was in doubt at first as to the identity of the hidden voice — as to whether it really came from the heavenly messenger whom he had seen in the mountains of Mecca or from an ordinary jinni . . .[15]

Muḥammad quietly preached his faith in One God for some time. He won a few converts: his best friend, Abū-Bakr, a wise, respected and rich merchant; later 'Uthmān and Ṭalḥah, equally important and well-to-do Makkan Qurayshīs; and a number of poor citizens and slaves. Then he received the command to preach in public: 'Thus We send you (O Muḥammad) to a nation, before whom other nations have passed away, that you may recite to them that which We have inspired in you . . . Thus have We revealed it, a decisive utterance (Qur'ān) in Arabic . . .'[16]

With this command from God, the Prophet went forward to warn his people against idol worship and to tell them to expect a resurrection and a day of judgement.

He stood for the first time on the Hill of Ṣafā opposite the Ka'bah, where the Makkan idols were glorified, and said to the people: 'Supposing I now told you that just behind the slopes of this hill there was

15. Andrae, op. cit., p. 47.
16. al-Qur'ān, 13: 30, 37.

an enemy cavalry force charging on you. Would you believe?'

'We never knew that you lied,' they replied.

Then he said, 'I warn you I have a Message from God, and I have come to you as a warner and as the forerunner of a dreadful punishment. I cannot protect you in this world, nor can I promise you anything in the next life, unless you declare that there is no God but the one God.'[17]

They mocked him and went away. Thus began his ten-year career of active struggle and persecution in Makka. He did not desist from preaching to his people of a punishment that would come upon the unbelieving city. He told them, in the fiery language of the early *Sūrahs,*[18] how God had punished the old tribes of the Arabs who would not believe in His messengers — how the flood had swallowed up the people who would not harken to Noah.

He swore unto them — by the wonderful sights of nature, by the noonday brightness, by the night when it spreads its view, by the day when it appears in glory — that a like destruction would assuredly come upon them if they did not turn away from their idols and serve God alone. He fired his Message with every resource of language and metaphor until it seared the ears of his people. And then he told them of the last day when a just reckoning would be made of the deeds they had done, and he spoke of Paradise and Hell with all the glow of Eastern imagery. The people were moved and terrified; conversions increased.

It was time for the Qurayshis to take action. If the idols were destroyed, what would become of them, the keepers of the idols, and their renown throughout the land? How would they retain the allegiance of the neighbouring tribes who came to worship their several divinities at the Ka'bah? That a few should follow the ravings of a mad man or magician who preferred one God above the beautiful deities of Makka was of small concern; but that some leading men of the city should join the sect, and that the magician should terrify the people in broad daylight with his denunciation of the worship which they superintended, was intolerable.

The chiefs were seriously alarmed, and resolved on a more active policy. Hitherto they had merely ridiculed the preacher of this new faith; now they would take stronger measures. Muhammad they dared not touch directly, for he belonged to a noble family which, though

17. 'Azzām, *op. cit.,* p. 16.
18. *Sūrah* means chapter of the Qur'ān.

reduced and impoverished, deserved well of the city and which, moreover, was now headed by a man who was revered throughout Makka and was none other than the adoptive father and protector of Muhammad himself. Nor was it safe to attack the other chief men among the Muslims, for blood revenge was no light risk.[19] They were thus compelled to content themselves with the invidious satisfaction of torturing the black slaves who had joined the 'obnoxious faction'.

The struggle grew in intensity. The Makkan oligarchy was seriously disturbed. Muhammad was in earnest: he was the Messenger of God, and was under His orders. The idols of Makka were not gods or partners with the Almighty; they were helpless and useless, and there was no god but Allah. This purest form of monotheism, which is the essence of Muhammad's faith, was an impossible doctrine for the Qurayshīs to accept. The polytheism of Makka had been established from time immemorial. It was not only the religion of their ancestors but the source of their distinction in all Arabia. If it went, with it would go their honour, power and wealth. Muhammad was the descendant of 'Abd-Manāf, Hāshim, and 'Abd al-Muttalib, who, generation after generation, had been the leading men of the Quraysh and had had its interest at heart; so why not try to settle with him, on whatever might satisfy his dream of power and ambition?

A prominent leader of the Makkan oligarchy, 'Utbah ibn-Rabī'ah, was authorized to negotiate with Muhammad. 'Utbah called Muhammad to the Ka'bah and there stated his proposals: 'O son of my brother, you know your place among us Qurayshīs. Your ancestors are high in our pedigree, and your clan is foremost and strong. You have shocked and disturbed your people. You have broken their unity; you have ridiculed their wisdom; you have insulted their gods; you have degraded their religion; and you have even denied piety and pure faith to their ancestors.'

Muhammad then said, 'I am listening.'

'Utbah continued, saying, 'If you want wealth, we will all contribute to make you the richest of us all. If your object is honour and power, we will make you our leader and promise to decide nothing without you. If, even, you think of royalty, we will elect you our king. If that which you experience and see' — meaning the revelation and the visitation of Gabriel — 'is beyond your control and you cannot defend yourself

19. Stanley Lane-Poole, *The Speeches and Table-Talk of the Prophet Mohammad,* (London: Macmillan & Co., 1882), p. xxxiii.

against it, we shall help cure you by spending money for medical care. It is possible for a man to be overcome by the force of an unseen power until he finds a way to a cure.'

Muḥammad's answer was frustrating to the great representative of the Makkan leaders. He said, with respect, 'Abū al-Walīd, listen to me, please,' whereupon he began to recite from the Qur'ān the basic tenets of his new creed.[20]

The negotiation was broken; a compromise was impossible. Muḥammad wanted nothing less than a complete submission to the new faith. He himself was only a Messenger, and he had to carry out his orders from God and fulfill His mission faithfully.

The situation became more serious. The Makkan oligarchy resorted to violence against the growing humble element of the new congregation. They appealed to Muhammad's dignity and to his aristocratic blood, rebuking him for being the leader of the slaves and the unworthy in the city: 'You are followed only by the contemptible and degraded people who do not think.'[21]

But Muḥammad was not sent to the aristocrats alone; he was a Messenger to all people. He was preaching what God ordered: 'O Mankind! Lo! We . . . have made you nations and tribes that ye may know one another (and be friends). Lo! the noblest of you, in the sight of Allah, is the best in conduct.'[22]

The persecution of those who listened to the Apostle of God continued. At last the Makkan leaders appealed to Muḥammad's sense of tribal solidarity. They explained the danger to which the Quraysh and the city were exposed by the humiliation of their idols and the dissolution of Arab religious tradition. They said, 'If we were to follow the right path with you, we would be torn out of our land (and dispersed).'[23] They meant that they would be no different from the nomads of Arabia and would not be secure in their homes.

For Muḥammad that danger did not exist. God Who commanded him would provide for the defense of the faithful and the victory of those who abided by His Law. They should know and recognize the truth that the idols were helpless stones, and that there was no God but the Almighty Allah, the Creator of all, who had no partners. They

20. 'Azzām, *op. cit.* p. 16. He called 'Utbah by the name Abū al-Walīd, Father of Walīd, who was his son; this was a customary sign of respect.
21. al-Qur'ān, 11: 27. This was also said to Noah by his people.
22. Ibid., 49: 13.
23. Ibid., 28: 57.

should recognize that there would be a resurrection and a day of judgement in which nothing would avail but devotion to God.

But they hated that menace of a judgement, and did not believe in a resurrection. A prominent leader, Umayyah ibn-Khalaf, took a decayed human bone from its grave and brought it to the Prophet, asking, 'You say that this will come to life again?'

'He Who has created it in the first instance can make it return,' the Prophet replied.

The arguments and disputes went on, accompanied by an intensive persecution of the Prophet's followers. Muhammad then advised them to migrate to the opposite side of the Red Sea, to Christian Abyssinia (Ethiopia). They were received there by the Negus (emperor), whose protection they asked. According to tradition, they appealed to him in these words: 'O King, we lived in ignorance, idolatry and impurity; the strong oppressed the weak; we spoke untruths; we violated the duties of hospitality. Then a Prophet arose, one whom we knew from our youth, whose decent conduct, good faith, and morality is well known to all of us. He told us to worship one God, to speak the truth, to keep good faith, to assist our relations, to fulfill the duties of hospitality, and to abstain from all things impure and unrighteous; and he ordered us to offer prayers, to give alms, and to fast. We believed in him, and we followed him. But our countrymen persecuted us, tortured us, and tried to cause us to forsake our religion. And now we throw ourselves upon your protection. Will you not protect us?'

The Muslim refugees recited parts of the Qur'ān which praise Jesus and the Virgin Mary. It is said that the Negus and bishops thought their belief to be derived from the same sources as those of Christianity. Meanwhile, the Makkans did not remain idle. They sent emissaries with presents to the Abyssinians and petitioned them for the surrender of their escaped slaves and the other emigrants; but they were refused.

In Makka, the Prophet and a few of his converts, who through tribal customs and clan usages could protect themselves, remained as adamant and as devoted as ever in preaching the faith and in praying publicly at the Ka'bah against its gods.

The leaders of the Quraysh had already tried to negotiate with Muhammad's kinsmen, the Banū-Hāshim, for the Prophet's death, offering payment of blood money in return, but the tribe had refused the offer. Finally, the Makkan oligarchy decided in desperation to take steps against Abū-Tālib. In their opinion, he was the real protector of the blasphemy, although still a revered upholder of Mak-

kan institutions and unconverted to Muḥammad's faith. They agreed
to send him an ultimatum. When he received their warning, the old
man was disturbed. He called in his nephew and told him that he had
been warned by his tribe. 'I am afraid that the masses of Arabs will
rally against me. Save yourself and me, and burden me not beyond the
possible.'

Muḥammad wept, and answered, 'May God be my witness, if they
were to place the sun in my right hand and the moon in my left, I would
not renounce my Message but would rather perish instead.' Then he
departed, but his uncle called him back and said, 'Go, my son. Say
what you believe; I shall never, under any circumstance, let you down.'

This stand taken by the uncle, who was never converted to the new
faith and who remained a leader in Makka with its pagan traditions
and codes of honour, constitutes a remarkable episode in history.
Abū-Ṭālib, though strictly a traditionalist and unwilling to part with
his ancestors' religion, had found it just as important or even more
important not to surrender to growing pressures or persecute his prot-
égé, of whose sincerity and righteousness he had no doubt.

The Makkan leaders were perplexed. Abū-Ṭālib's refusal to act
meant war. The Arabs were used to feuds and wars, but they could not
accept this challenge, for it would have involved fratricidal slaughter
in which Muḥammad's followers would be negligible. The staunch
traditionalists like themselves, including a majority of the Hāshimites,
Muṭṭalibites, and others, would fight for the Prophet's cause for family
reasons while sharing the Makkans' religion; and those who shared his
faith (Abū-Bakr, 'Uthmān, Ṭalḥah, 'Umar, and others) would be on
the other side against their kinsmen. The leaders backed down, waiting for Muḥammad to realize the dangerous situation toward which
he was leading his clan, its supporters and those who believed in him.

Muḥammad was not to seek any conciliation. He was in the hands of
God. He was sure that another, higher will was directing his destiny,
and that the only way out was for the Quraysh to see, despite all its
pride and vested interests, that its shame lay in worshipping useless
idols that could not direct men to piety and righteousness in this world
or save them in the next on the great day of judgement. He was sent
through the mercy of God to make the Arabs a worthy people dedicated to the cause of serving mankind and their Creator.

The Quraysh and its mass supporters heaped ridicule and contempt
upon the Prophet and his mission, and threw dirt on him wherever he
went, but to no avail. He still preached publicly, and went to the

Ka'bah to pray in his own way. Ultimately, they decided to take extreme measures against his family, the Hāshimites: they refused to have any contact with them, to marry with them, or even to trade with them. They pledged themselves to that end in a proclamation which they placed in the sacred Ka'bah.

Abū-Ṭālib wisely and quietly took stock of the situation, and decided to withdraw to a valley on the eastern outskirts of Makka, where he and the loyal Hāshimites entrenched themselves. He wanted to avoid bloodshed, and all Hāshimite supporters, except Abū-Lahab, felt the same way. The Muṭṭalib clan, cousins of the Hāshimites, followed suit, and also entrenched themselves in the *shi'b* (a short, closed valley). Deprived of everything for more than two years, the Hāshimites and their supporters endured extreme hardships. Food was scarce; there was not enough to meet their needs. Some of the merciful people of the city would now and then smuggle a camel-load of food and supplies to them.

Hardly any new converts were made during this period. Most of those converts who remained outside the *shi'b* took refuge in Abyssinia. Nevertheless, the Prophet's determination and courage never weakened. He continued to go to the Ka'bah and to pray publicly. He used every opportunity to preach to outsiders who visited Makka for business or on pilgrimage during the sacred months. He never doubted God's ultimate victory.

In the third year of boycott and siege, many Quraysh leaders began to feel guilty about isolating their kinsmen to perish in the *shi'b*. After all, the majority of those boycotted and besieged were not even converts; they were idol worshippers, like themselves, but they were going through these trials just the same, in keeping with their code of honour, for the protection of a kinsman who had always been a truthful and honest person.

The moderates found an excuse in that the proclamation suspended in the Ka'bah under the watchful eyes of the idol gods was eaten by worms. The merciful party thus took courage; their leaders put on their arms and went to the *shi'b,* where the exiles had been suffering, and extricated them.

And so, in the eighth year of the Prophet's mission, the converts, his uncle Abū Ṭālib, and the clan that had honoured its tribal tradition in giving protection to a faithful son went back to their homes.

That was not the end of the bad times and suffering. Muḥammad soon lost his uncle, the veteran Sheik of Banū-Hāshim. Abū Ṭālib was soon followed by the faithful Khadījah, the first convert of the Prophet, his beloved wife, adviser and comforter. Hearing of the respite from siege and boycott, many of the emigrants to Abyssinia came back, but they soon met an intensified persecution and were subjected to endless suffering.

To preach in Makka seemed hopeless, and to provoke the Qurayshīs was not the best of wisdom. The Prophet then turned his hopes away from his tribe and city to other cities and tribes. The nearest and strongest competitor of Makka was the city of al-Ṭā'if, fifty miles southeast of Makka. With his servant Zayd the Prophet walked up the rugged mountains to that city. He visited the tribal leaders, and quietly asked their help. He was refused and badly treated. Dismissed, and followed by vagabonds and street urchins who drove him on and would not allow him to rest, he became exhausted. His feet bleeding, he sat and appealed to the Almighty for His mercy. The prayer that ensued has become one of the cherished legacies of the faithful appealing to God in desperate circumstances.

He gathered strength and continued on his way back to Makka, reaching it three days later. Zayd was concerned, and asked the Prophet whether he did not fear thrusting himself into the hands of the Qurayshīs, who continued to plot against the powerless in the city. 'God will protect His religion and His Prophet,' was the reply. The Makkans had learned of the Prophet's reverses at al-Ṭā'if and were preparing a degrading reception for him. None of the Makkan chieftains from whom Muḥammad requested protection for safe entry into the city would extend him help; but a good-hearted pagan chief, al-Muṭ'im ibn-'Adī, took him under his protection and brought him home. Thus did Muḥammad re-enter Makka — guarded by a polytheist, scoffed at by his fellow citizens, and pitied for his lot by his helpless followers.

In that sad year of recurring calamities and gloom, when tragedy seemed about to engulf Muḥammad's mission, a gleam of hope came to sustain him. During the pilgrimage season and the sacred months, when the traditional laws forbade violence, the Prophet had by happy chance converted a few people from Yathrib, who swore allegiance to him. They returned to 'Aqabah in the spring of A.C. 621 with the good news that his faith was being accepted by many in Yathrib. They were accompanied by twelve representatives of the two principal tribes, Aws and Khazraj, who in Muslim history later became known as *Anṣār* (helpers). The Yathribite delegation told the Prophet that their people were willing to accept Islam and pledged, 'We will not worship save one God; we will not steal nor commit adultery nor kill our children; we will in no wise slander, nor will we disobey the Prophet in anything that is right.' This pledge was later called the first Bay'at al-'Aqabah (Pledge of Al-'Aqabah). The second came a year later, following the pilgrims' season, when seventy of the Yathribites came again to 'Aqabah, and secretly pledged themselves and their people to defend the Prophet as they would defend their own wives and children.

Makka was no longer a safe place for the Muslims to reside in. The Prophet then directed those who had returned from Abyssinia and other converts to emigrate and head for Yathrib. Quietly they started to move out. In a few months, more than a hundred families left their homes and migrated to Yathrib. The Qurayshīs were on their guard. The migration of the Prophet to a rival city was harmful to them and they were determined to prevent it at all costs. They decided to kill him, but collectively — representatives of all clans would plunge their swords into him — so that the Hashimites, faced with this joint responsibility, would be prevented from taking vengeance on a single clan.

The Trusted Abū-Bakr and 'Alī stayed behind in Makka with the Prophet. 'Alī sought to deceive the spies of the oligarchy by occupying the Prophet's bed, while the Prophet and Abū-Bakr went to hide out in a neglected cave a few miles south of Makka, on Mount Thawr. When the Makkans discovered that the Prophet had eluded them, they immediately instigated a search, but they failed to catch him, and after concealing himself in the cave for three days, Muhammad rode off to Yathrib.[24] With his arrival, a new era dawned. Conscious of this fact, the Muslims dated their new era from this year of the migration commonly called the Hijrah (or Hegira). It began on June 16, A.C. 622.[25]

When the Prophet entered Yathrib in the summer of that year, many leading Anṣār and a few hundred others were already converted. There were also the Muhājirūn (the Makkan Muslim emigrants), who greeted him on the outskirts of the city. The pagans and Jews gave him a good reception as well, each for a different reason. The Arab Jews were monotheists — they constituted three tribes, living as neighbours of the Arab pagan tribes who had originally come from the Yemen and

24. This city was later called Madīnat al-Rasūl (the City of the Prophet), or simply al-Madīnah (the City); it is modern Medīna.
25. Hijrah means literally emigration. The Muslim calendar dates from the Hijrah; that is A.C. 622 is 1 Anno Hegirae (A.H.).

had gradually gained supremacy in Yathrib. The Jews hoped that Muḥammad, as a monotheist, might become their ally against the pagan Arabs and even against the Christians in northern Arabia. As for the pagans, their reason for receiving Muḥammad was not religion but rather the competition between Makka and Yathrib. Furthermore, the Prophet was related to them on his maternal side — his great-grandmother was a member of Khazraj, the most important tribe in Yathrib — and 'the enemy of my enemy' was as good a reason as any!

Members of each group tried to direct Muḥammad's camel toward their quarters so that he would become their guest. He asked them to let the animal go freely and stop where it would be best for everybody. Where it stopped, he chose his abode. Today, it is the famous shrine where the Prophet's tomb stands, and it is visited yearly by thousands of Muslim pilgrims.

On that spot he lived, directed the affairs of the new nation and built the first *masjid* or mosque of Islam; and on that spot he died.

After thirteen years of intensive struggle to survive, the Prophet had at last found a friendly city where he could defend himself and base his future operation.

The Qurayshis in Makka were disturbed. They were powerful as owners of interests in all parts of Arabia, as guardians of polytheism and the idol gods of the tribes, and as leaders of the Arabian pilgrimage. Their city was a centre both of Arabian trade and of a banking system whose money-lenders granted usurious loans to the various tribes. Muḥammad, their rebellious kinsman, had now taken refuge in a rival town, and had created a rival base astride their important trade routes to Syria and the north. Moreover, many of their sons and daughters had migrated with him to the enemy camp. They knew that Muḥammad would never compromise in his religion, and that peace would be impossible with him.

Muḥammad, however, was not to seek refuge for safety. He was the Messenger of God in the world, and idol worship in his tribe and homeland must come to an end. His new nation would have to divorce itself from idolatry, usury, immorality, alcoholism and vain and sanguine pride in tribalism, and above all it would have to become muslim, that is, submissive to God, the almighty One, Who has no partners, and to Whom all will return to be judged for whatever they have been.

His first concern in Yathrib was to build his simple place of worship, the *masjid,* where the faithful could also meet to discuss the affairs of their world. We must remember that Islam, unlike other great religions, such as Buddhism, Hinduism and Christianity, subscribes to a political and social order which is to be carefully established and observed in the here and now as a road to the afterworld. The Kingdom of God in Heaven is achieved through piety and through a system of social and political order, namely, a Kingdom of God on earth.

The life of the Prophet in Makka had been primarily concerned with the fundamentals of his faith: the unity of God, resurrection, the day of judgement, worship and the purification of the soul. This concern continued in Yathrib, where the *ummah* — congregation or nation — could be organized as an independent entity. A constitution and a system of defense were needed. The new society had to engender a social order and a state. The Prophet, guided by revelation, was able to implement the political and social structure of the new *ummah,* despite exposure to a war of annihilation.

In meeting this challenge, the Prophet, with the guidance of God and his own personal aptitude, fused the Muslim congregation of various clans into a solid nation with one loyalty, Islam, and one brotherhood transcending tribal customs. The second task was an alliance with the neighbouring Jews and pagan Arabs for a common defense and for security and peace in Yathrib. This was accomplished through treaty. This was the famous Covenant of Yathrib, resembling in certain aspects that of the League of Nations or of the United Nations, which aimed at the maintenance of peace and security among the various tribes and the creation of a common system of security as a consequence of common responsibility.

The next problem was what kind of defense to erect, a mobile or static one. In nomadic Arabia, static defense was but the final resort in extreme necessity, as it meant isolation accompanied by hardships. More important, it would also mean a halt in the expansion of the new faith and in the growth of the new *ummah.* Muhammad was essentially the Prophet of God to mankind and the chosen instrument of the propagation of Islam, and whether in Makka or Yathrib, the faith was his fundamental objective; therefore, he decided against static defense.

In the second year of the Hijrah, the Prophet initiated mobile defense, which led in the third year to the famous Battle of Badr, located southwest of Yathrib. His forces were some three hundred infantrymen and three cavalrymen, with no armour but swords and limited supplies. His enemy, Quraysh, had three times his infantry, a hundred cavalrymen and a large supply caravan. The Prophet's force nevertheless defeated them. The causes of the victory lay in their superior discipline and leadership and the high morale which resulted from their great faith in God and the promise of afterlife.

The Battle of Badr was a great victory, especially because it established the Muslim community as a separate political and social as well as religious entity and confirmed the power of the Prophet, but it was not decisive. Muḥammad treated his Quraysh prisoners in a chivalrous and humane way. His prestige in the eyes of the pagan bedouins[26] around Yathrib rose considerably. During the Battle of Badr, these nomads waited like poised vultures, ready to sweep down on the defeated and carry off the loot. As the Qurayshīs were well established in Arabia, they would have been afraid to exploit them in adversity; however, the Prophet's party still lacked roots firm enough to survive misfortune and the Arab nomad's greed for plunder. But God saved His followers, who never boasted of their victory — it was God's victory, they all agreed; even the angels were reinforcing them against the pagans.

The first Muslim army came back to Yathrib with Makkan prisoners who were mostly of the same tribe as the Prophet, who treated them with mercy and sent them home.

In the third year of the Hijrah, while the Prophet was as usual absorbed in his worship and in his preaching, he consolidated the position of his *ummah* and looked after the defense of his city. Neither were his enemies idle. One year later they were ready, and again marched on Yathrib with a force three times as large as the one defeated at Badr. The Prophet moved to engage them, and they met on the slopes of Mount Uhud. The fierce battle ended with the retreat of the Muslim forces and the wounding of the Prophet; but through his endurance and his resourceful and courageous leadership, he managed to save his small army. Abū Sufyān, who was leading the Makkans, called from the top of the hill, saying, 'Uḥud for Badr; we call it even. We will meet again next year.' Both forces retired to their original bases. But that was not the end; Uḥud, like Badr, was not decisive.

Two years later, Quraysh built up a much larger force, allied itself to many tribes, and was able to mobilize an army of ten thousand men. It

26. The English word comes from the Arabic *badawī* (singular: badū), meaning nomads, as distinguished from settled population.

was well armed and equipped, and thus far greater than any force that the Prophet could muster. The attackers laid siege on Yathrib, and for two weeks pressed to break through; but they failed. The Prophet had introduced new defense tactics — digging trenches and raising barricades, at which he himself laboured with the men day and night. The Prophet's faith in God and the great zeal of his followers, particularly the *Muhājirūn* and *Ansār,* balanced the enemy's superiority in arms and numbers. A severe wind blew, accompanied by a dust storm. The morale of the *Ahzāb*[27] faltered with the evening; they argued among themselves, and ultimately broke camp and retired. The Muslims followed them a certain distance. That was the last Quraysh attempt to destroy its enemy's base in Yathrib.

A year later, that is, in the sixth year of the Hijrah, the Prophet moved in force toward his home city, Makka. He wanted to make his lesser pilgrimage (*'umrah*) to the Ka'bah, which, although it housed pagan idols, was still regarded by Muslims as sacred, because in the view of the Prophet the Ka'bah had been built by the Patriarch Abraham for the worship of God. It was in the vicinity of the Ka'bah, near the well of Zamzam, that Abraham had settled his Egyptian wife Hagar with her son Ishmael. The Qurayshīs and other northern Arab tribes were the descendants of Abraham through his son Ishmael. The Muslims therefore believed that they had the right to perform the pilgrimage initiated by their great father, Abraham, the first Arab to worship Allah, the only God.

But the Makkans disagreed with them, and sought to bar their entry. Finally, a ten-year truce[28] was concluded with Quraysh whereby the Prophet agreed, among other things, to postpone his pilgrimage to the following season.

The march on Makka and the truce that resulted therefrom constitute a turning point in Muslim history: for the first time, the right of every person to preach and practice his faith freely was recognized by a formal treaty. A year after the conclusion of the truce, the Prophet and two thousand men entered Makka, which, according to previous agreement, was evacuated temporarily of its inhabitants. The Muslims completed their pilgrimage in an admirable manner, and impressed the Makkans to such an extent that conversions to Islam in-

27. Literally, leagues, that is, a group banded in a general alliance against the Prophet and his men.

28. Known as the Truce of al-Ḥudaybiyah (a place near Makka). The date was A.D. 628.

creased by leaps and bounds. Delegations were sent by Arabian tribes from the four corners of the peninsula to pledge their loyalty to Muḥammad in Yathrib.

When two years later the Qurayshīs violated their treaty obligations and attacked the Khuzā'ah tribe, which was allied with the Muslims, the Prophet led a march on Makka on Wednesday, the tenth of Ramaḍān (in the eighth year of the Hijrah — A.D. 630), with ten thousand men. On that memorable day, the Prophet asked the Makkans, 'What do you think I will do to you?' They answered, 'You are a generous brother and the son of a generous brother.' 'Go,' the Prophet rejoined, 'you are freed.'

Lane-Poole writes:

. . . The day of Muḥammad's greatest triumph over his enemies was also the day of the grandest victory over himself. He freely forgave Quraysh all the years of sorrow and cruel scorn with which they had afflicted him, and gave an amnesty to the whole population of Mecca. Four criminals whom Justice condemned made up Muḥammad's proscription list, when as a conqueror he entered the city of his bitterest enemies. The army followed in his example, and entered quietly and peaceably; no house was robbed, no woman insulted. One thing alone suffered destruction. Going to the Ka'bah, Muḥammad stood before each of the three hundred and sixty idols, and pointed to them with his staff saying, 'Truth is come, and falsehood is fled away!' and at these words his attendants hewed them down and all the idols and household gods of Mecca and round about were destroyed.'[29]

After the conquest of Makka, Muḥammad had to march on another stubborn enemy, al-Ṭā'if, the important dwelling place of the much-exalted idol god Hubal. It was the city to which the Prophet had journeyed in his worst days of persecution, seeking refuge but receiving humiliation instead. Ten years had elapsed since then, and now he believed that the victory in Makka might persuade the inhabitants of al-Ṭā'if to sue for peace. On the contrary, they mobilized the great Hawāzin confederacy of tribes against him, and rallied the city people for a decisive day with the enemy of their god. The two forces met at Hunayn. The Muslims were then commanding the largest force in their history to date, but they were being routed and were retreating when the Prophet rallied the old *Anṣār* and *Muhājirūn* veterans. Fighting courageously, though Muḥammad was wounded, they won the day. The Prophet was so generous and forgiving to his old enemies and

29. Lane-Poole, *op. cit.* p. xlvii.

persecutors that some of his followers among the *Anṣār* objected. But the Prophet soothed them with wise and fair exhortations, and played upon their sympathies until they wept.

Upon returning to Yathrib, Muḥammad encountered delegations sent by tribes and settled peoples of Arabia. They came to pay homage to him and to profess the faith of Islam. Thus was Arabia won over to Islam.

But what about the rest of the world? Muḥammad always conceived of his mission as being directed to all people. Already he had sent his emissaries to Arabia's neighbouring emperors, the Persian and Roman (Byzantine), who ignored his Message or humiliated the messengers. The only courteous response was from the Coptic leader of Egypt.

In southern Syria (modern Jordan), certain of his emissaries were brutally murdered, which occasioned the battle at Mu'tah later.[30] For some years after their army's defeat at Mu'tah, the Muslims were in a state of war with the Byzantine emperor, Heraclius, who was said to be gathering together a large force in Syria to deal with the new Arab menace on his southern frontier and to liquidate the new Arab ruler who entertained such serious pretensions.

For this and other reasons, the Prophet decided to prepare a large army and march north. This was the last military expedition he was to plan. He had pointed out the direction. A short time after his death, his Companions marched north and four years later, they conquered both mighty empires, the East Roman and the Persian.

In the tenth year of the Hijrah, the Prophet made his last pilgrimage to Makka, and delivered his Farewell Speech at Minā to a congregation of forty thousand Muslims. He commenced, 'O people, listen to me; I may not ever meet you again here after this year.' Then, in a great sermon, he expressed his fears that they might lose the way of God and return to a lawless society and to tribal feuds. He ended a great law-giving speech by asking them if they thought that he had faithfully delivered his message. They answered with one voice, 'Yes!' He then said, 'God, You are my witness,' and descended from his camel.

The Muslims called that sermon the Farewell Speech and that pilgrimage the Farewell Pilgrimage. Since the Prophet's first call by the angel Gabriel twenty-three years earlier, revelation after revelation had continued. He had learned them by heart and inscribed them, and so had his friends. They formed together the glorious Book of Islam, the Qur'ān. At the end of this sermon, and as a final word, he recited in the

30. See pp. 159-160.

name of God this revelation: 'This day I (Allah) have perfected your religion for you and completed My favour unto you, and have chosen for you as religion AL-ISLAM.'[31]

His dear friends then wept. They felt that his end was near, that the Prophet had fulfilled his mission; and it was so.

The Prophet died of fever in Yathrib, which thereafter was called al-Madīnah. His life, suffering, and triumph will remain for Muslims and non-Muslims alike a symbol of modesty, faithful devotion, and dedicated service to God, a high example of manhood.

31. al-Qur'ān, 5: 3.

5

The Qur'ān and Its Impact on Human History*

Allahbukhsh. K. Brohi

THE Holy Qur'ān claims to be a Book of *Hidāyah,* i.e. Guidance, for man. It is a Book that is available to whole mankind — indeed it addresses itself, by and large, to the totality of mankind. Its message is relevant to different peoples living in different parts of the world. Further, its message is valid for all times to come — in other words, it is not a Book that will ever be out of date. Such a claim, in principle at least, as can be appreciated, should be capable of being substantiated by appeal to historical evidence. If the Qur'ān is at all a Book of Universal Guidance in the sense that its message is relevant to all peoples in all ages and climes, it must have had, in the course of these fourteen hundred years of its existence, a decisive impact on human history — in particular, it must have had a liberating and transforming influence on the lives of those who may have come under its spell. I submit that clear historical evidence in support of the claim of the Holy Qur'ān exists and I shall endeavour to offer a broad survey of it in these pages.

But before I do that, it is necessary to point out that over and above the test of historical evidence to which appeal could be made, there are within the Divine Book itself numerous indications which ought to enable a discerning and perceptive student to appreciate the truth of the claim of the Qur'ān, namely, that it presents a message of universal significance. These 'intrinsic' tests, it must be admitted, are valid within the framework of religious beliefs and practices sanctioned by Islam and are, therefore, available only to the faithful — that is to say,

---

* Taken from an address delivered on the occasion of the fourteen hundredth anniversary celebrations of the revelation of the Qur'ān.

they are valid only for those who believe in the Divine Word and hold that it has been authentically revealed to the Prophet of Islam and has been preserved down the ages without any alteration having been effected in its text. The 'extrinsic' test of history, however, which I propose to apply in an endeavour to outline the extent of the impact which the Holy Qur'ān has made upon human history, is a *sui juris* one, and, in my submission, if properly appreciated, it is bound to appeal even to those who, not being themselves believers, are nevertheless open to conviction upon the premises of an argument based on the unimpeachable historical evidence that is furnished to us when we examine impartially and contemplate objectively the remarkable revolution that has been wrought in human history by the message that is contained in the Holy Book.

From this perspective, I submit the whole post-Muhammadan era of human history would appear to be a commentary on the claim of the Qur'ān that it is a Book of Guidance for the whole of mankind and that its teaching is relevant for all time to come. After all, God is, according to the Holy Qur'ān, God both of the East and of the West and the Truth revealed by Him has percolated deep into the warp and woof of the thought-life of all the peoples of the world — be they the inhabitants of the eastern or the western regions. And the Qur'ān assures us that where the truth appears the lie disappears — for, verily it is in the nature of lie that, in its confrontation with truth, it disappears.

(1)

The birthplace of the Prophet and, therefore, the rise of Islam, is strategically placed in the 'geographical' middle of the then prevailing civilisations of the times — the Graeco-Roman civilisation of the West and the Egyptian, Babylonian, Phoenician and Persian civilizations of the Near East and the Indian and Chinese civilizations of the Far East. The emergence of Islam from the landscape of Arabia in the larger vista of history is to be likened to the radiant light emanating from a brilliantly lit lamp placed in the middle of a world that had sunk into thick and impenetrable darkness. The Prophet of Islam, no wonder, is described in the Qur'ān as *a shining lamp* and in that image is befittingly addressed as 'Mercy' to all the peoples. Mankind cannot be grateful enough to him for what he had done for it.

The greatest Divine favour to man is that he has been taught the Qur'ān: indeed, the claim that God is Merciful is attested by no other credential than the one which says that He has taught the Qur'ān to man (see al-Qur'ān, 55: 1 and 2). The whole Book, regarded from that point of view, is to be construed as a sort of Instruments of Instructions which has been issued to man in his capacity as God's vicegerent on earth to enable him to conduct his life's operations here below in such a manner that he is able to obtain success in this world and the reward of eternal bliss in the Hereafter.

The distinctive feature of the Qur'ān as a religious scripture lies in the undeniable fact that it *affirms and completes the total process of revelation which has come from the Divine for the guidance of the human race.* God says to the Prophet in the well-known *Sūrah al-Mā'idah,* a *Sūrah* which is one of the very last to be revealed to the Prophet: 'This day We have perfected your religion and completed My favour' (al-Qur'ān, 5: 3). Similarly, in *Sūrah al-A'lā* (87: 14-19), the Qur'ān declares that the truth mentioned by it was also contained in the earlier scriptures — even as in the scriptures of Abraham and Moses. The process of revelation has begun since times immemorial and has been brought to mankind through the Prophets of universal religions by, as it were, a process of periodic installments, to stimulate its growth and development.

The necessity for revelation is attested by the facts of life: the very condition of finitude, in which we find ourselves, calls for Divine help. In the short span of life that is ours, having regard to the limited range of our capabilities and powers of perception, it would be impossible for us without assistance from the Divine to understand our role here below and to plan wise and intelligent action with a view to servicing the essential needs of our being. In order to be meaningfully aware of the necessity for revelation, one has merely to think of the obvious facts of man's dependence on the outer environment in which his lot is cast. Indeed, the very possibility of man's survival depends upon food and shelter which he has to provide to himself from the resources that are available to him from the world outside. If earth did not produce for him the food on which he lives, how can man at all hope to survive? Similarly, man finds himself in a universe which he knows has been there over millions of years before he himself arrived and, what is more, he is fully cognizant of the fact that it will continue being there after his own little 'day will have been done' and he will have 'vanished into the night' leaving things pretty much the same as they have always been. It is clear then that the universe is necessary for his survival but he is not necessary for the life of the universe! What is the meaning of the drama in which man is called upon to play his part. In particular, is he expected to play any part at all — and if so, is his role significant or is it something that is inconsequential? To questions such as these man must find the answers, if he is at all going to fruitfully employ the opportunity and time that is at his disposal while his life lasts. Before the end overtakes him, he must learn to regard his moment as a serviceable means for the fulfilment of the purpose for which he has been created — that, of course, provided if there be any for which he has been created. Reflection shows that even the most trained philosophers, despite considerable bulk of time they have devoted in finding answers to these questions, have found it difficult to return convincing answers. And yet while solutions to these problems are being sought, the river of life of man is continually moving relentlessly on and every moment that elapses for the son of man seems to hurl him on to ever new vistas of experience and opportunity. A tragedy of life is that every moment that passes is gone, never to return. What must man do in order to fulfil the law of his being? Without knowing what that law is, what can he do? Such is the state of helplessness in which man finds himself that from all sides and quarters difficult questions crop up — questions to which there are no satisfactory answers available. The Qur'ān refers to this very situation of man when it says: 'Verily, We have created man in difficulty.' Hence the need of 'revelation'. Religion provides answers to these questions of life on the authority of the Prophets of universal religion. Man has been guided by the Lord himself — even as Merciful Sustainer of the Universe He has guided the whole of creation.

The Qur'ān as a Book of Guidance has itself commented upon the full implications of the concept of *Hidāyah*. *Hidāyah* literally means 'to guide' and 'to show the way'. In *Sūrah al-A'lā* of the Qur'ān reference is made to all the relevant aspects of the process of development through which all created beings pass. 'Praise the name of the Lord, the Most High, who has created and then *equiliberated* all things, Who has appointed their *destinies* and Who has *guided* them' (al-Qur'ān 87: 1-2). This *Hidāyah* in its wider sense, may be regarded as a principle of internal development of the species. To the lower animals have been given instincts and senses through which they are led on to balance or equiliberate themselves. And it is through seeing, hearing, feeling and smelling that they adapt themselves to their environment — and thus to sustain themselves and to procreate their species. With man, additionally, *Hidāyah* takes the form of conferment by God of the gift of Reason upon him, — a sort of a capacity which controls and limits the expression of instinctive life of the animal in him. It is by means of this control which reason enables man to impose over his lower nature that he is elevated to a higher status. Great as this gift of reason is, by itself it does not and cannot suffice — for reason only operates within the framework of instinctive life conditioned as it is by the sensory apparatus. It has, therefore, its own limits, and beyond those limits it is dangerous for it to go. Thus the Prophets have brought *Hidāyah* to man from the Divine in yet one more form. And this form has reference to the message concerning those injunctions, the disregard of which would involve man in wasteful friction with the universe, nay, in a veritable war against his own potentialities. Armed by this *Hidāyah* man is capable of being liberated from the narrower precincts in which his reason operates. He is able, thanks to this guidance, to contemplate his total destiny and regulate his individual conduct and the conduct of his fellow beings in the light of the revealed truth which has been brought to him by the Prophets of universal religions. It would appear that each succeeding phase of guidance is intended to limit the earlier one: thus senses correct the instincts, reason corrects the sense, and the revealed truth corrects the operation of reason itself. The prophetic consciousness mirrors for man the higher truth which it is incapable of being attained by the operations of unguided reason. Man is informed of the limits within the circle of which he must move if he is to be saved. He is thus educated and initiated into the scheme of things in which he is to strive for the fruition of his appointed destiny. The Qur'ān, no wonder, says: 'Truly, it is for Us to show the way to man and truly Ours is the future and truly the past' (al-Qur'ān, 2:12:13). Similarly, it goes on to assert: 'Whoso makes effort to follow in Our ways, We will *guide* them; for God is assuredly with those who do righteous deeds' (al-Qur'ān, 29: 69). Far more explicit than these references to man's dependence on Divine guidance are the following:

> Say, verily *guidance* is from God. That is the true *guidance*; and we are indeed to surrender ourselves to the Lord of all beings. (al-Qur'ān, 6: 71).

Then, again:

> But until you follow their religion, neither the Jews nor the Christians will be satisfied with you. Say, verily *guidance* is from God — that is the guidance. (al-Qur'ān, 2: 120)

The irreducible minimum requirements for the successful discovery of the solution of life's problems thus would appear to be two. *First* of all there is to be a *question* in the soul, a *craving* to find answers to the problems of life, a *prayer* at the altar of the Divine for the way being shown. And it is this that imparts to *Sūrah al-Fātihah* the importance that has been assigned to it by those who have thought deeply about the strategy of the Qur'ān: each time man has to pray: he asks: 'Show us the way' — in other words 'Grant us the guidance'. If a man with a pure soul, with a feeling heart, asks for guidance and proceeds to read that portion of the Qur'ān that is bound to issue forth from the Book he will get an answer to his question. And, *secondly,* one has to have the will to walk on the way that is revealed. For not the whole path would be shown to man if he would not even walk on that part of the way which is being shown to him: capacity to receive truth ultimately depends upon *man's efforts to implement the truth that comes to him.* He who sees the way, but would not negotiate it, will stay where he is — indeed, such is the law, the rest of the way will never be shown to him.

The strategy of religion precisely consists in this is that it enables man to find his way to the goal that counts. Man by the flickering light of his feeble powers — which is all that is furnished to him by his meagre resources — cannot be expected to discover the way on his own, much less have the *energy* and the *inclination* to follow the way. It is his faith in the revealed truth that has come to him from the Prophets of universal religion that is capable of coming to his rescue in this regard and this is so because the natural reach of his own personality is such that in respect of the essential questions of life it cannot, by itself, find any valid answers.

The process of revelation, as remarked earlier, has been consummated in the message that has been brought by the Prophet of Islam to mankind. So much is this true that it may be said that Islam itself provides for the education of the human race. Man has evolved and has been a witness to various phases of his own evolution. Different Prophets have brought different messages for their people, if only because, having regard to the different conditions in which humanity has found itself, the message in question could only be addressed to particular people in certain well-defined epochs of human history. Only by some such teaching was it possible to secure man's further development. In Islam religion has been perfected. That is another way of saying that with Islam the age of new revelation has come to a close, and that the age of realization of the principles of revealed religion has been inaugurated. That is why in all the earlier scriptures references are to be found to the advent of the Prophet of Islam. Students of Bible, for instance, know that Jesus had said: 'I have yet many things to say unto you, but ye cannot bear them now . . . He will guide you unto all truth: for he shall not speak of himself; but of whatsoever he shall hear, that shall he speak' (John 16: 12-13).

Further, the New Testament bears testimony to this very truth: 'Whom the heaven must receive until the times of restitution of all things, which God hath spoken by the mouth of all his holy prophets since the world began (Acts, 3: 21). The Holy Qur'ān itself affirms this reference in chapter 61, verse 6, when it says: 'And that Jesus, son of Mary, said: "O children of Israel, surely I am the messenger of Allah to you verifying that which is before me of Torah and giving the good news of a Messenger who will come after me, his name being Ahmad." '

That then is the meaning of the fundamental tenet of Islam which enjoins that the Prophet of Islam is the *last* Prophet. The Holy Qur'ān thus embodies the final-most communication from the Divine. After the Prophet of Islam came to mankind the need for continuing the process of Divine communication itself has come to an end. For Islam signifies in the history of mankind that phase of human development which corresponds to the period of majority in the life of the individual. A few words by way of explanation of this distinctive feature of the Holy Book which consists in its address being directed to fully grown-up individuals are called for — and are offered in all humility as an aid to those who would like to understand the grand strategy of the Qur'ān for bringing about the moral and mental regeneration of mankind on earth.

The very fact that the Qur'ān claims itself to be a Book of Guidance assumes that it is not a book of Ten Commandments as is, for instance, the Old Testament. The Prophet was called upon to purify the people, to teach them the Book, that is their destiny and to make them wise (al-Qur'ān, 2: 129 and 151; also 3: 163.). He was to warn and to guide. The Qur'ān unmistakably places the burden of making a choice between good and evil fully and squarely on the shoulders of man. It says: 'Have We not shown to you the two ways' — the easy way and the difficult way. The Qur'ān further declares that nothing belongs to man except his effort: that he is going to be judged by what he does here and now. Does this not suggest that the Qur'ān assumes man to have reached a level where he is regarded as being capable of choosing between the right and the wrong. The Qur'ān is also called *al-Furqān* — which merely means it is the book which helps one to discriminate —

between the scale of values, pointing out which acts are good, better, and best and which ones are bad, worse, and worst. All this shows that the Qur'ān addresses itself to people who can choose!

(2)

One way of demonstrating the indispensibility of the message contained in the Qur'ān to the modern world is to take up, one by one, the present-day standards of excellence — that is, values and ideals which are accepted and upheld by enlightened sections of contemporary humanity and to ask the question: What is the genesis of those values and ideals? Whence have they come? And, in particular, one must ask whether those values and ideals were at all commended or enjoined by pre-Islamic religious teaching. If we were to reach the conclusion that the present-day set of ideals and values which is considered worthy by a civilized man to adopt and accept was revealed for the *first time* by Islam, then the fact that even after fourteen hundred years that message continues, at least in priciple, to bto be followed still, would be proof positive of the claim that what the Qur'ān proclaims to the world is *even today the acceptable gospel.*

Negatively, if it could be shown that what the Qur'ān enjoins is out of date today so far as the practice of civilized people is in issue, or that some new values and ideals have gained currency in modern times which are not stressed by the Qur'ān, we will have to say that Qur'ān was an ephemeral book and its message is out of date today.

If I were asked to state what are the values which the enlightened consensus of mankind upholds in the mid-twentieth century, I would put them in the following order:

(1) Equality, dignity and brotherhood of man.
(2) Value of universal education with emphasis on spirit of free enquiry and the importance of scientific knowledge.
(3) Practice of religious tolerance.
(4) Liberation of the woman and her spiritual equality with man.
(5) Freedom from slavery and exploitation of all kinds.
(6) Dignity of manual labour.
(7) Integration of mankind in a feeling of oneness irrespective of their differences *qua* race and colour (that is, the programme of securing integration of mankind on the basis of moral and spiritual principles).

(8) The devaluation of arrogance and pride based on superiority of race, colour, wealth, etc., and the founding of society on the principle of justice.

(9) Rejection of the philosophy of asceticism.

Each one of these items on the agenda of modern man's heroic and noble endeavour, I submit, is fully and adequately supported by various injunctions of the Qur'ān and ably illustrated by the kind of life that the Prophet of Islam lived himself.

The Prophet of Islam is exemplary precisely because he is a man-prophet. The Qur'ān emphasises again and again that he is a man like any other man except to the extent that the *Waḥī,* that is the Holy Angel, brings revelation to him. He is the one Prophet who is not only not interested in performing miracles, but makes the non-performance of miracles as his passport to main distinction. He does not claim any Divine origin. For himself he is content to be just an ordinary human being. He lives a life of honest and earnest endeavour throughout his life. To the very end he preserves a high sense of moral rectitude and conducts the enterprises of life with a great human dignity. He is an able warrior, an excellent soldier, a loving husband, a reliable friend, a wise ruler. *He sanctifies life in all its aspects, omitting nothing from its embrace.* He treats the whole earth as a prayer carpet, denies that the Arabs have any superiority over the non-Arabs. He makes one and only one decisive test about the grandeur, the loftiness, and greatness of the human soul — which consists in its capacity to control itself so as to be able to practise righteousness. And even when he becomes the ruler of the whole of Arabia he never discards his old way of simple life and incessantly enjoins upon himself and upon his followers the supreme necessity of giving away of the good things of life to their fellow men who might need them. 'So give,' says he, 'that your left hand may not see what your right has given.' He forbids his followers from renouncing the world. Indeed, God is everywhere and His earth is very wide and man is to serve Him wherever he likes.

Adverting to the importance the Qur'ān attaches to the educational process, the matter is too obvious to need any elaboration. The Book itself begins with an imperative to read: 'Read in the name of your Lord Who created man from a blood-clot' (al-Qur'ān, 96: 1, 2). 'Read and your Lord is most generous who taught man by the pen' (al-Qur'ān, 96: 3 and 4). It emphasises the value of *the ink and the pen and what they write* (al-Qur'ān, 68: 1). The Qur'ān is full with repeated emphasis on the value of thinking, of pondering, of rationalization, of discrimination. In a way, it would not be an exaggeration to say that the whole of the Book is concerned with outlining the methodology and technique by which man is to read the Book of Nature and to witness within himself the Signs of the Divine. All universe is one and man is called upon to look at it and to learn from it. How many times does not the Qur'ān call upon us to look at the various phenomena in nature — and challenges us to throw our glance at the creation of the Lord and to say if we find any flaw therein. Not content with asking us to throw our first glance at the universe, we are invited to throw a second glance at the universe. We are told that: Verily our vision will return weary upon us and that we shall not be able to see any flaw in the Master's creation (see al-Qur'ān, 67: 3 and 4). Then we are called upon to see the Signs of the Lord in the rhythm of change that is discoverable in nature — between the night and the day, as though one is chasing the other. We are asked to notice the way in which the dead earth is brought to life by the rainfall. We are asked to consider the motions of the seasons, the sun and the moon, each one running its course. The Qur'ān enjoins that there are signs in nature for people who reflect (al-Qur'ān, 13: 3-4). In the magical words of the Qur'ān: 'And He it is who spread the earth, made in it firm mountains and rivers. And of all fruits, He has made it in pairs, two (of every kind). He makes the night cover the day. Surely there are signs in this for people who reflect. And in the earth are tracts side by side and gardens of vines and corn and palm trees growing from one root and distinct roots — they are watered with one water and we make some of them excel others in fruit. Surely there are signs in these for people who understand.'

It was this constant call to see nature and to understand the secret of its operations which enabled the earlier Arabs to become pioneers of science and scientific methods. Nowadays, of course, everything is attempted to be explained by the historians of human culture as though Arabian science did not so much as exist. Everything is supposed to have been found for us by the Greeks!

The moral and intellectual flowering of the European culture and civilization has had a source other than the one that is generally invoked by scholar. European civilization itself is a 'post-Protestantism' product. Of course, every school-boy in Europe is today taught to believe that Reformation was the result of Renaissance which in its turn is supposed to have been ushered in, thanks to the revival of learning that took place after the fall of Constantinople. Somehow, the dark ages of Europe suddenly ceased and the light of Renaissance came to be.

That is all taught in the universities of civilized Europe and America in the name of liberal education; and as to the origin of this 'Renaissance' itself all kinds of false explanations exist and continue to be concocted — but an honest attempt at historical analysis will in the wise words of Robert Briffault, show that:

It was under the influence of the Arabian and Moorish revival of culture, and in the fifteenth century, that the real Renaissance took place. Spain, not Italy, was the cradle of the rebirth of Europe. After steadily sinking lower and lower into barbarism, it had reached the darkest depth of ignorance and degradation when the cities of the Saracenic world, Baghdad, Cairo, Cordova, Toledo were growing centres of civilization and intellectual activity. It was there that the new life arose which was to grow into a new phase of Human Evolution. From the time when the influence of their culture made itself felt, began the stirring of a new life.

It is highly probable that but for the Arabs modern European civilization could never have arisen at all; it is absolutely certain that, but for them, it would not have assumed that character which has enabled it to transcend all previous phases of evolution. For although there is not a single aspect of European growth in which decisive influence of Islam is not traceable, nowhere is it so clear and momentous as in the genesis of that power which constitutes the paramount distinctive force of the Modern World and the Supreme Source of its Victory — Natural Science and the Scientific Spirit. (*The Making of Humanity,* pp. 183-90).

Not merely in the direction of intellectual evolution of Modern Europe alone is the influence of Islam to be acknowledged and understood. 'To the intellectual culture of Islam', says the same author, 'which has been fraught with consequences of such moment, corresponded an ethical development not less notable in the influence which it has exercised. The fierce intolerance of Christian Europe was indeed more enraged than humiliated by the spectacle of the broad tolerance which made no distinction of creed and bestowed honour and position of Christian and Jew alike, and whose principles are symbolized in the well-known apologue of the Three Rings popularized by Boccacio and Lessing. It was, however, not without far-reaching influence on the more thoughtful minds of those who came in contact with Moorish civilization. But barbaric Europe confessed itself impressed and was stung to emulation by the lofty magnanimity and the ideals of chivalrous honour presented to it by the knights of Spain, by gentlemen like the fierce soldier, Al-Mansūr, who claimed that, though he had slain many enemies in battle, he had never offered an insult to any — an ideal of knightly demeanour and dignity which twentieth-century England might with profit perpend. The ruffiantly crusaders were shamed by the grandeur of conduct and generosity of Saladin and his chivalry. The ideal of knightly virtue was adopted, the tradition of *Noblesse Oblige* was established. Poetry and Romances deeply tinged with Arabian ideas formed the only secular literature which circulated and appealed to the popular imagination; and a new conception of the place and dignity of women passed into Europe through the Courts of Provence from the Moorish world, where she shared the intellectual interests and pleasures of man . . . Thus, shocking as the paradox may be to our traditional notions, it would probably be only strict truth to say that Mohammadan culture has contributed at least as largely as to the actual practical, concrete morality of Europe as many as more sublimated ethical doctrine' (see ibid., pp. 307-9).

Similarly, the position of the woman in the pre-Islamic era was so pathetic that it is impossible to get the modern man to realise how much of advance has Islam made in enjoining upon humanity the necessity of respecting and honouring the woman. The Arabs found it difficult to let daughters grow up in their house. This was supposed to be something derogatory to their status. They used to bury them alive. With Islam all this was prohibited. The *daughter* was admitted to be a sharer with her brother in the law relating to inheritance. This is rather significant considering that in as civilized a country as England, not until 1922, was a married woman entitled to own property. Islam gave to the woman not only the right to inherit property but to own it even against her husband, so much so that if a husband is guilty of misappropriating her property she is entitled to obtain a divorce from him on that account alone. As a widow she gets a share in her husband's property. The rights of wives are to be acknowledged by her husband and are clearly mentioned (see al-Qur'ān, 2: 228; 4: 34; and 2: 229). She was given a right to claim a divorce fourteen hundred years ago whereas under the Ecclesiastical law sanctioned by the Church of Christ it is impossible for her to obtain a divorce even now. The modern secular legislation which recognizes divorce in Christian countries is an indirect acceptance of the wisdom of the Qur'ān on this subject.

There was a time when of woman, it was said: 'He for God and she for God in him.' But now with Islam woman has been declared an independent personality as she has been made directly accountable to God. The Qur'ān has honoured woman so much that there is a chapter in it entitled 'Woman' and numerous references to her status and dignity are to be found therein. This was a radical departure from the position of pre-Islamic woman — and, indeed, if only a comparative study upon that subject were made it would seem that her position in the framework of Qur'ānic teaching is much above even the present status of woman anywhere in the world. Such triumphs as the cause of the liberation of woman has made in the annals of human history, I submit, are directly traceable to the impact of the Qur'ān.

Similarly, Islam came to terminate the age of slavery. Indeed, the freeing of the slave is the highest point of honour to which the Qur'ān invites man (al-Qur'ān, 90: 13). The Qur'ān deals with the question of the emancipation of man so very comprehensively that it can be called the *Testament of Human Liberty*. Man is declared free and he is brought in such a direct relationship with God that even 'priesthood' has been thrown overboard. How can man worship God freely unless he be free from political, economic, social and religious exploitation? God says: He is nearer to us than the veins of our necks . . . how can anyone intervene to interpret His will to us. Man is to be made free to be able freely to worship the Lord!

The whole world today believes in religious tolerance, and whatever be the extent of its conformity to the ideal postulated by religious and intellectual tolerance, all civilized countries the world over subscribe to man's inherent right to pursue, in the light of his own feeble powers and resources, the goal which he has kept before himself. Indeed, the Qur'ān is the only religious Book, I know, which has, on the one hand, commanded the followers of Islam to *spread* their faith by resort to the use of beautiful words of persuasion and, on the other hand, *prohibited* them against the vice of being intolerant of other people's religious beliefs and practices. It candidly says that there is no compulsion in religion. Further, it enjoins the Prophet say: 'Your God and my God is one God'; still further, when all arguments fail and the detractor of Islam refuses to listen to reason, the Muslim is admonished to say, even as the Prophet said to his detractors: 'You have your own religion and I have my religion.' Indeed, the Qur'ān has gone farthest in this direction when it declares: 'Revile not those whom they call on besides God, lest they, in their ignorance, despitefully revile Him. We have so fashioned the nature of man that they like the deeds they do. After all they shall return to their Lord and He will declare to them what their actions have been' (al-Qur'ān, 6: 109). This sort of religious tolerance preached by Islam and practised by Muslims stems from, and is the consequence of, a larger truth — the truth that the *Dīn*, that is, the *way of life commanded by God to be revealed by the Prophets to mankind* has been in essential aspect one and the same. 'To each amongst you,' declares the Qur'ān, 'Have We prescribed the law and an open way. If God had willed He would have made you all of one pattern; but He would test you by what He has given to each. Be emulous then in good deeds' (al-Qur'ān, 5: 48). Similarly, the Holy Qur'ān points out the great truth, namely, 'To every people We have appointed observances which they deserve. Therefore let them not dispute this matter with you; but bid them to their Lord for you are on the right way' (al-Qur'ān, 22: 67).

To various peoples in different climes various Prophets have been sent, all of whom have revealed the same *Dīn* (the way of life) to them, although the observances sanctioned for the realization of the *Dīn* in their own time have been different. 'There has not been people who have not been visited by the warners,' says the Qur'ān (al-Qur'ān, 35: 24). 'And, indeed, the Prophet of Islam himself is nothing more than a warner and a guide.' (al-Qur'ān, 13: 7). 'Several of these Prophets the Lord has sent amongst the people as of old' (al-Qur'ān, 63: 6). Some of these Prophets have been mentioned by name in the Qur'ān and of others, says the Lord to the Prophet, 'We have told thee nothing' (al-Qur'ān, 40: 78).

Indeed, the tolerance preached by Islam reaches its high water-mark when the Qur'ān declares 'Verily, those who believe (that is Muslims) and they who follow the Jewish religion, Christians and the Sabians . . . whosoever believes in God and the Last Day and does that which is right shall have their reward with the Lord. Fear shall not come upon them, nor shall they grieve.' (al-Qur'ān, 2: 62). Could spirit of religious toleration go any further?

The greatest contribution which the Qur'ān has made to human history, in my submission, concerns the clarification it has offered of the only foundational principle on which mankind as a whole can be brought to live together in peace and harmony. The Qur'ān has emphasised over and over again the supreme necessity of mankind getting together, for after all 'Have We not,' says the Lord, 'created mankind as though it were one self.' The internecine warfares that have gone on between groups and groups, communities and communities, nations and nations, and sects and sects appear to stem from man's inveterate desire to uphold not *what* is Right, but merely to decide *who* is Right. The Qur'ān invites all of us to adhere to the Law of God with a happy and apt metaphor, of sticking to one and the same rope of the Lord. The Qur'ān admonishes us against forming cliques and being privies to schisms and developing spirit of partisanship. Indeed, the Qur'ān mercilessly denounces those who form sects and *sponsor group formations* and as to those who split up their religion and become parties to the founding of sects, it tells the Prophet: 'You have nothing to do with them. Their affair is with God. Hereafter shall We tell them what they have been' (al-Qur'ān, 6: 160). It goes on to enjoin in another place: 'But men have rent their great concern (the one religion which was made for all mankind), one among another, into sects and every party rejoicing in that which is their own' (al-Qur'ān, 23: 53).

These internal divisions and schisms which have disrupted the peace of the world result from mankind disregarding the supreme fact of its own constitution, namely, that all of us are from God and to God is our return. Similarly, the racial pride is discounted by the Qur'ān when it proclaims that *all mankind is from Adam and Adam is made from dust.* Satan is exhibited as an accursed one precisely because he argues, for the superiority of his *high* origin as contrasted from what he believes in the *lowly* origin of man. 'Man, after all,' says he, 'was created of dust whereas I am created of a fire.' This sort of sense of exclusivism which also comes to a people purely out of a desire to claim superior and high quality of blood in their being has been denounced by the Qur'ān in no unmistakable terms and no matter what the detractors of the Prophet might say, the supreme fact of post-Islamic history is that Islam alone of all possible creeds has successfully devalued the importance of race, colour and privilege. It has admonished its followers not to organize mankind into groups based on principles of blood or geographical contiguity or particular privilege which they might claim for themselves. According to Islam, he alone is exalted who is a *muttaqī*—that is, one who is a self-controlled individual, one who lets the law of God rule him. All other trimmings and trappings of individual life are false credentials and mean nothing.

Today in a world, divided by all manner of groupings, and accursed

as it is, by the worship of a false God called 'nationalism', the realization has come to mankind that the brotherhood of man is capable of
being founded only upon a spiritual principle — not on the basis of
colour, race, privilege. That spiritual principle highlights the importance of organizing the brotherhood of man upon the only basis that he
is a man — not because of *what he has* but because of *who he is*. Those
who believe in the superiority of race are being roundly condemned
everywhere: those who believe that greatness of a nation is measured
by its economic and industrial potential are being hated everywhere
and, what is worse, they are not even at peace with themselves. The
institution of pilgrimage sanctioned by Islam is the only illustration I
know of the operation of the spiritual principle for securing integration
of mankind; gathering of Muslims in Makka every year is the only
model upon which a move towards a supra-national synthesis of
mankind can be stimulated.

The spiritual principle upon which mankind can be grouped,
according to Islam, takes the form of devotion to the ideal of justice.
There are innumerable references in the Qur'ān to the supreme necessity of establishing a *just* society, a *just* order. We, the individual men
and women, are invited to be just, to hold scales of justice evenly, and
are forbidden from employing false measures in weighing things or
artificially tilting the balance in our favour. We are called upon to
advance the cause of justice by offering testimony should the need to
do so arise, even against our own kith and kin, our own near ones and
dear ones. There was a time when the highest ideal for man was to
extend hope and offer comfort to persons who were suffering because of
the iniquitous and unjust conditions to which they were subject. The
religious duty was merely to *comfort* the victims of injustice with the
assurance that God is with the lowly and humble and that because of
their suffering they will be rewarded in the Hereafter. The Qur'ān
would not accept any organizational synthesis of mankind which is not
based on the ideal of justice — which consists in giving to each nation
or community what is its due. The Christian society in the conception
of its present professions could only be founded by upholding the value
of meekness, or rendering unto Caesar what is Caesar's and to God
what is of God — of charity, of compassion — not upon the foundation
of justice which consists in the enforcement of just laws by just people.
Islam enjoins upon its votaries to inflict duly sanctioned punishments
on the transgressors of the law and admonishes us to call upon the
perpetrators of the wrong to compensate those who have been wrong-

ed by the unjust exercise of their power. It says all power is God's and anyone who has it must exercise it not for his *personal aggrandizement but in His holy name for the advancement of His purpose.*

(3)

The Qur'ān manifesto is thus there for all to see. Willy-nilly, it has been accepted in principle by the whole world. The world swears by its ideals and in fact cherishes the values sponsored by it. It is true that here, as elsewhere, there is a great deal of discord between our 'professions' and 'performance'. It is also true that in the sphere of practice, the teaching of the Qur'ān is least followed by those who call themselves Muslims. No book in the world down the ages has been adored more than the Holy Qur'ān has been by the Muslims. The respect they show for the Book, however, is not the only response that is demanded by the Book. Far more important is the claim of the Qur'ān that the guidance furnished by it should be *understood* and *applied* to the details of our daily conduct.

If the Qur'ān is a Book of *Hidāyah* is it not obligatory for all of us to know what is contained in it, and what it has enjoined upon us. And how can we, I ask, know what it has enjoined upon us unless we are able to understand what it says. This is not the place to indicate in any measure of details what are the pre-conditions which have to be fulfilled before the Qur'ān can have appeal to the heart of man. A great deal of discipline in the nature of internal purity and a great deal of devotion to the Lord Who has revealed it to mankind is required before mere knowledge of Arabic can be serviceable. It is true that knowledge of Arabic is necessary and the more we know Arabic the better will it be — but then, knowledge of Arabic is not to be confused with a close study of its syntax, of its grammar, and of its lexicographical superfine distinctions. The Arabic of the Qur'ān is simple — therefore such is its miracle that it cannot be understood easily by the sophisticated ones!

The Qur'ān is the best evidence that there is for all of us to believe that God exists, that Muḥammad is His Prophet. It is also a Book of Hope in the sense that it presents to us the image of our Maker Who forgives us and protects us against our own follies.

PART III

The Islamic System

6

---

*Islam and Social Responsibility**

T. B. Irving

ONE of the serious facts of this present age is that the old norms have failed to convince and hold our youth, and we are facing a new time of Ignorance, a fresh *Jāhiliyya,* as the Arabs or Muslims would state it. Whether this is because Western values are basically false or that some form of dry rot has infected our communications media, the fact remains that we are facing a real crisis throughout the Western world.

This process is the opposite of the great eighteenth-century movement which was called the Enlightenment, when Western Europe and North America seemed to be shaking off their age-old prejudices. For Muslims, it also forms a contrast to the startling period when the Prophet Muḥammad led his arid peninsula out of chaos, both political and social, into the leadership of the then known world. In fact, wherever Islam entered during its earliest youth, the middle ages, especially as Western Europe knew this dark period in human history, simply ceased to exist.

THE ISLAMIC ERA

The Prophet Muḥammad (peace be upon him) established religion, and then, Islamic state or commonwealth developed slowly, somewhat challengingly, during the decade from the year 622 or the *Hijra* as it is called, the Zero year in the Islamic calendar, until his death in 632, only ten years later. By that time, instead of being a peninsula of

* This is based on a paper presented by the author to a Muslim-Baptist Dialogue Conference held at Toledo, Ohio, U.S.A., and published in *Impact International,* August, 1974.

mutually raiding tribes, Arabia had become a commonwealth which raised new standards for the world to adopt. All this occurred within the ten years after the *Hijra* or 'Transfer' of the Prophet and his Muslim community from trying circumstances in Makkah to its new capital of Yathrib, or Madīna as this city came to be called, two hundred miles to the north in an oasis on the ancient caravan route to Syria.

The life of the Prophet thus lasted from around the year 570 of the Christian era, when he was born, until 632. He was called *an-Nabī al-Ummī* or 'the Unlettered Prophet' in the Qur'ān (7: 157-158). What does this term mean? It means simply that Muḥammad (peace be upon him) was not college trained, as we might expect him to be today; nevertheless he led his people formally and sincerely to a better way of life. He was the most cultured and concerned individual yet he had never been to school, only trained to speak good Arabic by living as an infant out on the desert, where they spoke the best Arabic in that day. Or even since.

Almost immediately following his death, Islam burst upon the Near Eastern and the world scene, to take over the whole Sassanid empire of Persia plus the southern tier of the Byzantine empire as far West as Spain and Morocco on the Atlantic. This covered less than one century: by the year 711, or only eighty years after the Prophet's death, Muslims were on the borders of France in the far West, and they were entering India to the East . . . Islam was termed the 'middling nation' (al-Qur'ān, 2: 143), the community which was to follow the Happy Medium in all matters, that aim of both Greek and Islamic society, and of any moderate one on earth.

BASIC PURPOSE

The Muslim's basic purpose in life is to worship God in His Oneness, *bi-at-Tawḥīd,* and not through the trinity of the Christians, nor the duality and idolatry of other religions. The Muslim works through the power of God's transcendence; in the words of King Arthur, as this Celtic leader was preparing to enter the next world, he admonished his Knights of the Round Table:

> For what are men better than sheep or goats, that nourish a blind life within the brain, if, knowing God, they lift not hands in prayer both for themselves and those that call them friend?

God is thus Transcendent, *al-Ghanī* as the Qur'ān teaches us; while mere man is only 'rich' or 'wealthy' when this same adjective is applied to him. Divine service or worship means giving 'worth' or value to what we respect and revere. We Muslims know God; we meet Him five times a day at least, and while we are on our knees before Him.

Today our New World is helping to lift the dead hand which opposed these concepts, and to spread the universal message of Islam. If we all are willing to listen, then we may clear up some of the misunderstanding which has hindered Western appreciation of Middle Eastern ethics and values, especially since Islam itself is now pushing into the cities of North America, Great Britain and continental Europe.

THE SPIRIT OF ISLAMIC CIVILIZATION

'Read!' our Prophet was told at the beginning of Chapter 96 (al-'Alaq), which bears this simple title and thus sets an early standard for Islamic society. Islam demanded from its very inception a fully literate tradition. Human records must be preserved if civilization is to function satisfactorily. We call this need statistics, which form the basis for economics and sociology, and especially for taxation and planning. Our great preoccupation as Muslims has thus always been with the matter or substance of civilized living, so that we can attain both spiritual and intellectual values, and thereby function usefully within our society.

What is civilization? At first Islam seemed to have started in a cultural backwater, almost a vacuum; but immediately, within the first decade of the Prophet's passing, it became a focus for cultural energy within the civilized world.

The Islamic way of viewing these values or standards is different. In the first place, it is based upon a clear vision of the world and the Deity which is Responsible for its creation and existence. The Arabic word for 'religion' is dīn, which means something we 'owe' to God, much like the Latin concept of religio meaning something 'binding (us) back' to God. Similarly the word for 'standard' is furqān which gives the title to Chapter 25 (Al-Furqān) in the Qur'ān. Our three capital or mortal sins are designed to ensure the pure worship of God Alone; these are:

1. Kufr, which means 'disbelief' as well as 'ingratitude'; while a kāfir, which is the present participle of the same root, is the ungrateful pagan or atheist who refuses to concede that God has any role within His creation;
2. Shirk or 'association', which means giving God a partner of any

sort, so that we no longer trust in Him Alone. Christian translators of the Qur'ān often call this 'polytheism' or 'idolatry', hoping thereby to divert criticism from themselves, although the trinity can be considered a variation on this theme, as can the dualism of the ancient Persians, or the cruder forms of paganism;

3. *Ṭughyān* or 'arrogation', which is the sin of refusing to trust in God implicitly, and acting in a tyrannous or bullying manner. When water, for instance, is arrogant, it overflows and floods us out, as happened in the case of Noah (al-Qur'ān, 69: 11).

The Muslim's reaction to these concepts must be reinforced with practice, with the liturgy or ritual that develops with any religion. In Islam we call this underpinning of our faith the Five Pillars, which are: (1) Our belief or creed; (2) Prayer, which sustains daily practice; (3) Fasting; (4) the Welfare Tax which redistributes wealth within society; and finally (5) the Pilgrimage to Makka, when we have the means to do so, and not leave our families in want. These practices are summed up in the great hymn to Light in the chapter of that same name; note the eloquence of the Qur'ān which has convinced millions of Muslims through fourteen glorious centuries:

God is the Light of Heaven and Earth!
His light may be compared to a niche in which there is a lamp; the lamp is in a glass; the glass is just as if it were a glittering star kindled from a blessed olive tree (which is) neither Eastern nor Western, whose oil will almost glow though fire has never touched it. Light upon light, God guides anyone He wishes to His light.
God sets up parables for mankind;
God is Aware of everything!

There are houses God has permitted to be built where His name is mentioned; in them He is glorified morning and evening by men whom neither business nor trading distract from remembering God, keeping up prayer, and paying the welfare tax. They fear a day when their hearts and eyesight will feel overcome unless God rewards them for the finest things they may have done, and gives them even more out of His bounty.
God provides for anyone He wishes without any reckoning! Those who disbelieve (will find) their deeds are like a mirage on a desert: the thirsty man will reckon it is water till as he comes up to it, he finds it is nothing. Yet he finds God (stands) beside him and he must render Him his account; God is Prompt in reckoning!

Or like darkness on the unfathomed sea;
one wave covers up another wave over which (hang) clouds;
layers of darkness, one above the other!
When he stretches out his hand he can scarcely see it.
Anyone to whom God does not grant light will have no light!

(al-Qur'ān, 24: 35-40).

Thus Islam sets up its value system plainly concerning our necessity to think clearly about the Deity, and to worship Him sincerely. Only after we accomplish this, and establish His pure worship, do we consider the other sins or crimes which might be committed against society or our fellow men, such as murder, theft, lying, slander, adultery, etc. Of the big three disbeliefs, association and arrogation are much more serious, since they strike directly at basic belief and one's clear vision of God Alone.

SOCIAL RESPONSIBILITY

Thus we are faced with social responsibility. Everyone has obligations to his own family, and we also have them towards society. Individual responsibility here becomes clear, since the commanding presence of God Alone makes each one of us acutely aware of his duty throughout the world. The welfare tax redistributes wealth among the poor and needy so that society can function in a just manner. Muḥammad (peace be upon him) was an orphan, and so he knew from his childhood how necessary some form of public charity was, and is. Parenthood is a serious obligation and must be assumed in a responsible manner too. Sections on moral behaviour are traced out in like manner. Good manners in both private and public are likewise considered to be important. However no duty is overwhelming: 'God only assigns a soul something it can cope with; it is credited with whatever it has earned, while it is debited with whatever it has brought upon itself.' (al-Qur'ān, 2: 286). What one might call our Major Commandments or our responsibilities are well set forth:

SAY: 'Come close, I will list what your Lord has forbidden you:

I   Do not associate anything with Him:

II   And (show) kindness towards both (your) parents.

III   Do not kill your children because of poverty; We shall provide for you as well as for them.

IV   Do not indulge in shocking acts which you may practise openly or keep secret.

V   Do not kill any person whom God has forbidden except through
     (due process of) law. He has instructed you with this so that you
     may use your reason.

VI   Do not approach an orphan's estate before he comes of age
     except to improve it.

VII Give full measure and weight in all fairness. We do not assign
     any person to do more than he can cope with.

VIII Whenever you speak, be just even though it concerns a close
     relative.

IX   Fulfil God's agreement. Thus has He instructed you so that you
     may bear it in mind.

X   This is My Straight Road, so follow it and do not follow paths
     which will separate you from His path. Thus has He instructed
     you so that you may heed.

     (al-Qur'ān, 6: 151-153).

Economic life must likewise be taken care of in an ethical fashion,
especially matters like usury or taking interest, which has always led to
abuse. The law and the state must thus be able to function on a basis of
justice for everyone. The ancient nation of Thamūd was warned that
even a thirsty camel has its drinking rights (al-Qur'ān, 54: 23-30). Each
nation is responsible for what it does (al-Qur'ān, 2: 134); the matter of
collective responsibility is stated in the verse: 'God is no one to alter any
favour He has granted any folk until they alter what they themselves
have.' (al-Qur'ān, 8: 53 & 13: 11). The principle of collective defence
has been bewildering to those people who have attacked an Islamic
community: Islam does not preach the idealistic doctrine of the Other
Cheek, but instead prefers self-defence tempered with compassion and
an attempt at reconciliation, as we learn in the following passage:

Who is finer in speech than someone who appeals to God, acts
honourably and says: 'I am a Muslim.'?

A good deed and an evil deed are not alike: repay (evil) with
something that is finer, and notice how someone who is separated
from you by enmity will become a bosom friend!

Yet only those who discipline themselves will attain it; only the
very luckiest will achieve it!

Nevertheless if some impulse from Satan should prompt you,
seek refuge with God: He is the Alert, Aware! (al-Qur'ān, 41:
33-36).

On an individual level, responsible action is encouraged: positive behaviour is preferred over negative or destructive conduct; we are promised: 'Anyone who comes with a fine deed will have ten more like it, while anyone who comes with an evil deed will only be rewarded with its like; they will not be harmed.' (al-Qur'ān, 6: 161). Thus we are encouraged to be constructive in our conduct; with our close relatives first of all, with women, children and especially orphans, and with the poor and feebleminded, and the wayfarer, all of whom need care and compassion. The hospitality of Muslim countries has become proverbial: 'They offer food to the needy, the orphan and the captive out of love for Him: "We are only feeding you for God's sake. We want no reward from you nor any thanks." ' (al-Qur'ān, 76: 8-9).

Much of this attitude was worked out in its details by following the example of Prophetic practice or *Sunnah* as it is called in Arabic. The science of *Ḥadīth* or 'Traditions' was established for this purpose, and its rigorous application is one of the glories of historical method which was developed in a painstaking fashion by Muslim scholars aiming at ascertaining the truth of past events and statements. Through all of this the personality of the Prophet can be seen working with the intense sincerity which forms the basis for our *Ḥadīth* or Islamic traditions.

Ours is a proud tradition which has bound the middle belt of countries that stretch from Morocco through Africa and southern Asia into Indonesia together into a cultural whole. Despite the inroads of the West, the Islamic world is once more arising to assert itself as the 'Middling Community' on the present world scene. Its ethics and its expression in art and society have given it a dignity which even the French were unable to destroy in North Africa, although the Spanish did this in Granada and Valencia. Here however is the message which the religion of Islam brings to the present century as the Western world gropes for its values, and seeks once more for what man should worship or give worth to. Islam steps forward with clear values to guide us to renewed social responsibility.

7

*The Islamic Concept of Worship**

Muṣṭafā Aḥmad al-Zarqā

WORSHIP, according to Islam, is a means for the purification of man's soul and his practical life.

The basis of *'ibādah* (worship) is the fact that human beings are creatures and thus bond-servants of God, their Creator and their Lord, to Whom they are destined to return. Thus Man's turning towards God, in intimate communion, reverence, and in the spirit of devotion and humble submission, is termed *'ibādah.*

Worship is an indispensable part of all religions, including the idolatrous ones. It is motivated, however, in each religion by different objectives, assumes different forms and is performed under a different set of rules.

In some religions worship is a means to develop in man the attitude of asceticism and isolation from life. In these religions it seeks to develop a mentality which anathematizes the enjoyment of the pleasures of this world.

Then, there are other religions which consecrate certain places for the sake of worship and prohibit its performance at any other place. There are also religions which are of the view that worship can be performed only under the leadership of a particular class of people — the ordained priests. People may, therefore, perform worship under the leadership of priests and only at the places consecrated for it. Thus the nature as well as the forms of worship differ from one religion to the other.

* This article was originally published in *al-Muslimūn,* Beirut. Translated from Arabic by Dr. Zafar Isḥaq Ansari.

As for Islam, its conception of worship is related to its fundamental view that the true foundations of a good life are soundness of belief and thinking, purity of soul, and righteousness of action.

Through belief in the unity of God, Who is invested with all the attributes of perfection, Islam seeks to purge human intellect of the filth of idolatry and superstitious fancies. In fact, polytheism and idolatry which are opposed by Islam degrade man to a level which is incompatible with his dignity. Islam fights against idolatry and polytheism in whichever forms and to whatever extent they might be found. In its concern to eradicate idolatry Islam takes notice even of the imperceptible forms of idolatry. It takes notice even of those beliefs and practices which do not appear to their adherents as tainted with idolatry. One of the manifestations of this concern is that Islam does not permit the performance of ritual prayer (ṣalāt) in front of a tomb, nor does it permit man to swear in the name of anyone except God. All this is owing to the uncompromising hostility of Islam to idolatry When Caliph 'Umar saw that people had begun to sanctify the tree beneath which the Companions of the Holy Prophet (peace be upon him) had pledged to lay down their lives in the way of God on the occasion of Hudaybiyah, he feared that its sanctification might corrupt the beliefs of the people. He, therefore, had it cut down. By destroying everything which might blur the distinction between the creature and the Creator, Islam brought man out of the darkness of superstition and ignorance to the full daylight of realities.

Coming back to 'worship' in Islam, it serves as a means to purge man's soul and his practical life of sin and wickedness. It has been so regulated as to suffice for the purpose of this purification, provided it is performed in earnest and if sufficient care is taken to preserve its true spirit.

DISTINGUISHING FEATURES

The characteristic features of worship as propounded by Islam may be stated as the following:

(a) Freedom from Intermediaries.

First of all, Islam has liberated 'worship' from the bondage of intermediaries between man and his Creator. Islam seeks to create a direct link between man and his Lord, thus rendering the intercession of intermediaries unnecessary.

Religious scholars in Islam, it may be pointed out, are neither intermediaries between man and God nor are they considered to be entitled to accept or reject acts of worship on behalf of God. Instead, they are equal to ordinary human beings in the sight of God. Rather, they have been burdened with the additional duty of imparting knowledge to those who lack knowledge. They will be deemed guilty if they hold it back from the seekers after knowledge. In other words, the Islamic *Shari'ah* does not impose the domination of religious scholars on the rest of the people. The function of these scholars is merely to guide people in the right direction. This is amply borne out by what Allah said to the Holy Prophet:

'Remind them, for you are but a remembrancer; you are not at all a warder over them.' (al-Qur'ān, 88: 21-22).

The Prophet (peace be on him) also addressed the following words to his own daughter Fāṭimah, which show that all human beings stand on a footing of complete equality before God:

'O Fātimah, daughter of Muḥammad:
I shall be of no help to you before Allah.'

(b) *Not Confined to Specific Places.*

Secondly, Islam has not only liberated man's *'ibādah* from the bondage of intermediaries; it has also liberated it from confinement to specific places. Islam regards every place — whether it is one's dwelling place, the back of an animal, the board of a vessel on the surface of the sea, or a mosque specifically built for worship — as pure enough for the performance of worship. Wherever a man might be, he can turn towards his Lord and enter into communion with Him. The Holy Prophet has expressed this idea beautifully:

'The (whole of the) earth has been
rendered for me a mosque: pure and clean.'

(c) *All-Embracing View.*

Thirdly, Islam has also considerably widened the scope of worship. In Islam, worship is not confined to specified prayers and litanies which are to be performed on particular occasions. Rather, Islam considers every virtuous action which has been sincerely performed and with the view to carry out the commandments of God and in order to seek His Pleasure, an act of worship for which man will be rewarded. The fact is that even eating, drinking, sleeping and enjoyment of innocent recreation, even those worldly actions which satisfy man's physical needs and even yield sensuous pleasures, become acts of worship provided they are performed with true religious motives. Yes, even those acts become acts of worship if the intention underlying them is to comply with the will of God: that is, if one tries to satisfy one's needs within legitimate means so as to keep oneself in check against indulging in things which are prohibited. It is also an act of worship to try to strengthen one's body by providing it with its due of nourishment and sleep; by making it undertake exertion as well as giving it rest and recreation so as to enable it to shoulder the responsibilities which have been placed on man by God. In fact, if one does all that with the above-mentioned intention, one's action would be in harmony with the following saying of the Holy Prophet (peace be upon him): 'A believer who is possessed of strength is better and dearer to God than a believer who is weak.' In short, it is simply by purification of motives that the actions which are part of worldly life become acts of devotion and worship.

Thus, it is possible that a man should advance spiritually even while he is fully enjoying the pleasures of worldly life. The reason is that during all this enjoyment his heart will be in communion with God by virtue of the purity of his intentions, and owing to his having yoked himself completely to the service of God. It will enable him to remain perpetually in the state of submission, obedience and devotion to God — even during his working pursuits — and this is the very essence of worship.

For Islam, unlike other religions, does not anathematize gratification of man's instinctive bodily appetites.

Islam does not even consider abstention from the satisfaction of these desires to be in any way an act of greater piety and virtue than satisfying them. Islam wants man to enjoy the pleasures and good things of life provided he does not transgress the limits of legitimacy or the rights of others, nor trample upon moral excellence, nor injure the larger interests of society.

There is a profound wisdom and an important reason for this extension of the scope of worship. The reason is that Islam wants man's heart to remain in perpetual communion with his Lord. Islam also wants that man should observe ceaseless vigilance over his desires so that his life may become a source of his welfare in the life to come as the Qur'ān says: 'Seek the abode of the hereafter in that which Allah has given to you and neglect not your portion of the world.' (al-Qur'ān, 28: 77). Now, when a person knows that even his enjoyments and pleasures can become acts of worship merely by virtue of purity of intention and motive, it becomes easy for him to render obedience to God continually and to direct all his attention in seeking Divine pleasure. For he knows well that this devotion to God does not necessarily mean abandonment of worldly life, and misery and wretchedness.

What does good intention lead to? It will prevent man from forgetting God because of excessive self-indulgence. The Holy Prophet has said that (even) when a person affectionately puts a piece of food in the mouth of his wife in order to strengthen bonds of matrimonial love, he is rewarded for it. This is understandable for he is trying to fulfil the purpose of living together with love and affection, the purpose which, as the Qur'ān says is the *raison d'etre* of family life.

> 'And of His signs is this: He created for you your partners that you might find rest in them and He ordained between you love and mercy.' (al-Qur'ān, 30: 21).

INTENTIONS AND MOTIVES

It is because of this basis that Muslim jurists and scholars have proclaimed that good intention changes acts of habit (*ʿādah*) into acts of worship (*ʿibādah*). Good intention creates a world of difference in human life. It is owing to the absence of purity of intention that there are people who eat and drink and satisfy their animal desires and while so doing they simply live on the same plane as the animals do. The reason for this is that their actions are actuated by no other motive than the gratification of animal desires. On the contrary there are also people who are, apparently, similar to the aforementioned people in so far as they also satisfy their desires and enjoy the pleasures of life. Nevertheless, thanks to the noble intention which motivates their actions, even their physical self-fulfilment becomes an act of worship for which they merit reward. The reason is that the motive behind all their actions is to live in compliance with the Will of God. Their sublimity of motive becomes manifest in their conduct in day-to-day life in so far as it reflects the fact that they distinguish between good and evil.

On the contrary, those whose lives are shorn of good intentions are liable to be overwhelmed by their lusts and are likely to slide into a life of sin and moral decadence. On the contrary, the purity of intention and high thinking are likely, with regard to people of the second category, to stand in the way of their slipping into degradation. And thanks to the positive attitude of Islam towards life, all this is ensured without depriving man of a wholesome enjoyment of life. The real basis of this difference lies in the fact that while the one is always mindful of God and remembers Him, the other is altogether negligent. It is this that makes the former a pious, worshipful being, and the latter a heedless, self-indulgent animal. It is for the people of this kind that the Holy Qur'ān has said: '. . . Those who disbelieve, take their comfort in this life and eat even as the cattle eat, and the Fire is their habitation.' (al-Qur'ān, 47: 12).

Then, what a great loss indeed do people suffer by not rectifying their orientation of life and purifying their intentions. For it is this alone which transforms even their pursuits of pleasure and enjoyment into acts of worship. What a tragedy that people spoil the prospects of their eternal life although they could have been attained so easily, without necessarily losing their share in this world.

This is the Islamic philosophy of worship. Without saying 'no' to any of his legitimate physical needs and desires, Islam seeks to elevate humanity to a place which befits its dignity and status.

POSITION OF SPECIFIC RITUALS

The wide jurisdiction of worship — i.e. its incorporation of all acts which are performed with the intention of complying with the Will of God, including fulfilment of legitimate pleasures, is sometimes utilized as a pretext to support the erroneous view that the obligatory rituals of worship such as prayers, fasting, zakāt and pilgrimage can be dispensed with; or that they are not very important. The truth, however, is quite contrary to this. In Islam, they are the chief means for strengthening man's attachment with God. Thus absolutely misconceived is the view of those who are given to laxity in religious matters with regard to the obligatory acts of worship, and imagine that true faith does not consist of ṣalāt (prayers) and ṣawm (fasting); that the basis of true faith is merely purity of heart, goodness of intention and soundness of conduct. This constitutes misrepresentation of Islamic teachings.

So far as the intention to live a life of righteousness is concerned, it does not lend itself to external observation. Hence the intention to do good alone does not mark off the true men of faith from the rest. Religion, after all, has an external aspect in the same way as it has an internal aspect.

This attitude of deliberate disregard of ritual obligations is destructive of the very foundations of religion. For, were that viewpoint to be adopted, everyone, even those who are in fact opposed to religion, could claim to be the devoutest of all worshippers! The prayers and all other prescribed forms of worship for that matter, serve to distinguish the ones who do really have faith and wish sincerely to serve God from those who are content with lip-service. So important indeed is prayer that the Prophet has said: *'Salāt* (prayer) is the pillar of the Islamic religion and whosoever abandons it, demolishes the very pillar of religion.'

A PRACTICAL IDEAL

The real purpose of Islam in declaring that *'ibādah* embraces the total life of man is to make religious faith play a practical and effective role in reforming human life, in developing in man an attitude of dignified patience and fortitude in the face of hardships and difficulties and in creating in him the urge to strive for the prevalence of good and extirpation of evil.

All this makes it amply evident that Islam, the standard-bearer of the above-stated concepts and ideals, is opposed to those defeatist and isolationist philosophies which scholars have termed as asceticism. This is that erroneous kind of asceticism which is based on world-renunciation, on resignation from the resources of life, on withdrawal from the life of action and struggle, on sheer stagnation and decadence. These things have nothing to do with Islam. Rather, they are the symbols of defeatism and escape from the struggle of life. For life requires strength, material resources and active habits. The role of Islam in the struggle of life is a positive one. It is through this attitude that Islam ensures the channelization of man's powers and resources in such a manner as to lead eventually to general good. The Islamic system of worship is a means to ensure this soundness of orientation.

An event may be narrated here to illustrate the Islamic attitude to the question under discussion, and to disabuse minds of wrong notions of spiritual life. It is reported that 'Ā'ishah, the mother of the faithful, once saw a person walking with his body stooped down and his back bent with weakness, appearing as if he were not fully alive, attracting thereby the glances of those around him. She inquired about him and was informed that he was a saintly person. 'Ā'ishah denounced this kind of saintliness and said: ' 'Umar son of Khattāb, was the saintliest of people. But when he said something, he made himself heard; when he walked, he walked fast; and when he beat, his beating caused pain.'

8

*Islamic Approach to Social Justice**

by Syed Qutb

WE cannot comprehend the nature of social justice in Islam until we have first studied the Islamic concept of Divinity, the universe, life and humanity. For, social justice is only a branch of that great principle on which all Islamic teachings are based.

Now the faith of Islam which undertakes the organization of the whole of human life does not treat the different aspects of that life at random, nor does it consider them as unrelated parts. That is to say Islam has a perfect, comprehensive concept of Divinity, of the universe, of life and humanity — a concept on which are based all the myriad details; and from which are drawn the basis of its laws and juridical thought, its modes of worship and patterns for social behaviour. All these matters are based on this fundamental and all-embracing concept, so that for every situation we need not falter in the darkness to seek its solution, nor is every problem required to be dealt with in isolation from all other problems. The scheme of life envisaged by Islam is a complete whole that revolves round the central concept of Divinity, i.e. *Tawḥīd.*

A knowledge of this universal Islamic concept will enable the student to understand the principles and laws of Islam and to relate the

---

* This article is taken from the author's *al-'Adālah al-ijtimā 'īyah fī'l-Islām* (seventh edition). This is a new translation by Mi'rāj Muhammad, published in *The Criterion,* vol. 3, No. 4, July-August, 1968. The translator has not modified the style of the original which represents one of the finest literary styles of the Arabic language. Some of the Western readers may not be familiar with this style. We would request them to concentrate more on the substance of the argument. Editor.

particulars to the fundamental rules. This will also help him study its features and directions with interest and with depth of perception. He will thus be able to see that this concept is both coherent and comprehensive, and that it is a whole which cannot be divided. He will also observe that its application to human life cannot bear fruit unless it is applied as a whole and not in pieces.

So the best method of studying Islam is to start by understanding its all-embracing concept of Divinity, the universe, life and humanity before going on to study its views on politics or economics or the relationship between society and man. For such questions as these are in fact based on that comprehensive concept and they cannot be truly and deeply understood except in its light.

Now the true Islamic concept is not to be sought in Ibn Sīna (Avicenna) or Ibn Rushd (Averroes) or al-Fārābī or the like who are known as 'the philosophers of Islam'; for their philosophy is no more than a shadow of the Greek philosophy which is in its essence foreign to the spirit of Islam. The faith of Islam has its own native, perfect concept which is to be sought in its own authentic sources: The Qur'ān and the Traditions, and in the life of its Prophet (upon whom be the blessings and the peace of God). These sources are sufficient for every student who wants to obtain a deep understanding of the universal Islamic concept on which are based all the teachings and the laws of Islam.

FOUNDATIONS OF SOCIAL JUSTICE

Islam as a faith has dealt with the nature of the relation between the Creator and His creation, the nature of man's relation to the universe and to life in general in this world, and of man's relation to his own self. It has also discussed the nature of the relationship of individual to society and to state, and of the relation between different human societies, and of the relation between one nation and another. Islam has based all these relations on the one universal, comprehensive concept which is always kept in view in the formulation of all the particular rules.

The detailed study of this concept is beyond the scope of this treatise; it rather forms the subject of another work of the author, 'The Characteristics of the Islamic Concept and its Fundamentals'.[1] So here we shall merely indicate the main outlines of the general scheme, in order to facilitate our study of social justice in Islam.

1. See Muhammad Quṭb.*Khaṣā' is al-Taṣawwur al-Islāmī wa Muqawwimātuh,* Cairo, 1965.

Humanity remained for long ages devoid of a comprehensive concept of the Creator and His creation, or of the universe, life and mankind.

Whenever a messenger brought a certain form (of religion) from God to mankind a few of them accepted it, and a great majority of them turned away from it. Then humanity as a whole abandoned the true religion and returned to misleading, distorted concepts of Ignorance. Then came Islam with the most perfect concept and the most comprehensive *Sharī'ah* (legal system) both of which were connected with each other. Islam established a realistic way of life in which the concept and the *Sharī'ah* both are represented in a practical form.

The relation between the Creator and His creation (i.e. the universe, life and mankind) is to be found in the power of the Word, the Active Will from which all creation came:

'His command, when He desires a thing, is to say to it "Be", and it is.' (al-Qur'ān, 36: 82).

So there is no intermediary in the form of power or matter between the Creator and His creation. It is from His absolute will that all existing things directly proceed; and it is by that absolute Will that all things are sustained, organized and conducted:

'He conducts the affairs, He distinguishes the signs . . .' (al-Qur'ān, 13: 2).

'It is not for the sun to overtake the moon, nor does the night outstrip the day. They float each in an orbit.' (al-Qur'ān, 36: 40).

'Blessed be He in whose hand is the Kingdom, and He is powerful over everything.' (al-Qur'ān, 67: 1).

So all creation, issuing as it does from one absolute Will, forms a perfect unity in which each individual part is in harmonious order with the remainder. And thus, too, every form of existence is based on a wisdom which agrees with this perfect order:

'. . . And He created everything, then He ordained for it a measure.' (al-Qur'ān, 25: 2).

'Surely We have created everything in measure.' (al-Qur'ān, 54: 49).

'. . . Who created seven heavens in harmony. You do not see in the creation of the Beneficient any incongruity. Return your gaze; do you see any rifts? Then return your gaze again, and again your gaze will come back to you dazzled, aweary.' (al-Qur'ān, 67: 34).

'God is He who sends the winds, that stir up clouds, and He spreads them in the sky how He will, and shatters them; then you see the rain coming forth from them, and when He makes it to fall on whomsoever of His servants He will, lo, they rejoice . . .' (al-Qur'ān, 30: 48).

All these Qur'ānic verses make it obvious that every existing being is based on a wisdom which is in perfect harmony with the purpose of creation; and that the Will from which all creation first proceeds, and by which it is then continually sustained and directed, makes every existing being harmonious with and universally advantageous to all creation.

Having directly proceeded from a single, absolute, perfect Will, all creation is a unity which is perfect in all its parts, and harmonious in its nature, its organization and its directions. Because of these characteristics the whole creation is suitable for, helpful in, and conducive to, the existence of life in general, and to the existence of man, the highest form of life, in particular. So the universe cannot be hostile to life, or to man: nor can 'Nature' be held to be antagonistic to man, opposed to him, or striving against him. Being a creation of God, she is rather a friend whose aims are one with those of life and mankind. Nor is it a function of living beings to contend with Nature, for they have grown up in her bosom, and she and they together form a part of the universe which has proceeded from the single Will. Thus, basically man lives in a purely friendly environment, among the powers of a friendly universe. So God, when He created the earth, 'set therein firm mountains over it, and He blessed it, and He ordained therein its diverse sustenance.' [2] 'And He cast on the earth firm mountains, that it shake not with you . . .' [3] 'And the earth, He has set it down for all beings.' [4] 'It is He who made the earth submissive to you, so walk in its tracts, and eat of His provision.' [5] 'It is He who created for you all that is in the earth.' [6] Moreover, the heaven with its stars is a part of the universe which is perfect with all its parts, and everything that is in the heaven and in the earth is friendly, co-operative and harmonious with all the remaining parts. God says:

2. al-Qur'ān, 41: 10.
3. ibid., 16: 15.
4. ibid., 55: 10.
5. ibid., 67: 15.
6. ibid., 2: 29.

'Have We not made the earth a flat expanse and the mountains as pegs? And We have created you in pairs, and have appointed your sleep for a rest; and We have appointed the night for a garment, and have appointed the day for a livelihood. And We have built above you seven strong ones, and We have appointed a blazing lamp and have sent down out of the rain-clouds water cascading that We may bring forth thereby grain and vegetation, and gardens luxuriant.' (al-Qur'ān, 78: 6-16).

The creed of Islam has thus established that God, the Nourisher of man, has created all these forces as friends and helpers of man. In order to gain the friendship of these forces it is necessary for man to study them, to make himself acquainted with them, and to co-operate with them. If any of these forces harms man, it is because he has not approached it properly and is ignorant of the law that governs it.

The Creator has, however, not left living beings and men to the friendly universe without giving them His direct attention and constant care, for His direct Will is constant throughout all the universe, constant, too, over its every individual existing being at all times. (God says:)

'God holds the heavens and the earth, lest they remove; and if they were to remove there is not one that could hold them after him.' (al-Qur'ān, 35: 41)

'No creature is there crawling on the earth, but its provision rests on God; He knows its habitation and its repository.' (al-Qur'ān, 11: 6).

'We indeed created man; and We know what his soul whispers within him, and We are nearer to him than his jugular vein.' (al-Qur'ān, 50: 16).

'Your Lord has said, "Call upon Me and I will answer you." ' (al-Qur'ān, 40: 60).

'. . . and slay not your children because of poverty; We provide for you and for them . . .' (al-Qur'ān, 6: 152).

Now, since the unified universe has emanated from a single Will; because man is himself a part of the Universe, co-operative with and harmonious to all the other parts; and because individuals are as atoms, co-operative with and harmonious to the world; therefore all of these are bound to be co-operative with and harmonious to one another. Hence the Islamic concept that humanity is an essential unity; its parts separate only to join in, they vary from one another only to create a harmony and they adopt different ways merely to help one another in the end. For thus and only thus can man be able to co-operate with the unified creation: 'O mankind, We have created you male and female, and have made you races and tribes, that you may know one another.' (al-Qur'ān, 49: 13).

There can be no sound system in human life until this co-operation and harmony have taken place in the manner that God has ordained. Its realization is necessary for the welfare of all humanity, so that forceful efforts may be made to bring back those who have deviated from the right path: 'The only reward of those who wage war against God and His Messenger, and strive after corruption in the land, is that they shall be killed, or crucified, or their hands and feet shall alternately be cut off, or they shall be banished from the land.'[7] 'If two parties of the Believers fight, make peace between them; then, if one of them oppresses the other, fight the oppressing one till it returns to God's commandment. If it returns, make peace between them equitably, and be just.'[8] 'And if God had not repelled some men by others, the earth would have been corrupted.'[9]

Accordingly, the fundamental thing is this co-operation, mutual understanding, acquaintance and harmony on the lines set by the Divine law, and whoever deviates from this principle must be brought back to it. For the Divine law is worthier to be followed than the desires of individuals and of societies. Such mutual responsibility among all is in keeping with the purpose of the unified universe and the aims of its Creator.

Now when we come to consider man as a race and as an individual, we fiwd him a perfect unity; man's faculties which are so diverse in appearance are essentially one in purpose. In this respect man is comparable to the universe in its entirety, since its power too is a unity, though diverse in appearance.

Man lived for ages without arriving at any comprehensive concept of human and universal powers. He continued to differentiate between spiritual and material powers, he denied one of these in order to establish the other, or he admitted the existence of both in a state of opposition and antagonism. He based all his sciences on the presumption

7. al-Qur'ān, 5: 33.
8. Ibid, 48: 9.
9. ibid., 2: 251.

that there was a basic conflict between these two types of power, and that the superiority of one depended on belittling the other. He held that such superiority on the one side and inferiority on the other was inevitable, because in his opinion such conflict was inherent in the nature of the universe and man.

Christianity — the form which the Church and the Holy Synods gave to it — is one of the clearest examples of this conflict in man. And in this respect it agrees to some extent with Hinduism and Buddhism, though the latter two religions differ from each other on a number of essentials. For, according to them, the salvation of the soul is to be gained by humiliating the body, by tormenting it, or even by annihilating it, or at the least by neglecting it and abstaining from its enjoyments.

In the distorted (creed of) Christianity and in other similar faiths this is the cardinal principle on which are based their doctrines on life and its enjoyment, on the duties of the individual on the one hand and of society on the other, and on man and the different powers and abilities which exist in his nature.

Thus the conflict between the two types of power continued, and man remained torn by it. He continued to be perplexed, and failed to arrive at a decision. Then came Islam which brought with it a perfect, coherent theory in which there was neither any crookedness nor any confusion, neither any contradiction nor any conflict. Islam came to unify all powers and abilities, to fuse together spiritual aspirations and bodily desires, and to harmonize their directions, and thus to create a comprehensive unity in the universe, life and man. Its aim was to unite earth and Heaven in the system of this world, to join the present world and the Hereafter in the doctrines of the faith; to link spirit and body in the person of man; to correlate worship and work in the system of life. It sought to bring all these into one path — the path which led to God. It aimed at subjecting all these to one authority — the authority of God.

The universe is, therefore, a unity, composed of things which are visible and can be perceived, and of things which are invisible and imperceptible. Life is, likewise, a unity, consisting of material abilities and spiritual powers which can never be separated from each other as this will result in disorder and confusion. Similarly man is a unity composed of spiritual aspirations soaring towards Heaven, and of (material) desires which cling to the earth. No separation can be made between these two aspects of human nature, because there is no disunity between Heaven and earth, or between things perceptible and things imperceptible in the universe, and because in this religion (of Islam) there is no isolation between this world and that to come, or between daily life and worship, or between the creed and the law.

Beyond all this, there does exist one eternal, everlasting power, which has no beginning that can be known and no end that can be attributed to it. This power ultimately bears sway over the whole universe, life and mankind. It is the power of God.

As for the mortal human individual, he is capable of having himself connected with this eternal, everlasting Power which guides him in life, and from which he seeks help in his misfortunes. He can get in touch with this power when he is abroad in the world, busy in earning his livelihood, just as he comes in contact with it when he is in the mosque at prayer.

Similarly, the human individual can strive for the Hereafter, not only when he fasts and denies himself all kinds of pleasurable things, but also when he breaks his fast and enjoys all the good things of life — so long as he does either of these two things with his heart firmly directed towards God.

And thus the life of this world, with all its prayer and its work, all its enjoyments and its deprivations, is the only way to the next world, with its Heaven and its Hell, its punishment and its reward.

This is the true unity between various parts of the universe and its powers, between all the diverse potentialities of life, between man and his soul, between his actualities and his dreams. This is the unity which can establish a lasting harmony between the universe and life, between life and living beings, between society and the individuals, between man's spiritual aspirations and his bodily desires, and finally between the world and the faith, between the temporal and the spiritual.

This harmony is not established at the expense of the physical side of man, nor yet at the expense of the spiritual side, rather it gives freedom of action to both of them in order to unify their activities and direct them towards welfare, goodness and growth. Similarly this harmony is not established at the expense of the individual, or of society; nor to the advantage of one group and to the disadvantage of the other, nor in favour of one people over another. But each of these is held to have its own rights and its own responsibilities according to the principle of justice and equality. For the individual and society, the party and the community, the people and all other peoples — all are bound by one law which has but one aim: namely, that the freedom of action should be given to both the individual and society without any mutual conflict; and that the people, one and all, should work together for the growth and progress of human life, and for its orientation towards the Creator of life.

Islam, then, is a faith of the unity of all the powers of the universe; and beyond doubt it is a faith which stands for unity — the unity of God, the unity of all religions in the Divine Faith, and the unity of all the prophets in their preaching of this one Faith since the dawn of time:[10] 'Surely this community of yours is one community, and I am your Lord; so serve Me.'[11]

So also Islam stands for the unity of worship and social intercourse, of creed and law, of spiritual and material realities, of economic and spiritual values, of the present world and the world to come, of earth and Heaven. On this all-embracing unity are based all the laws and duties prescribed in Islam, all its instructions and restrictions, as well as its precepts for administering political and financial matters, and its teachings of the distribution of profits and liabilities, and on rights and responsibilities. In short, this fundamental principle of unity embraces all the details and particular rules of life.

When we have studied this comprehensiveness which is inherent in the nature of the Islamic theory of Divinity, the universe, life and humanity, we can easily understand the fundamental features and outlines of social justice in Islam.

THE SPIRIT OF ISLAMIC SOCIAL JUSTICE

For one thing, it is a comprehensive human justice embracing all sides and basic factors of human life. It is not merely a limited economic justice. It, therefore, deals with all aspects of life and its activities, even as it is concerned with the mind and attitude, with heart and conscience. The values with which this justice deals are not only economic values, nor are they merely material values in general; rather they are a mixture of these values and moral and spiritual values together.

The distorted version of Christianity looks at man only from the stand-point of his spiritual aspirations, and attempts to crush his bodily desires in order to give the reins to his aspirations. On the other hand, Communism looks at man only from the stand-point of his

10. See the chapter on *al-qissah fi'l-Qur'ān* (History in the Qur'ān) in the *al-Taṣwīr al-Fannī fi'l-Qur'ān* (Literary Artistry of the Qur'ān) by the present writer (Cairo, Dār al-Maʿārif, n.d., pp. 111-164).
11. al-Qur'ān, 21: 92).

material needs; it looks not only at humanity — but also at the whole creation and the universe — from a purely material point of view. But Islam looks at man as forming a unity whose spiritual aspirations cannot be separated from his bodily desires, and whose spiritual needs cannot be divorced from his material needs. It looks at the universe and at life with this all-embracing view which permits no separation or division. This is the point where the ways of Communism, Christianity and Islam diverge. This divergence is due to the fact that Islam is purely a divine religion, whereas in Christianity human distortions have crept in and Communism is purely a product of man's fantasy.

Secondly, in the Islamic view, life consists of established, well-defined forms of mutual love and respect, co-operation and mutual responsibility between Muslims in particular, and between all human beings in general. The same view of life is held by Christianity, but there these forms are not based on codified, well-defined, explicit laws, nor on the realities and facts of life. On the other hand in the Communist view, life is a continual strife and struggle between classes, a struggle which must end in one class overcoming the other; at which point the Communist dream is realized. This makes manifest that Christianity is the dream of an abstract world of ideas and imagination, a dream which is to be realized only in the Kingdom of Heaven; and that Islam is the perpetual dream of humanity, embodied in a reality which exists on earth; and that Communism is hatred of mankind harboured by a people.

These are, then, two main features — the absolute, just, and coherent unity, and the general, mutual responsibility of individuals and societies — by which is marked the concept of social justice in Islam which takes into consideration the basic elements of human nature, and does not, at the same time, disregard human abilities.

The Glorious Qur'ān says of man that 'surely he is violent in his love for benefit:'[12] his love for benefit for himself and for his belongings. It says, also, describing that greed which is in the nature of man that 'souls are prone to avarice,'[13] so it is always present in their minds. So also there occurs in the Qur'ān a wonderfully artistic description of this remarkable human trait: 'Say: "If you possessed the treasures of the Lord's mercy, yet would you hold them back for fear of expending; and man is ever niggardly." '[14] On the other hand the Qur'ān affirms that

12. al-Qur'ān, 100: 8.
13. ibid., 4: 128.
14. ibid., 17: 100.

the mercy of God (is so vast that it) embraces all things.[15] So by indicating the vastness of Divine mercy and that of human stinginess the Qur'ān shows the extent of avarice in the nature of man if he is left without discipline or instructions.

Accordingly, when Islam comes to lay down its rules and laws, its exhortations and instructions, it does not disregard that natural love for self-interest, nor does it neglect that deep natural avarice; it rather cures this sordid selfishness and avarice by instructions and laws, and charges man only to his capacity. At the same time Islam does not ignore the needs and the welfare of society, nor does it overlook the high ideals of life both in individuals and society in every age and among different peoples.

Islam affirms that, just as encroachments upon society by the cupidity and ambition of the individual are a kind of social oppression which is inconsistent with justice, similarly encroachments upon the nature and ability of the individual by society are also a kind of injustice. It is an injustice, not to the individual alone, but to the society also. For the evil effects of suppressing the activity of the individual by crushing his (natural) trends and propensities do not only result in the deprivation of that one individual of his due; but also results in precluding the whole society from availing itself of his maximum abilities. When the social system vouches for the rights of the community in the efforts and abilities of the individual, and lays down curbs and limitations on the freedom, the desires, and the ambitions of the individual, it should not, therefore, ignore the right of the individual concerning the freedom of action within the limits which safeguard the welfare of the community and of the individual himself, and which prevent his actions from coming in conflict with the high objectives of life. As such life is a matter of co-operation and mutual responsibility according to Islam, and not a constant warfare to be lived in a spirit of struggle and hostility. Likewise, it stands for the freedom of individual and collective abilities, and not for repression, deprivation and imprisonment. According to it, everything that is not legally forbidden is perfectly permissible; and a man is rewarded for his salutary deeds which he performed observing the boundaries set by the Divine law, and for seeking the pleasure of God alone, and which are conducive to the achievement of the high ideals of life that God approves of.

This breadth of vision in the Islamic view of life, together with the fact that it goes beyond merely economic values to those other values

15. ibid., 7: 156.

on which life depends — these things render the Islamic faith more capable of striking balance and equity in society, and of establishing justice in the whole of the human sphere. It also relieves Islam from the narrow interpretation of justice as understood by Communism. For justice, according to the Communist theory, is an equality in wages, in order to prevent economic disparity; but when this theory was faced with practical application, Communism found itself unable to establish this mechanical, arbitrary equality. On the other hand, justice in Islam is a human equality envisaging the adjustment of all values, of which the economic forms a part. To be precise, justice in Islam means equality in opportunity and freedom of talents which work within the limits that do not come into conflict with the high ideals of life.

Since values, talents and resources are manifold and inter-blended, and it is only in the light of the varied context that justice can be established, Islam does not want to impose a compulsory economic equality in the narrow literal sense of the term. This kind of equality is against nature, and is opposed to the basic fact that individuals are endowed with differing talents. This type of equality arrests the development of outstanding ability, and makes it equal to lesser ability; it prevents talented people from using their talents to their own advantage and to that of the community. Consequently, the community as well as entire humanity is deprived of the fruits of these talents.

It is of no avail to stick to the fallacy that the natural endowments are equal. For we may distort this fact in respect of mental and spiritual endowments (though there is no possibility of distorting this fact when practical life takes its course), but we cannot falsify the fact that some individuals are born with different natural endowments of health, perfection and potentiality. In fact, there is no possibility of establishing equality in respect of all abilities and endowments until a machine is not invented for casting them into one mould after the fashion of standardized products.

It is, therefore, foolish and useless to deny the existence of outstanding endowments of personality, intellect and spirit. This hardly needs a discussion. As such we must reckon with all these endowments, and to all of them we must give the opportunity to produce their maximum results. Then we should try to take from these results that which appears to be necessary for the welfare and benefit of society. On no account must we close the outlet for such endowments, or discourage them by making them equal with regard to lesser abilities. In no respect should we shackle such gifts, or hinder them from free action, thereby frittering them away and depriving of their fruits the community and the human race.

Islam does, of course, recognize the principle of equality in opportunity, and the principle of justice among all. It leaves the door open for achievement of pre-eminence through hard work. Then it establishes in the Muslim society values other than the economic. (God says:)

> 'Surely the noblest among you in the sight of God is the most godfearing of you.' (al-Qur'ān, 49: 13).
>
> 'God raises up in rank those of you who believe and have been given knowledge.' (al-Qur'ān, 58: 11).
>
> 'Wealth and children are an ornament of life of the world; but the abiding things, the deeds of righteousness, are better in thy Lord's sight for reward, and better in hope.' (al-Qur'ān, 18: 46).

From this it is apparent that there are values other than the merely economic on which Islam counts, and regards them as the real values. It is through these values that Islam aims at establishing balance in society despite the disparity in the financial resources of the individuals which is due to the reasonable differences in their struggle and endowments, and is not a result of adopting the means and methods prohibited in Islam.

Islam, then, does not prescribe a literal equality of wealth, because the acquisition of wealth depends on men's abilities, which are not uniform. Hence absolute justice demands that men's incomes and rewards should also vary, and that some have more than others — so long as human justice is upheld by the provision of equal opportunity for all. Thus status or upbringing, origin or race, or any kind of restriction which stifles enterprise should not stand in the way of any individual. Justice must also be upheld by the inclusion of other real values in the reckoning, and by the freeing of the human mind completely from the pressure of the purely economic values, and by the relegation of these to their true and reasonable place. Economic values must not be given an intrinsically high standing, such as they enjoy in those human societies which lack the perception of religious values, or which minimize their importance and assign supreme and fundamental value to wealth alone.

Islam refuses to give this value to wealth. It disdains to consider life in terms of a mouthful of bread, carnal desires, or a handful of money. Yet at the same time it prescribes a competence for every individual, and at times more than a competence. It prefers to provide this competence by means of individual property and through such enterprises as are conducive to that kind of economic system which recognizes private ownership, in order to remove the fear of destitution on the one hand, and to eliminate the tyranny of the authority which appropriates the sources of income on the other. At the same time Islam forbids that unbridled luxury which gives the reins to a scramble for lucre and carnal desires, and which results in creating gross disparity in the standards of living. Islam recognizes the claims of the poor upon the wealth of the rich, according to their needs, and to the same extent as is suitable for society; and thus guarantees its equivalence, balance and growth. As such Islam does not neglect any of the various aspects of life, material, intellectual, religious and worldly. It rather organizes them all, that they may be related together and thus furnish an all-embracing unity in which it will be difficult to neglect any one of its various harmonious, integral parts, and that this unity may harmonize with the unity of the great universe, and with that of life, and of all mankind.

9

---

*Woman in Islam**

Gamal A. Badawi

THE status of women in society is neither a new issue nor is it a fully
settled one. The position of Islam on this issue has been among the
subjects presented to the Western reader with the least objectivity.
This paper is intended to provide a brief and authentic exposition of
what Islam stands for in this regard. The teachings of Islam are based
essentially on the Qur'ān (God's revelation) and *Ḥadīth* (elaborations
by Prophet Muḥammad). The Qur'ān and *Ḥadīth,* properly and un-
biasedly understood, provide the basic source of authentication for
any position or view which is attributed to Islam.

The paper starts with a brief survey of the status of women in the
pre-Islamic era. It then focuses on these major questions:

What is the position of Islam regarding the status of woman in
society? How similar or different is that position from 'the spirit of the
time', which was dominant when Islam was revealed? How would this
compare with the 'rights' which were finally gained by woman in
recent decades?

One major objective of this paper is to provide a fair evaluation of
what Islam contributed towards the restoration of woman's dignity
and rights. In order to achieve this objective, it may be useful to review
briefly how women were treated in general in previous civilizations
and religions, especially those which preceded Islam (Pre-610 C.E.) [1]
Part of the information provided here, however, describes that status

* This chapter is taken from the author's booklet published by the Muslim
Students' Association of the United States and Canada, Gary, Indiana, U.S.A.
1. 'C.E.' throughout the paper stands for Christian Era (A.D.).

of woman as late as the nineteenth century, more than twelve centuries after Islam.

WOMAN IN OTHER CIVILIZATIONS

Describing the status of a Hindu woman, an authority on the subject states:

> In India, subjection was a cardinal principle. Day and night must women be held by their protectors in a state of dependence, says Manū. The rule of inheritance was agnatic, that is descent traced through males to the exclusion of females. [2]

In Hindu scriptures, the description of a good wife is as follows: 'a woman whose mind, speech and body are kept in subjection, acquires high renown in this world, and, in the next, the same abode with her husband.' [3]

In Athens, women were not better off than either the Indian or the Roman women.

'Athenian women were always minors, subject to some male — to their father, to their brother, or to some of their male kin.' [4]

Her consent in marriage was not generally thought to be necessary and 'she was obliged to submit to the wishes of her parents, and receive from them her husband and her lord, even though he were stranger to her.' [5]

A Roman wife was described by an historian as : 'a babe, a minor, a ward, a person incapable of doing or acting anything according to her own individual taste, a person continually under the tutelage and guardianship of her husband.' [6]

In the *Encyclopaedia Britannica,* we find a summary of the legal status of women in the Roman civilization: [7]

> In Roman Law a woman was even in historic times completely dependent. If married she and her property passed into the power of her husband . . . the wife was the purchased property of her husband and like a slave acquired only for his benefit. A woman could

2. *The Encyclopaedia Britannica,* 11th ed., 1911, Vol. 28, p. 782.
3. In Mace, David and Vera, *Marriage East and West,* Dolphin Books, Double-day and Co., Inc., N.Y., 1960.
4. Allen, E.A., *History of Civilization,* Vol. 3, p. 444.
5. Ibid., p. 443.
6. Ibid., p. 550.
7. *The Encyclopaedia Britannica,* 11th ed., 1911, op. cit., Vol. 28, p. 782.

not exercise any civil or public office . . . could not be a witness, surety, tutor, or curator; she could not adopt or be adopted, or make will or contract.

Among the Scandinavian races women were:

under the perpetual tutelage, whether married or unmarried. As late as the Code of Christian V, at the end of the 17th Century, it was enacted that if a woman married without the consent of her tutor he might have, if he wished, administration and usufruct of her goods during her life.[8]

According to the English Common Law:

. . . all real property which a wife held at the time of a marriage became a possession of her husband. He was entitled to the rent from the land and to any profit which might be made from operating the estate during the joint life of the spouses. As time passed, the English courts devised means to forbid a husband's transferring real property without the consent of his wife, but he still retained the right to manage it and to receive the money which it produced. As to a wife's personal property, the husband's power was complete. He had the right to spend it as he saw fit.[9]

Only by the late nineteenth century did the situation start to improve. 'By a series of acts starting with the Married Women's Property Act in 1870, amended in 1882 and 1887, married women achieved the right to own property and to enter contracts on a par with spinsters, widows, and divorcees.'[10] As late as the nineteenth century an authority in ancient law, Sir Henry Maine, wrote: 'No society which preserves any tincture of Christian institutions is likely to restore to married women the personal liberty conferred on them by the Middle Roman Law.'[11]

In his essay *The Subjection of Women*, John Stuart Mill wrote:

We are continually told that civilization and Christianity have restored to the woman her just rights. Meanwhile the wife is the actual bondservant of her husband; no less so, as far as the legal obligation goes, than slaves commonly so called.[12]

8. Ibid., p. 783.
9. *The Encyclopaedia Americana* (International Edition), Vol. 29, p. 108.
10. *The Encyclopaedia Britannica*, 1968, Vol. 23, p. 624.
11. Quoted in Mace, *Marriage: East and West*, op. cit., p. 81.
12. Ibid., pp. 82-83.

Before moving on to the Qur'ānic decrees concerning the status of woman, a few Biblical decrees may shed more light on the subject, thus providing a better basis for an impartial evaluation. In the Mosaic Law, the wife was betrothed. Explaining this concept, the *Encyclopaedia Biblica* states: 'To betroth a wife to oneself meant simply to acquire possession of her by payment of the purchase money; the betrothed is a girl for whom the purchase money has been paid.' [13] From the legal point of view, the consent of the girl was not necessary for the validation of her marriage. 'The girl's consent is unnecessary and the need for it is nowhere suggested in the Law.' [14]

As to the right of divorce, we read in the *Encyclopaedia Biblica*: 'The woman being man's property, his right to divorce her follows as a matter of course.' [15] The right to divorce was held only by man. 'In the Mosaic Law divorce was a privilege of the husband only . . .' [16]

The position of the Christian Church until recent centuries seems to have been influenced by both the Mosaic Law and by the streams of thought that were dominant in its contemporary cultures. In their book, *Marriage: East and West,* David and Vera Mace wrote: [17]

Let no one suppose, either, that our Christian heritage is free of such slighting judgements. It would be hard to find anywhere a collection of more degrading references to the female sex than the early Church Fathers provide. Lecky, the famous historian, speaks of 'These fierce incentives which form so conspicuous and so grotesque a portion of the writing of the Fathers . . . woman was represented as the door of hell, as the mother of all human ills. She should be ashamed at the very thought that she is a woman. She should live in continual penance on account of the curses she has brought upon the world. She should be ashamed of her dress, for it is the memorial of her fall. She should be especially ashamed of her beauty, for it is the most potent instrument of the devil.' One of the most scathing of these attacks on woman is that of Tertullian: 'Do you know that you are each an Eve? The sentence of God on this sex of yours lives in this age: the guilt must of necessity live too. You are the devil's gateway:

13. *Encyclopaedia Biblica,* 1902, Vol. 3, p. 2942.
14. Ibid., p. 2942.
15. Ibid., p. 2947.
16. *The Encyclopaedia Britannica,* 11th ed., *op. cit.,* p. 782. It should be noted here that such interpretations by religious institutions do not necessarily conform to what the Muslim believes to be the original version of all revealed religions, which is believed to be essentially the same throughout history.
17. D. and V. Mace, *Marriage East and West, op. cit.,* pp. 80-81.

you are the unsealer of that forbidden tree; you are the first deserters of the divine law; you are she who persuades him whom the devil was not valiant enough to attack. You destroyed so easily God's image, man. On account of your desert — that is death — even the Son of God had to die.' Not only did the church affirm the inferior status of woman, it deprived her of legal rights she had previously enjoyed.

WOMAN IN ISLAM

In the midst of the darkness that engulfed the world, the divine revelation echoed in the wide desert of Arabia with a fresh, noble and universal message to humanity[18]: 'O Mankind, keep your duty to your Lord who created you from a single soul and from it created its mate (of same kind) and from them twain has spread a multitude of men and women.' (al-Qur'ān, 4: 1).[19]

A scholar who pondered about this verse states: 'It is believed that there is no text, old or new, that deals with the humanity of the woman from all aspects in such an amazing brevity, eloquence, depth and originality as this divine decree.'[20]

Stressing this noble and natural conception, the Qur'ān states:

He (God) it is who did create you from a single soul and therefrom did create his mate, that he might dwell with her (in love) . . . (al-Qur'ān, 7: 189).

The Creator of heavens and earth: He has made for you pairs from among yourselves. (al-Qur'ān, 42: 11).

And God has given you mates of your own nature, and has given you from your mates, children and grandchildren, and has made provision of good things for you. Is it then in vanity that they believe and in the grace of God that they disbelieve? (al-Qur'ān, 16: 72).

The rest of this paper outlines the position of Islam regarding the status of woman in society from its various aspects — spiritually, socially, economically and politically

18. Al-Sibā'ī, M., Al-Mar'ah Bayna'l-Fiqh Wa'l-Qānūn, 2nd ed., 1966, 0. 20.

19. 'From it' here refers to the kind, i.e. 'from the same kind, or of like nature, God created its mate.' There is no trace in the Qur'ān to a parallel of the Biblical concept that Eve was created from one of Adam's ribs.' See Yūsuf 'Alī, The Holy Qur'ān, note No. 504.

20. Al-Khūlī, Al-Bahī, Min Usūs Qadiyyah al-Mar'ah, Al-Wa'iy Al-Islāmī, Ministry of Wakf, Kuwait, Vol. 3, No. 27, June 9, 1967, p. 17. Translated by the writer.

THE SPIRITUAL ASPECT

The Qur'ān provides clear-cut evidence that woman is completely equated with man in the sight of God in terms of her rights and responsibilities. The Qur'ān states:

> Every soul will be (held) in pledge for its deeds. (al-Qur'ān, 74: 38).

It also states:

> '. . . So their Lord accepted their prayers, (saying): I will not suffer to be lost the work of any of you whether male or female. You proceed one from another . . .' (al-Qur'ān, 3: 195).

> Whoever works righteousness, man or woman, and has faith, verily to him We give a new life that is good and pure, and We will bestow on such their reward according to the best of their actions. (al-Qur'ān, 16: 97, see also 4: 124).

Woman according to the Qur'ān is not blamed for Adam's first mistake. Both were jointly wrong in their disobedience to God, both repented, and both were forgiven. (al-Qur'ān, 2: 36-37; 7: 20-24). In one verse in fact (al-Qur'ān, 20: 121), Adam specifically, was blamed.

In terms of religious obligations, such as the Daily Prayers, Fasting, Poor-due and Pilgrimage, woman is no different from man. In some cases, indeed, woman has certain advantages over man. For example, the woman is exempted from the daily prayers and from fasting during her menstrual periods and forty days after childbirth. She is also exempted of fasting during her pregnancy and when she is nursing her baby if there is any threat to her health or her baby's. If the missed fasting is obligatory (during the month of Ramadān), she can make up for the missed days whenever she can. She does not have to make up for the missed prayers because of one of the above reasons. Women used to go to the mosque during the days of the Prophet and thereafter attendance at the Friday congregational prayers is optional for them while it is mandatory for men (on Friday):

This is clearly a tender touch of the Islamic teachings for they are considerate of the fact that a woman may be nursing her baby or caring for him, and thus may be unable to go out to the mosque at the time of the prayers. They also take into account the physiological and psychological changes associated with her natural female functions.

THE SOCIAL ASPECT

(a) *As a child and an adolescent.*

Despite the social acceptance of female infanticide among some Arabian tribes, the Qur'ān forbade this custom, and considered it a crime like any other murder.

'And when the female (infant) buried alive — is questioned, for what crime she was killed.' (al-Qur'ān, 81: 8-9).

Critcizing the attitudes of such parents who reject their female children, the Qur'ān states:

'When news is brought to one of them, of (the Birth of) a female (child), his face darkens and he is filled with inward grief! With shame does he hide himself from his people because of the bad news he has had! Shall he retain her on (sufferance) and contempt, or bury her in the dust? Ah! What an evil (choice) they decide on?' (al-Qur'ān, 16: 58-59).

Far from saving the girl's life so that she may later suffer injustice and inequality, Islam requires kind and just treatment for her. Among the sayings of Prophet Muḥammad (peace be upon him) in this regard are the following:

Whosoever has a daughter and he does not bury her alive, does not insult her, and does not favour his son over her, God will enter him into Paradise. (Ibn Ḥanbal, No. 1957).

Whosoever supports two daughters till they mature, he and I will come in the day of judgement as this (and he pointed with his two fingers).

A similar *Hadīth* deals in like manner with one who supports two sisters. (Ibn Ḥanbal, No. 2104).

The right of females to seek knowledge is not different from that of males. Prophet Muḥammad (peace be upon him) said: 'Seeking knowledge is mandatory for every Muslim.' (Al-Bayhaqī). Muslim as used here including both males and females.[21]

(b) *As a wife.*

The Qur'ān clearly indicates that marriage is sharing between the

21. Some less authentic versions add 'male and female'. The meaning, however, is sound etymologically even as it is consistent with the over-all nature of Islamic duties in applying equally to males and females unless special exemptions are specified.

two halves of the society, and that its objectives, beside perpetuating human life, are emotional wellbeing and spiritual harmony. Its bases are love and mercy.

Among the most impressive verses in the Qur'ān about marriage is the following:

'And among His signs is this: That He created mates for you from yourselves that you may find rest, peace of mind in them, and He ordained between you love and mercy. Lo, herein indeed are signs for people who reflect.' (al-Qur'ān, 30: 21).

According to Islamic Law, women cannot be forced to marry anyone without their consent.

Ibn 'Abbās reported that a girl came to the Messenger of God, Muḥammad (peace be upon him), and she reported that her father had forced her to marry without her consent. The Messenger of God gave her the choice (between accepting the marriage or invalidating it). (Ibn Ḥanbal No. 2469). In another version, the girl said: 'Actually I accept this marriage but I wanted to let women know that parents have no right (to force a husband on them).' (Ibn Mājah, No. 1873).

Besides all other provisions for her protection at the time of marriage, it was specifically decreed that woman has the full right to her *Mahr,* a marriage gift, which is presented to her by her husband and is included in the nuptial contract, and that such ownership does not transfer to her father or husband. The concept of *Mahr* in Islam is neither an actual or symbolic price for the woman, as was the case in certain cultures, but rather it is a gift symbolizing love and affection.

The rules for married life in Islam are clear and in harmony with upright human nature. In consideration of the physiological and psychological make-up of man and woman, both have equal rights and claims on one another, except for one responsibility, that of leadership. This is a matter which is natural in any collective life and which is consistent with the nature of man.

The Qur'ān thus states:

'And they (women) have rights similar to those (of men) over them, and men are a degree above them.' (al-Qur'ān, 2: 228).

Such degree is *Qiwāma* (maintenance and protection). This refers to that natural difference between the sexes which entitles the weaker sex to protection. It implies no superiority or advantage before the law. Yet, man's role of leadership in relation to his family does not mean the husband's dictatorship over his wife. Islam emphasizes the importance of taking counsel and mutual agreement in family decisions. The Qur'ān gives us an example:

'. . . If they (husband wife) desire to wean the child by mutual consent and (after) consultation, there is no blame on them . . .' (al-Qur'ān, 2: 233).

Over and above her basic rights as a wife comes the right which is emphasized by the Qur'ān and is strongly recommended by the Prophet (P); kind treatment and companionship.

The Qur'ān states:

'. . . But consort with them in kindness, for if you hate them it may happen that you hate a thing wherein God has placed much good.' (al-Qur'ān, 4: 19).

Prophet Muḥammad (P) said:

The best of you is the best to his family and I am the best among you to my family.

The most perfect believers are the best in conduct and the best of you are those who are best to their wives. (Ibn Ḥanbal No. 7396).

Behold, many women came to Muḥammad's wives complaining against their husbands (because they beat them) . . . those (husbands) are not the best of you.

As the woman's right to decide about her marriage is recognized, so also her right to seek an end for an unsuccessful marriage is recognized. To provide for the stability of the family, however, and in order to protect it from hasty decision under temporary emotional stress, certain steps and waiting periods should be observed by men and women seeking divorce. Considering the relatively more emotional nature of women, a good reason for asking for divorce should be brought before the judge. Like the man, however, the woman can divorce her husband without resorting to the court, if the nuptial contract allows that.

More specifically, some aspects of Islamic Law concerning marriage and divorce are interesting and are worthy of separate treatment.[22]

22. It is sufficient to say here that polygamy existed in almost all nations and was even sanctioned by Judaism and Christianity until recent centuries. The Qur'ān is the only revealed scripture that explicitly limited polygamy and discouraged its practice by various stringent conditions. One reason for not categorically forbidding polygamy is that in different places at different times, there may exist individual or social exigencies which make polygamy a better solution than either divorce or a hypocritical pretence of morality.

When the continuation of the marriage relationship is impossible for any reason, men are still taught to seek a gracious end for it.

The Qur'ān states about such cases:

> When you divorce women, and they reach their prescribed term, then retain them in kindness and retain them not for injury so that you transgress (the limits). (al-Qur'ān, 2: 231). (See also al-Qur'ān, 2: 229, and 33: 49).

(c) As a mother:

Islam considered kindness to parents next to the worship of God.

'Your Lord has decreed that you worship none save Him, and that you be kind to your parents . . .' (al-Qur'ān, 17: 23).

Moreover, the Qur'ān has a special recommendation for the good treatment of mothers:

'And we have enjoined upon man (to be good) to his parents: His mother bears him in weakness upon weakness . . .' (al-Qur'ān, 31: 14). (See also al-Qur'ān, 46: 15; 29: 8).

A man came to Muḥammad (P) asking, 'O Messenger of God, who among the people is the most worthy of my good company?' The Prophet said, 'Your mother.' The man said, 'Then who else?' The Prophet (P) said, 'Your mother.' The man said, 'Then who else?' The Prophet (P) said, 'Your mother.' The man said, 'Then who else?' Only then did the Prophet (P) say, 'Your father.' (Al-Bukhārī and Muslim).

A famous saying of the Prophet is 'Paradise is at the feet of mothers.' (In Al-Nisā'ī, Ibn-Mājah, Ibn Ḥanbal).

'It is the generous (in character) who is good to women, and it is the wicked who insults them.'

THE ECONOMIC ASPECT

Islam decreed a right of which woman was deprived both before Islam and after if (even as late as this century),[23] the right of independent

---

23. For example, it was not until 1938 that the French Law was amended so as to recognize the eligibility of women to contract. A married woman, however, was still required to secure her husband's permission before she could dispense with her private property. See for example Al-Sibā'ī, op. cit., pp. 31-37.

ownership. According to Islamic Law, woman's right to her money, real estate, or other properties is fully acknowledged. This right undergoes no change whether she is single or married. She retains her full rights to buy, sell, mortgage or lease any or all her properties. It is nowhere suggested in the Law that a woman is a minor simply because she is a female. It is also noteworthy that such right applies to her properties before marriage as well as to whatever she acquires thereafter.

With regard to the woman's right to seek employment, it should be stated first that Islam regards her role in society as a mother and a wife as the most sacred and essential one. Neither maids nor babysitters can possibly take the mother's place as the educator of an upright, complex-free, and carefully-reared child. Such a noble and vital role, which largely shapes the future of nations, cannot be regarded as 'idleness'.

However, there is no decree in Islam which forbids woman from seeking employment whenever there is a necessity for it, especially in positions which fit her nature and in which society needs her most. Examples of these professions are nursing, teaching (especially for children), and medicine. Moreover, there is no restriction on benefitting from woman's exceptional talent in any field. Even for the position of a judge, there may be a tendency to doubt the woman's fitness for the post due to her more emotional nature, we find early Muslim scholars such as Abū-Ḥanīfa and al-Ṭabarī holding there is nothing wrong with it. In addition, Islam restored to woman the right of inheritance in some cultures. Her share is completely hers and no one can make any claim on it, including her father and her husband.

'To men (of the family) belongs a share of that which parents and near kindred leave, and to women a share of that which parents and near kindred leave, whether it be a little or much — a determinate share.' (al-Qur'ān, 4: 7).

Her share in most cases is one-half of the man's share, with no implication that she is worth half a man! It would seem grossly inconsistent after the overwhelming evidence of woman's equitable treatment in Islam, which was discussed in the preceding pages, to make such an inference. This variation in inheritance rights is only consistent with the variations in financial responsibilities of man and woman according to the Islamic Law. Man in Islam is fully responsible for the maintenance of his wife, his children, and in some cases of his needy relatives, especially the females. This responsibility is neither waived nor reduced because of his wife's wealth or because of her access to any personal income gained from work, rent, profit, or any other legal means.

Woman, on the other hand, is far more secure financially and is far less burdened with any claims on her possessions. Her possessions before marriage do not transfer to her husband and she even keeps her maiden name. She has no obligation to spend on her family out of such properties or out of her income after marriage. She is entitled to the *Mahr* which she takes from her husband at the time of marriage. If she is divorced, she may get an alimony from her ex-husband.

An examination of the inheritance law within the overall framework of the Islamic Law reveals, not only justice, but also an abundance of compassion for woman.[24]

THE POLITICAL ASPECT

Any fair investigation of the teachings of Islam or into the history of Islamic civilization will surely find a clear evidence of woman's equality with man in what we call today 'political rights'.

This includes the right of election as well as the nomination to political offices. It also includes woman's right to participate in public affairs. Both in the Qur'ān and in Islamic history we find examples of women who participated in serious discussions and argued even with the Prophet (P) himself (see al-Qur'ān, 58: 1; and 60: 10-12).

During the Caliphate of 'Umar Ibn al-Khaṭṭāb, a woman argued with him in the mosque, proved her point, and caused him to declare in the presence of people: 'A woman is right and 'Umar is wrong.'

Although not mentioned in the Qur'ān, one *Hadīth* of the Prophet is interpreted to make woman ineligible for the position of head of state. The *Hadīth* referred to is roughly translated: 'A people will not prosper if they let a woman be their leader.' This limitation, however, has nothing to do with the dignity of woman or with her rights. It is rather, related to the natural differences in the biological and psychological make-up of men and women.

According to Islam, the head of the state is no mere figure-head. He leads people in the prayers, especially on Fridays and festivities; he is continuously engaged in the process of decision making pertaining to

24. For a good discussion of this point, also of the acceptance of women's witness according to Islamic Law, see 'Abd al-Atī, Hammūdah, *Islam in Focus,* pp. 117-118, and Al-Sibā'ī, Mustafā, *Al-Mar'ah Bayn al-Fiqh wa'l-Qānūn* (in Arabic).

the security and well-being of his people. This demanding position, or any similar one, such as the Commander of the Army, is generally inconsistent with the physiological and psychological make-up of woman in general. It is a medical fact that during their monthly periods and during their pregnancies, women undergo various physiological and psychological changes. Such changes may occur during an emergency situation, thus affecting her decision. The excessive strain during these periods has other effects as well. Moreover, some decisions require a maximum of rationality and a minimum of emotionality — a requirement which may not coincide with the instinctive nature of women.

Even in modern times, and in the most developed countries, it is rare to find a woman in the position of a head of state acting as more than a figurehead, a woman commander of the armed services, or even a proportionate number of women representatives in parliaments, or similar bodies. One can not possibly ascribe this to backwardness of various nations or to any constitutional limitation on woman's right to be in such a position as a head of state or as a member of the parliament. It is more logical to explain the present situation in terms of the natural and indisputable differences between man and woman, a difference which does not imply any 'supremacy' of one over the other. The difference implies rather the 'complementary' roles of both the sexes in life.

CONCLUSION

The first part of this paper deals briefly with the position of various religions and cultures on the issue under investigation. Part of this exposition extends to cover the general trend as late as the nineteenth century, nearly 1300 years after the Qur'ān set forth the Islamic teachings.

In the second part of the paper, the status of women in Islam is briefly discussed. Emphasis in this part is placed on the original and authentic sources of Islam. This represents the standard according to which degree of adherence of Muslims can be judged. It is also a fact that during some of our moments of decline, such teachings were not strictly adhered to by many people who professed to be Muslims.

Such deviations were unfairly exaggerated by some writers, and the worst of these were superficially taken to represent the teachings of Islam to the Western reader without taking the trouble to make any original and unbiased study of the authentic sources of these teachings. Even with such deviations three facts are worth mentioning:

1. The history of Muslims is rich with women of great achievements in all walks of life from as early as the seventh century (C.E.).[25]
2. It is impossible for anyone to justify any mistreatment of woman by any decree of rule embodied in the Islamic Law, nor could anyone dare to cancel, reduce or distort the clearcut legal rights of women given in Islamic Law.
3. Throughout history, the reputation, chastity and maternal role of Muslim women were objects of admiration by impartial observers.

It is also worthwhile to state that the status which women reached during the present era was not achieved due to the kindness of men or due to natural progress. It was rather achieved through a long struggle and sacrifice on woman's part and only when society needed her contribution and work, more especially during the two world wars, and due to the escalation of technological change.

In the case of Islam such compassionate and dignified status was decreed, not because it reflects the environment of the seventh century, nor under the threat or pressure of women and their organization, but rather because of its intrinsic truthfulness.

If this indicates anything, it would demonstrate the divine origin of the Qur'ān and the truthfulness of the message of Islam, which, unlike human philosophies and ideologies, was far from proceeding from its human environment, a message which established such humane principles as neither grew obsolete during the course of time and after these many centuries, nor can become obsolete in the future. After all, this is the message of the All-Wise and All-Knowing God whose wisdom and knowledge are far beyond the ultimate in human thought and progress.

25. See, for example, Nadvi, A. Sulaiman, *Heroic Deeds of Muslim Women,* Islamic Publications Ltd., Lahore, Pakistan. Siddiqui, *Women in Islam,* Institute of Islamic Culture, Lahore, Pakistan, 1959.

BIBLIOGRAPHY

The Holy Qur'ān: Translation of verses is heavily based on A. Yūsuf 'Alī's translation, *The Holy Qur'ān Text, Translation and Commentary,* The American International Printing Company, Washington, D.C., 1946.

'Abd Al-'Atī, Hammūdah, *Islam in Focus,* The Canadian Islamic Center, Edmonton, Alberta, Canada, 1963.

Allen, E. A., *History of Civilization,* General Publishing House, Cincinnati, Ohio, 1889, Vol. 3.

Al-Sibā'ī, Muṣṭafā, *Al-Mar'ah Baynal-Fiqh Wa'l-Qānūn* (in Arabic), 2nd ed., Al-Maktabah al-'Arabiyyah, Ḥalab, Syria, 1966.

Al-Khulī, Al-Bahī *'Min Usūs Qadiyyah Al-Mar'ah'* (in Arabic), *Al-Wa'ī Al-Islāmī,* Ministry of Wakf, Kuwait, Vol. 3 (No. 27) June 9, 1967.

Encyclopaedia Americana (International Edition), American Corp. N.Y., 1969, Vol. 29.

Encyclopaedia Biblica (Rev. T. K. Cheynene and J. S. Black, editors), The Macmillan Co., London, England, 1902, Vol. 3.

The Encyclopaedia Britannica (11th ed.), University Press, Cambridge, England, 1911, Vol. 28.

The Encyclopaedia Britannica, The Encyclopaedia Britannica Inc., Chicago, Ill., 1968, Vol. 23.

Ḥadīth. Most of the quoted *aḥādīth* were translated by the writer. They are quoted in various Arabic sources. Some of them, however, were translated directly from the original sources. Among the sources checked are *Musnad* of Ahmad Ibn Hanbal, Dār Al-Ma'ārif, Cairo, U.A.R., 1950 and 1955, Vol. 4 and 3, *Sunan* of Ibn-Mājah, Dār Iḥyā' al-Kutub al-'Arabiyyah, Cairo, U.A.R., 1952, Vol. 1, *Sunan* of al-Tirmidhī, Vol. 3.

Mace, David and Vera, *Marriage: East and West,* Dolphin Books, Doubleday and Col, Inc., N.Y., 1960.

Mawdūdī, Abūl 'Alā, *Purdah and the Status of Woman in Islam,* Islamic Publications Ltd., Lahore, 1973.

10

Political Theory of Islam[*]

Abū'l A'lā Mawdūdī

WITH certain people it has become a sort of fashion to somehow identify Islam with one or the other system of life in vogue at the time. So at this time also there are people who say that Islam is a democracy, and by this they mean to imply that there is no difference between Islam and the democracy as in vogue in the West. Some others suggest that Communism is but the latest and revised version of Islam and it is in the fitness of things that Muslims imitate the Communist experiment of Soviet Russia. Still some others whisper that Islam has the elements of dictatorship in it and we should revive the cult of 'obedience to the *Amīr'* (the leader). All these people, in their misinformed and misguided zeal to serve what they hold to be the cause of Islam, are always at great pains to prove that Islam contains within itself the elements of all types of contemporary social and political thought and action. Most of the people who indulge in this prattle have no clear idea of the Islamic way of life. They have never made nor try to make a systematic study of the Islamic political order — the place and nature of democracy, social justice, and equality in it. Instead they behave like the proverbial blind men who gave altogether contradictory descriptions of an elephant because one had been able to touch only its tail, the other its legs, the third its belly and the fourth its ears only. Or perhaps they look upon Islam as an orphan whose sole hope for survival lies in winning the patronage and the sheltering care of some

* This chapter is taken from the author's *Islamic Law and Constitution*. It was originally presented as a paper before a gathering of graduate and undergraduate students of the Punjab University, Lahore, in October, 1939 — Editor.

dominant creed. That is why some people have begun to present apologies on Islam's behalf. As a matter of fact, this attitude emerges from an inferiority complex, from the belief that we as Muslims can earn no honour or respect unless we are able to show that our religion resembles the modern creeds and it is in agreement with most of the contemporary ideologies. These people have done a great disservice to Islam; they have reduced the political theory of Islam to a puzzle, a hotchpotch. They have turned Islam into a juggler's bag out of which can be produced anything that holds a demand! Such is the intellectual plight in which we are engulfed. Perhaps it is a result of this sorry state of affairs that some people have even begun to say that Islam has no political or economic system of its own and anything can fit into its scheme.

In these circumstances it has become essential that a careful study of the political theory of Islam should be made in a scientific way, with a view to grasp its real meaning, nature, purpose and significance. Such a systematic study alone can put an end to this confusion of thought and silence those who out of ignorance proclaim that there is nothing like Islamic political theory, Islamic social order and Islamic culture. I hope it will also bring to the world groping in darkness the light that it urgently needs, although it is not yet completely conscious of such a need.

II

FUNDAMENTALS OF ISLAM

It should be clearly understood in the very beginning that Islam is not a jumble of unrelated ideas and incoherent modes of conduct. It is rather a well-ordered system, a consistent whole, resting on a definite set of clear-cut postulates. Its major tenets as well as detailed rules of conduct are all derived from and logically connected with its basic principles. All the rules and regulations that Islam has laid down for the different spheres of human life are in their essence and spirit a reflexion, an extension and corollary of its first principles. The various phases of Islamic life and activity flow from these fundamental postulates exactly as the plant sprouts forth from its seed. And just as even though the tree may spread in all directions, all its leaves and branches remain firmly attached to the roots and derive sustenance from them and it is always the seed and the root which determine the nature and form of the tree, similar is the case with Islam. Its entire scheme of life also flows from its basic postulates. Therefore whatever aspect of the Islamic ideology one may like to study, he must, first of all, go to the roots and look to the fundamental principles. Then and then alone he can have a really correct and satisfactory understanding of the ideology and its specific injunctions and a real appreciation of its spirit and nature.

THE MISSION OF THE PROPHETS

The mission of a prophet is to propagate Islam, disseminate the teachings of Allah and establish the divine guidance in this world of flesh and bones. This was the mission of all the divinely inspired Prophets who appeared in succession ever since man's habitation on earth up to the advent of Muḥammad (peace be upon him). In fact the mission of all the prophets was one and the same — the preaching of Islam. And Prophet Muḥammad (peace be upon him) was the last of their line. With him prophethood came to an end and to him was revealed the final code of human guidance in all its completeness. All the prophets conveyed to mankind the guidance which was revealed to them and asked it to acknowledge the absolute sovereignty of God and to render unalloyed obedience to Him. This was the mission which each one of the prophets was assigned to perform.

At first sight this mission appears to be very simple and innocuous. But if you probe a little deeper and examine the full significance and the logical and practical implications of Divine Sovereignty and the concept of *Tawḥīd* (the Unity of Godhead), you will soon realize that the matter is not so simple as it appears on the surface, and that there must be something revolutionary in a doctrine which roused such bitter opposition and sustained hostility on the part of the non-believers. What strikes us most in the long history of the prophets is that whenever these servants of God proclaimed that 'There is no *ilāh* (object of worship) except Allah', all the forces of evil made common cause to challenge them. If it were merely to call to bow down in the places of worship before one God with perfect freedom outside these sacred precincts to owe allegiance to and carry out the will of the powers that be, it would have been the height of folly on the part of the ruling classes to suppress the religious liberties of its loyal subjects for a minor matter which had no bearing on their attitude towards the established government. Let us therefore try to explore the real point of dispute between the Prophets and their opponents.

There are many verses of the Qur'ān which make it absolutely clear that the non-believers and polytheists too, who opposed the Prophets, did not deny the existence of God, nor that He was the sole Creator of heavens and earth and man, nor that the whole mechanism of nature operated in accordance with His commands, nor that it is He who pours down the rain, drives the winds and controls the sun, the moon, the earth, and everything else. Says the Qur'ān:

'Say to whom (belongs) the earth and whoso is in it, if you have knowledge? They will say, to Allah. Say: Will you not then remember? Say: Who is Lord of the seven heavens, and Lord of the tremendous Throne? They will say, to Allah (all that belongs). Say: Will you not then keep duty (to Him)? Say: In whose hands is the dominion over all things and He protects, while against Him there is no protection, if you have knowledge? They will say: to Allah (all that belongs). Say: How then are you bewitched?'[1] 'And if you were to ask them: Who created the heavens and the earth, and constrained the sun and the moon (to their appointed task)? They would say: Allah. How then are they turned away? . . . And if you were to ask them: who causes water to come down from the sky, and therewith revives the earth after its death? They verily would say: Allah.'[2]

'And if you asked them who created them, they will surely say: Allah. How then are they turned away.'[3]

These verses make it abundantly clear that the dispute was not about the existence of God or His being the Creator and Lord of heavens and earth. All men acknowledged these truths. Hence there was no question of there being any dispute on what was already admitted on all hands. The question arises, then what was it that gave rise to the tremendous opposition that every prophet without any exception had to face when he made this call? The Qur'ān states that the whole dispute centred round the uncompromising demand of the prophets that the non-believers should recognize as their *rabb* (Lord) and *ilāh* (Master and Law-giver) also the very Being whom they acknowledged as their Creator and that they should assign this position to none else. But the people were not prepared to accept this demand of the prophets.

Let us now try to find out the real cause of this refusal and what the

1. al-Qur'ān, 23: 84-89.
2. Ibid., 29: 61, 63.
3. Ibid., 43: 87.

terms *ilāh* and *rabb* mean. Furthermore, why did the prophets insist that Allah alone should be recognized and acknowledged as *ilāh* and *rabb* and why did the whole world range itself against them upon this apparently simple demand?

The Arabic word *ilāh* stands for *ma'būd* (i.e. the object of worship) which in itself is derived from the word *'abd,* meaning a servant or slave. The relationship which exists between man and God is that of 'worshipper' and 'the worshipped'. Man is to offer *'ibādah* to God and is to live like His *'abd.*

And *'ibādah* does not merely mean ritual or any specific form of prayer. It means a life of continuous service and unremitting obedience like the life of a slave in relation to his Lord. To wait upon a person in service, to bow down one's head in acknowledgement of his elevated position, to exert oneself in obedience to his commands, to carry out his orders and cheerfully submit to all the toil and discipline involved therein, to humble oneself in the presence of the master, to offer what he demands, to obey what he commands, to set one's face steadily against the causes of his displeasure, and to sacrifice even one's life when such is his pleasure — these are the real implications of the term *'ibādah* (worship or service) and a man's true *Ma'būd* (Object of worship) is he whom he worships in this manner.

And what is the meaning of the word *rabb*? In Arabic it literally means 'one who nourishes and sustains and regulates and perfects'. Since the moral consciousness of man requires that one who nourishes, sustains, and provides for us has a superior claim on our allegiance, the word *rabb* is also used in the sense of master or owner. For this reason the Arabic equivalent for the owner of property is *rabb al-māl* and for the owner of a house, *rabb al-dār.* A person's *rabb* is one whom he looks upon as his nourisher and patron; from whom he expects favour and obligations; to whom he looks for honour, advancement and peace; whose displeasure he considers to be prejudicial to his life and happiness; whom he declares to be his Lord and master; and lastly, whom he follows and obeys.[4]

Keeping in view the real meaning of these two words *ilāh* and *rabb* it can be easily found who is it that may rightfully claim to be man's *Ilāh* and *Rabb* and who can, therefore, demand that he should be served, obeyed and worshipped. Trees, stones, rivers, animals, the sun, the

4. for a detailed discussion over the meaning and concept of *ilāh* and *rabb* see: Abūl A'lā Maudūdī, *Qur'ān Kī Chār Bunyādī Iṣṭilāhen.* (Four basic terms of the Qur'ān). Lahore.

moon and the stars, none of them can venture to lay claim tó this position in relation to man. It is only man who can, and does, claim godhood in relation to his fellow-beings. The desire for godhood can take root only in man's mind. It is only man's excessive lust for power and desire for exploitation that prompts him to project himself on other people as a god and extract their obedience; force them to bow down before him in reverential awe, and make them instruments of his self-aggrandisement. The pleasure of posing as a god is more enchanting and appealing than anything else that man has yet been able to discover. Whoever possesses power or wealth or cleverness or any other superior faculty, develops a strong inclination to outstep his natural and proper limits, to extend his area of influence and thrust his godhood upon such of his fellow men as are comparatively feeble, poor, weak-minded or deficient in any manner.

Such aspirants to godhood are of two kinds and accordingly they adopt two different lines of action. There is a type of people who are comparatively bold or who possess adequate means of forcing their claim on those over whom they wield power and who consequently make a direct claim to godhood. For instance, there was Pharaoh who was so intoxicated with power and so proud of his empire that he proclaimed to the inhabitants of Egypt: *'Anā rabbukum al-a'lā'* (I am your highest Lord) and *'Mā 'alimtu lakum min ilāhin ghayrī'* (I do not know of any other *ilāh* for you but myself). When Prophet Moses approached him with a demand for the liberation of his people and told him that he too should surrender himself to the Lord of the Universe, Pharoah replied that since he had the power to cast him into the prison, Moses should rather acknowledge him as *ilāh.* [5] Similarly, there was another king who had an argument with Prophet Abraham. Ponder carefully over the words in which the Qur'ān has narrated this episode. It says:

> 'Are you not aware of that king who had an argument with Abraham about his Lord because Allah had given him the kingdom? When Abraham said: My Lord is He who gives life and death, he answered: I give life and cause death. Abraham said: Allah causes the sun to rise in the East; cause it, then, to rise in the West. Then was the disbeliever confounded.' [6]

5. al-Qur'ān, 26: 29; 28: 38; 79: 24.
6. Ibid., 2: 258.

Why was the unbelieving king confounded? Not because he denied
the existence of God. He did believe that God was the ruler of the
universe and that He alone made the sun rise and set. The question at
issue was not the dominion over the sun and the moon and the universe
but that of *the allegiance of the people;* not that who should be regarded as
controlling the forces of nature, but that *who should have the right to claim
the obedience of men.* He did not put forth the claim that he was Allah;
what he actually demanded was that no objection should be cast over
the absoluteness of his authority over his subjects. His authority as the
ruler should not be challenged. This claim was based on the fact that
he held the reins of government: he could do whatever he liked with the
property or the lives of his people: he had absolute power to punish his
subjects with death or to spare them. He, therefore, demanded from
Abraham that the latter should recognize him as his master, serve him
and do his bidding. But when Abraham declared that he would obey,
serve and accept no one but the Lord of the Universe, the king was
bewildered and shocked and did not know how to bring such a person
under his control.

This claim to godhood which Pharaoh and Nimrod had put forth
was by no means peculiar to them. Rulers all over the world in ages
past and present have advanced such claims. In Iran the words *Khudā*
(Master) and *Khudāwand* (Lord) were commonly employed in relation
to the king, and all the ceremonies indicative of servility were performed before him, in spite of the fact that no Iranian looked upon the
king as the lord of the universe, that is to say God, nor did the king
represent himself as such. Similarly, the ruling dynasties in India
claimed descent from the gods; the solar and lunar dynasties are well
known down to this day. The *rāja* was called *an-dāta* (the provider of
sustenance) and people prostrated themselves before him although
never recognized him as such. Much the same was, and still is, the state
of affairs in all other countries.

Words synonymous with *ilāh* and *rabb* are still used in direct reference to rulers of many places. Even where this is not customary, the
attitude of the people towards their rulers is similar to what is implied
by these two words. It is not necessary for a man who claims godhood
that he should openly declare himself to be an *ilāh* or *rabb*. All persons
who exercize unqualified dominion over a group of men, who impose
their will upon others, who make them their instruments and seek to
control their destinies in the same manner as Pharaoh and Nimrod did
in the hey-day of their power, are essentially claimants to godhood,

though the claim may be tacit, veiled and unexpressed. And those who serve and obey them, admit their godhood even if they do not say so by word of mouth.

In contrast to these people who directly seek recognition of their godhood there is another type of men who do not possess the necessary means or strength to get themselves accepted as *ilāh* or *rabb*. But they are resourceful and cunning enough to cast a spell over the minds and hearts of the common people. By the use of sinister methods, they invest some spirit, god, idol, tomb, plant, or tree with the character of *ilāh* and dupe the common people successfully into believing that these objects are capable of doing them harm and bringing them good; that they can provide for their needs, answer their prayers and afford them shelter and protection from evils which beset them all around. They tell them in effect: 'If you do not seek their pleasure and approval, they will involve you in famines, epidemics and afflictions. But if you approach them in the proper way and solicit their help they will come to your aid. We know the methods by which they can be propitiated and their pleasure can be secured. We alone can show you the means of access to these deities. Therefore, acknowledge our superiority, seek our pleasure and entrust to our charge your life, wealth and honour.' Many stupid persons are caught in this trap and thus, under cover of false gods, is established the godhood and supremacy of priests and shrine-keepers.

There are some others belonging to the same category who employ the arts of soothsaying, astrology, fortune-telling, charms, incantations, etc. There are yet others who, while owing allegiance to God, also assert that one cannot gain direct access to God. They claim that they are the intermediaries through whom one should approach his threshold; that all ceremonials should be performed through their mediation; and that all religious rites from one's birth to death can be performed only at their hands. There are still others who proclaim themselves to be the bearers of the Book of God and yet they deliberately keep the common people ignorant of its meaning and contents. Constituting themselves into mouthpieces of God, they start dictating to others what is lawful (*ḥalāl*) and what is unlawful (*ḥarām*). In this way their word becomes law and they force people to obey their own commands instead of those of God. This is the source of Brahmanism and Papacy which has appeared under various names and in diverse forms in all parts of the world from times immemorial down to the present day, and in consequence of which certain families, races and classes have imposed their will and authority over large masses of men and women.

If you were to look at the matter from this angle, you will find that the root-cause of all evil and mischief in the world is *the domination of man over man,* be it direct or indirect. This was the origin of all the troubles of mankind and even to this day it remains the main cause of all the misfortunes and vices which have brought untold misery on the teeming humanity. God, of course, knows all the secrets of human nature. But the truth of this observation has also been confirmed and brought home to humanity by the experiences of thousands of years that man cannot help setting up someone or other as his 'god', *ilāh* and *rabb,* and looking up to him for help and guidance in the complex and baffling affairs of his life and obeying his commands. This fact has been established beyond question by the historical experience of mankind that if you do not believe in God, some artificial god will take His place in your thinking and behaviour. It is even possible that instead of one real God, a number of false gods, *ilāhs* and *rabbs* may impose themselves upon you.

Even today man is enchained in the slavery of many a false god. May he be in Russia or America, Italy or Yugoslavia, England or China, he is generally under the spell of some party, some ruler, some leader or group, some money-magnate or the like in such a manner that man's control over man, man's worship of man, man's surveillance of man continue unabated. Modern man has discarded nature-worship, but man-worship he still does. In fine, wherever you turn your eyes, you will find that one nation dominates another, one class holds another in subjection, or a political party having gained complete ascendancy, constitutes itself as the arbiter of men's destiny, or again in some places a dictator concentrates in his hands all power and influence setting himself up as the lord and master of the people. Nowhere has man been able to do without an *ilāh*!

What are the consequences of this domination of man by man, of this attempt by man to play the role of divinity? The same that would follow from a mean and incompetent person being appointed a police commissioner or some ignorant and narrow-minded politician being exalted to the rank of a prime minister. For one thing, the effect of godhood is so intoxicating that one who tastes this powerful drink can never keep himself under control. Even assuming that such self-control is possible, the vast knowledge, the keen insight, the unquestioned impartiality and perfect disinterestedness which are required for carrying out the duties of godhood, will always remain out of the reach of man. That is why tyranny, despotism, intemperance, unlawful exploitation, and inequality reign supreme, whenever man's over-lordship and domination (*ilāhiyyah* and *rabūbiyyah*) over man are esta-blished. The human soul is inevitably deprived of its natural freedom; and man's mind and heart and his inborn faculties and aptitudes are subjected to such vexatious restrictions that the proper growth and development of his personality is arrested. How truly did the Holy Prophet observe:

'God, the Almighty, says: "I created men with a pliable nature; then the devils came and contrived to lead them astray from their faith and prohibited for them what I had made lawful for them." '[7]

As I have indicated above, this is the sole cause of all the miseries and conflicts from which man has suffered during the long course of human history. This is the real impediment to his progress. This is the canker which has eaten into the vitals of his moral, intellectual, political and economic life, destroying all the values which alone make him human and mark him off from animals. So it was in the remote past and so it is today. The only remedy for this dreadful malady lies in the repu-diation and renunciation by man of all masters and in the explicit recognition by him of God Almighty as his sole master and lord (*ilāh* and *rabb*). There is no way to his salvation except this; for even if he were to become an atheist and heretic he would not be able to shake himself free of all these masters (*ilāhs* and *rabbs*).

This was the radical reformation effected from time to time by the Prophets in the life of humanity. They aimed at the demolition of man's supremacy over man. Their real mission was to deliver man from this injustice, this slavery of false gods, this tyranny of man over man, and this exploitation of the weak by the strong. Their object was to thrust back into their proper limits those who had over-stepped them and to raise to the proper level those who had been forced down from it. They endeavoured to evolve a social organization based on human equality in which man should be neither the slave nor the master of his fellow-beings and in which all men should become the servants of one real Lord. The message of all the Prophets that came into the world was the same, namely:

7. *Ḥadīth Qudsī.*

'O my people, worship Allah. There is no *ilāh* whatever for you
except He.'[8]

This was precisely what Noah said; this is exactly what Hūd
declared; Sālih affirmed the same truth; Shu'ayb gave the same message, and the same doctrine was repeated and confirmed by Moses,
Jesus and by Prophet Muhammad (peace be upon them all). The last
of the Prophets, Muhammad (God's blessing and peace be upon him)
said:

'I am only a warner, and there is no God save Allah, the One, the
Absolute Lord of the heavens and the earth and all that is between
them.'[9]

'Your Lord is Allah who created the heavens and the earth in six
days, then sat Himself upon the Throne. He covers the night with
the day, which is in haste to follow and has made the sun and the
moon and the stars subservient by His command. His is all creation
and (His is the) command.'[10]

'Such is Allah, your Lord. There is no God save Him, the Creator
of all things, so worship Him. And He takes care of all things.'[11]

'And they are not enjoined anything except that they should
serve Allah, being sincere to Him in obedience.'[12]

'Come to a word common between us and between you, that we
shall worship none but Allah, and that we shall ascribe no partner
to Him and that none of us shall take others for lords beside Allah.'[13]

This was the proclamation that released the human soul from its
fetters and set man's intellectual and material powers free from the
bonds of slavery that held them in subjection. It relieved them of the
burden that weighed heavily upon them and was breaking their backs.
It gave them a real charter of liberty and freedom. The Holy Qur'ān
refers to this marvellous achievement of the Prophet of Islam when it
says:

'And he (the Prophet) relieves them of their burden and chains
that were around them.'[14]

8. al-Qur'īan 7: 59, 65, 73, 86; also 11: 50, 61, 84.
9. ibid., 38: 65-66.
10. ibid., 7: 54.
11. ibid., 6: 102.
12. ibid., 98: 5.
13. ibid., 3: 64.
14. ibid., 7: 157.

III
FIRST PRINCIPLE OF ISLAMIC POLITICAL THEORY

The belief in the Unity and the sovereignty of Allah is the foundation of the social and moral system propounded by the Prophets. It is the very starting-point of the Islamic political philosophy. The basic principle of Islam is that human beings must, individually and collectively, surrender all rights of overlordship, legislation and exercizing of authority over others. No one should be allowed to pass orders or make commands *in his own right* and no one ought to accept the obligation to carry out such commands and obey such orders. None is entitled to make laws on his own authority and none is obliged to abide by them. This right vests in Allah alone:

> 'The Authority rests with none but Allah. He commands you not to surrender to any one save Him. This is the right way (of life).'[15]
> 'They ask: "have we also got some authority?" Say: "all authority belongs to God alone".'[16]
> 'Do not say wrongly with your tongues that this is lawful and that is unlawful.'[17]
> 'Whoso does not establish and decide by that which Allah has revealed, such are disbelievers.'[18]

According to this theory, sovereignty belongs to Allah. He alone is the law-giver. No man, even if he be a Prophet, has the right to order others *in his own right* to do or not to do certain things. The Prophet himself is subject to God's commands:

> 'I do not follow anything except what is revealed to me.'[19]

Other people are required to obey the Prophet because he enunciates not his own but God's commands:

> 'We sent no messenger save that he should be obeyed by Allah's command.'[20]

15. al-Qur'ān, 12: 40.
16. ibid., 3: 154.
17. ibid., 16: 116.
18. ibid., 5: 44.
19. ibid., 6: 50.
20. ibid., 4: 64.

'They are the people to whom We gave the Scripture and Command and Prophethood.'[21]

'It is not (possible) for any human being to whom Allah has given the Scripture and the Wisdom and the Prophethood that he should say to people: Obey me instead of Allah. Such a one (could only say): be solely devoted to the Lord.[22]

Thus the main characteristics of an Islamic state that can be deduced from these express statements of the Holy Qur'ān are as follows: —

(1)   No person, class or group, not even the entire population of the state as a whole, can lay claim to sovereignty. God alone is the real sovereign; all others are merely His subjects;

(2)   God is the real law-giver and the authority of absolute legislation vests in Him. The believers cannot resort to totally independent legislation nor can they modify any law which God has laid down, even if the desire to effect such legislation or change in Divine laws is unanimous;[23] and

(3)   An Islamic state must, in all respects, be founded upon the law laid down by God through His Prophet. The government which runs such a state will be entitled to obedience in its capacity as a political agency set up to enforce the laws of God and only in so far as it acts in that capacity. If it disregards the law revealed by God, its commands will not be binding on the believers.

IV

THE ISLAMIC STATE:

ITS NATURE AND CHARACTERISTICS

The preceding discussion makes it quite clear that Islam, speaking from the view-point of political philosophy, is the very antithesis of secular Western democracy. The philosophical foundation of Western

21. ibid., 6: 90.
22. ibid., 3: 79.
23. Here the *absolute right of legislation* is being discussed. In the Islamic political theory this right vests in Allah alone. As to the scope and extent of human legislation provided by the *Sharī'ah* itself please see Mawdūdī, A.A., *Islamic Law and Constitution*, Chapter II: 'Legislation and Ijtihād in Islam' and Chapter VI: 'First Principles of Islamic State.' — Editor.

democracy is the sovereignty of the people. In it, this type of absolute powers of legislation — of the determination of values and of the norms of behaviour — rest in the hands of the people. Law-making is their prerogative and legislation must correspond to the mood and temper of their opinion. If a particular piece of legislation is desired by the masses, howsoever ill-conceived, it may be from religious and moral viewpoint, steps have to be taken to place it on the statute book; if the people dislike any law and demand its abrogation, howsoever just and rightful, it might be, it has to be expunged forthwith. This is not the case in Islam. On this count, Islam has no trace of Western democracy. Islam, as already explained, altogether repudiates the philosophy of popular sovereignty and rears its polity on the foundations of the sovereignty of God and the vicegerency (*Khilāfah*) of man.[24]

A more apt name for the Islamic polity would be the 'kingdom of God' which is described in English as a 'theocracy'. But Islamic theocracy is something altogether different from the theocracy of which Europe has had a bitter experience wherein a priestly class, sharply marked off from the rest of the population, exercises unchecked domination and enforces laws of its own making in the name of God, thus virtually imposing its own divinity and godhood upon the common people.[25] Such a system of government is satanic rather than divine. Contrary to this, the theocracy built up by Islam is not ruled by any particular religious class but by the whole community of Muslims including the rank and file. The entire Muslim population runs the state in accordance with the Book of God and the practice of His Prophet. If I were permitted to coin a new term, I would describe this system of government as a 'theo-democracy', that is to say a divine democratic government, because under it the Muslims have been given a limited popular sovereignty under the suzerainty of God. The

24. Here it must be clearly understood that democracy as a 'philosophy' and democracy as a 'form of organization' are not the same thing. In the form of organization, Islam has its own system of democracy as is explained in the following pages. But as a philosophy, the two, i.e. Islam and Western democracy, are basically different, rather opposed to each other. — Editor.

25. 'Theocracy: a form of government in which God (or a deity) is recognized as the king or immediate ruler, and his laws are taken as the statute book of Kingdom, these laws being usually administered by a priestly order as his ministers and agents; hence (loosely) a system of government by a sacerdotal order claiming a divine commission. *The Shorter Oxford Dictionary*, Vol. II, Oxford, 1956, S.V. *Theocracy*.

executive under this system of government is constituted by the general will of the Muslims who have also the right to depose it. All administrative matters and all questions about which no explicit injunction is to be found in the *shari'ah* are settled by the consensus of opinion among the Muslims. Every Muslim who is capable and qualified to give a sound opinion on matters of Islamic law, is entitled to interpret the law of God when such interpretation becomes necessary. In this sense the Islamic polity is a democracy. But, as has been explained above, it is a theocracy in the sense that where an explicit command of God or His Prophet already exists, no Muslim leader or legislature, or any religious scholar can form an independent judgement, not even all the Muslims of the world put together have any right to make the least alteration in it.

Before proceeding further, I feel that I should put in a word of explanation as to why these limitations and restrictions have been placed upon popular sovereignty in Islam, and what is the nature of these limitations and restrictions. It may be said that God has, in this manner, taken away the liberty of human mind and intellect instead of safeguarding it as I was trying to prove. My reply is that God has retained the right of legislation in His own hand not in order to deprive man of his natural freedom but to safeguard that very freedom. His purpose is to save man from going astray and inviting his own ruin.

One can easily understand this point by attempting a little analysis of the so-called Western secular democracy. It is claimed that this democracy is founded on popular sovereignty. But everybody knows that the people who constitute a state do not all of them take part either in legislation or in its administration. They have to delegate their sovereignty to their elected representatives so that the latter may make and enforce laws on their behalf. For this purpose, an electoral system is set up. But as a divorce has been effected between politics and religion, and as a result of this secularization, the society and particularly its politically active elements have ceased to attach much or any importance to morality and ethics. And this is also a fact that only those persons generally come to the top who can dupe the masses by their wealth, power, and deceptive propaganda. Although these representatives come into power by the votes of the common people, they soon set themselves up as an independent authority and assume the position of overlords (*ilāhs*). They often make laws not in the best interest of the people who raised them to power but to further their own sectional and class interests. They impose their will on the people by virtue of the authority delegated to them by those over whom they rule. This is the situation which besets people in England, America and in all those countries which claim to be the haven of secular democracy.

Even if we overlook this aspect of the matter and admit that in these countries laws are made according to the wishes of the common people, it has been established by experience that the great mass of the common people are incapable of perceiving their own true interests. It is the natural weakness of man that in most of the affairs concerning his life he takes into consideration only some one aspect of reality and loses sight of other aspects. His judgements are usually one-sided and he is swayed by emotions and desires to such an extent that rarely, if ever, can he judge important matters with the impartiality and objectivity of scientific reason. Quite often he rejects the plea of reason simply because it conflicts with his passions and desires. I can cite many instances in support of this contention but to avoid prolixity I shall content myself with giving only one example: the Prohibition Law of America. It has been rationally and logically established that drinking is injurious to health, produces deleterious effects on mental and intellectual faculties and leads to disorder in human society. The American public accepted these facts and agreed to the enactment of the Prohibition Law. Accordingly the law was passed by the majority vote. But when it was put into effect, the very same people by whose vote it had been passed, revolted against it. The worst kinds of wine were illicitly manufactured and consumed, and their use and consumption became more widespread than before. Crimes increased in number. And eventually drinking was legalized by the vote of the same people who had previously voted for its prohibition. This sudden change in public opinion was not the result of any fresh scientific discovery or the revelation of new facts providing evidence against the advantages of prohibition, but because the people had been completely enslaved by their habit and could not forgo the pleasures of self-indulgence. They delegated their own sovereignty to the evil spirit in them and set up their own desires and passions as their *ilāhs* (gods) at whose call they all went in for the repeal of the very law they had passed after having been convinced of its rationality and correctness. There are many other similar instances which go to prove that man is not competent to become an absolute legislator. Even if he secures deliverance from the service of other *ilāhs,* he becomes a slave to his own petty passions and exalts the devil in him to the position of a supreme Lord. Limitations on human freedom, provided they are appropriate and do not deprive him of all initiative are absolutely necessary in the interest of man himself.[26]

That is why God has laid down those limits which, in Islamic phraseology, are termed 'divine limits' (*Hudūd-Allāh*). These limits consist of certain principles, checks and balances and specific injunctions in different spheres of life and activity, and they have been prescribed in order that man may be trained to lead a balanced and moderate life. They are intended to lay down the broad framework within which man is free to legislate, decide his own affairs and frame subsidiary laws and regulations for his conduct. These limits he is not permitted to overstep and if he does so, the whole scheme of his life will go awry.

Take for example man's economic life. In this sphere God has placed certain restrictions on human freedom. The right to private property has been recognized, but it is qualified by the obligation to pay *Zakāh* (poor dues) and the prohibition of interest, gambling and speculation. A specific law of inheritance for the distribution of property among the largest number of surviving relations on the death of its owner has been laid down and certain forms of acquiring, accumulating and spending wealth have been declared unlawful. If people observe these just limits and regulate their affairs within these boundary walls, on the one hand their personal liberty is adequately safeguarded and, on the other, the possibility of class war and domination of one class over another, which begins with capitalist oppression and ends in working-class dictatorship, is safely and conveniently eliminated.

Similarly in the sphere of family life, God has prohibited the unrestricted intermingling of the sexes and has prescribed *Pardah*, recognized man's guardianship of woman, and clearly defined the rights and duties of husband, wife and children. The laws of divorce and separation have been clearly set forth, conditional polygamy has been permitted and penalties for fornication and false accusations of adultery have been prescribed. He has thus laid down limits which, if observed by man, would stabilize his family life and make it a haven of peace and happiness. There would remain neither that tyranny of male over female which makes family life an inferno of cruelty and oppression,

26. The question however is: Who is to impose these restrictions? According to the Islamic view it is only Allah, the Creator, the Nourisher, the All-Knowing Who is entitled to impose restrictions on human freedom and not any man. No man is entitled to do so. If any man arbitrarily imposes restrictions on human freedom, that is despotism pure and simple. In Islam there is no place for such despotism. — Editor.

nor that satanic flood of female liberty and licence which threatens to destroy human civilization in the West.

In like manner, for the preservation of human culture and society God has, by formulating the law of *Qiṣāṣ* (Retaliation) commanding to cut off the hands for theft, prohibiting wine-drinking, placing limitations on uncovering of one's private parts and by laying down a few similar permanent rules and regulations, closed the door of social disorder for ever. I have no time to present to you a complete list of all the divine limits and show in detail how essential each one of them is for maintaining equilibrium and poise in life. What I want to bring home to you here is that through these injunctions God has provided a permanent and immutable code of behaviour for man, and that it does not deprive him of any essential liberty nor does it dull the edge of his mental faculties. On the contrary, it sets a straight and clear path before him, so that he may not, owing to his ignorance and weaknesses which he inherently possesses, lose himself in the maze of destruction and instead of wasting his faculties in the pursuit of wrong ends, he may follow the road that leads to success and progress in this world and the hereafter. If you have ever happened to visit a mountainous region, you must have noticed that in the winding mountain paths which are bounded by deep caves on the one side and lofty rocks on the other, the border of the road is barricaded and protected in such a way as to prevent travellers from straying towards the abyss by mistake. Are these barricades intended to deprive the wayfarer of his liberty? No, as a matter of fact, they are meant to protect him from destruction; to warn him at every bend of the dangers ahead and to show him the path leading to his destination. That precisely is the purpose of the restrictions (*ḥudūd*) which God has laid down in His revealed Code. These limits determine what direction man should take in life's journey and they guide him at every turn and pass and point out to him the path of safety which he should steadfastly follow.

As I have already stated, this code, enacted as it is by God, is unchangeable. You can, if you like, rebel against it, as some Muslim countries have done. But you cannot alter it. It will continue to be unalterable till the last day. It has its own avenues of growth and evolution, but no human being has any right to tamper with it. Whenever an Islamic State comes into existence, this code would form its fundamental law and will constitute the mainspring of all its legislation. Everyone who desires to remain a Muslim is under an obligation

to follow the Qur'ān and the Sunnah which must constitute the basic
law of an Islamic State.

THE PURPOSE OF THE ISLAMIC STATE

The purpose of the state that may be formed on the basis of the Qur'ān
and the *Sunnah* has also been laid down by God. The Qur'ān says:

> 'We verily sent Our messengers with clear proofs, and revealed
> with them the Scripture and the Balance, that mankind may
> observe right measure; and We revealed iron, wherein is mighty
> power and (many) uses for mankind.[27]

In this verse steel symbolizes political power and the verse also
makes it clear that the mission of the Prophets is to create conditions in
which the mass of people will be assured of social justice in accordance
with the standards enunciated by God in His Book which gives explicit
instructions for a well-disciplined mode of life. In another place God
has said:

> '(Muslims are) those who, if We give them power in the land,
> establish the system of *Ṣalāh* (worship) and *Zakāh* (poor dues) and
> enjoin virtue and forbid evil and inequity.[28]
> 'You are the best community sent forth to mankind; you enjoin
> the Right conduct and forbid the wrong; and you believe in
> Allah.' [29]

It will readily become manifest to anyone who reflects upon these
verses that the purpose of the state visualized by the Holy Qur'ān is not
negative but positive. The object of the state is not merely to prevent
people from exploiting each other, to safeguard their liberty and to
protect its subjects from foreign invasion. It also aims at evolving and
developing that well-balanced system of social justice which has been
set forth by God in His Holy Book. Its object is to eradicate all forms of
evil and to encourage all types of virtue and excellence expressly mentioned by God in the Holy Qur'ān. For this purpose political power
will be made use of as and when the occasion demands; all means of
propaganda and peaceful persuasion will be employed; the moral
education of the people will also be undertaken; and social influence as
well as the force of public opinion will be harnessed to the task.

27. al-Qur'ān, 57: 25.
28. ibid., 22: 41.
29. ibid., 3: 110.

ISLAMIC STATE IS UNIVERSAL AND ALL-EMBRACING

A state of this sort cannot evidently restrict the scope of its activities. Its approach is universal and all-embracing. Its sphere of activity is coextensive with the whole of human life. It seeks to mould every aspect of life and activity in consonance with its moral norms and programme of social reform. In such a state no one can regard any field of his affairs as personal and private. Considered from this aspect the Islamic state bears a kind of resemblance to the Fascist and Communist states. But you will find later on that, despite its all-inclusiveness, it is something vastly and basically different from the modern totalitarian and authoritarian states. Individual liberty is not suppressed under it nor is there any trace of dictatorship in it. It presents the middle course and embodies the best that the human society has ever evolved. The excellent balance and moderation that characterize the Islamic system of government and the precise distinctions made in it between right and wrong — elicit from all men of honesty and intelligence the admiration and the admission that such a balanced system could not have been framed by anyone but the Omniscient and All-Wise God.

ISLAMIC STATE IS AN IDEOLOGICAL STATE

Another characteristic of the Islamic State is that it is an ideological state. It is clear from a careful consideration of the Qur'ān and the *Sunnah* that the state in Islam is based on an ideology and its objective is to establish that ideology. The state is an instrument of reform and must act likewise. It is a dictate of this very nature of the Islamic State that such a state should be run only by those who believe in the ideology on which it is based and in the Divine Law which it is assigned to administer. The administrators of the Islamic state must be those whose whole life is devoted to the observance and enforcement of this Law, who not only agree with its reformatory programme and fully believe in it but thoroughly comprehend its spirit and are acquainted with its details. Islam does not recognize any geographical, linguistic or colour bars in this respect. It puts forward its code of guidance and the scheme of its reform before all men. Whoever accepts this programme, no matter to what race, nation or country he may belong, can join the community that runs the Islamic state. But those who do not accept it are not entitled to have any hand in shaping the fundamental policy of the state. They can live within the confines of the State as non-Muslim citizens (*Dhimmīs*). Specific rights and privileges have been accorded to them in the Islamic Law. A *Dhimmī's* life, property and honour will be fully protected, and if he is capable of any service, his services will also be made use of. He will not, however, be allowed to influence the basic policy of this ideological state. The Islamic state is based on a particular ideology and it is the community which believes in the Islamic ideology which pilots it. Here again, we notice some sort of resemblance between the Islamic and the Communist states. But the treatment meted out by the Communist states to persons holdings creeds and ideologies other than its own bears no comparison with the attitude of the Islamic state. Unlike the Communist state, Islam does not impose its social principles on others by force, nor does it confiscate their properties or unleash a reign of terror by mass executions of the people and their transportation to the slave camps of Siberia. Islam does not want to eliminate its minorities, it wants to protect them and gives them the freedom to live according to their own culture. The generous and just treatment which Islam has accorded to non-Muslims in an Islamic State and the fine distinction drawn by it between justice and injustice and good and evil will convince all those who are not prejudiced against it, that the prophets sent by God accomplish their task in an altogether different manner — something radically different and diametrically opposed to the way of the false reformers who strut about here and there on the stage of history.[30]

---

30. This paper was written in 1939 and in it the author has dealt with the theoretical aspect of the problem only. In his later articles he has discussed the practical aspect as well. In his article on the 'Rights of Non-Muslims in Islamic State' (see *Islamic Law and Constitution,* Chapter VIII, pp. 316-317). He writes:

'However, in regard to a parliament or a legislature of the modern conception, which is considerably different from *Shūrā* in its traditional sense, this rule could be relaxed to allow non-Muslims to become its members provided that it has been fully ensured in the Constitution that:
(i)   It would be *ultra vires* of the parliament or the legislature to enact any law which is repugnant to the Qur'ān and the *Sunnah.*
(ii)   The Qur'ān and the *Sunnah* would be the chief source of the public law of the land.
(iii)   The head of the state or the assenting authority would necessarily be a Muslim. With these provisions ensured, the sphere of influence of non-Muslims would be limited to matters relating to the general problems of the country or to the interests of minorities concerned and their participation would not damage the fundamental requirements of Islam.'

The non-Muslims cannot occupy key-posts — posts from where the ideologi cal policy of the state can be influenced — but they can occupy general administrative posts and can act in the services of the state.   Editor.

V

THE THEORY OF THE CALIPHATE AND THE
NATURE OF DEMOCRACY IN ISLAM

I will now try to give a brief exposition of the composition and structure of the Islamic state. I have already stated that in Islam, God alone
is the real sovereign. Keeping this cardinal principle in mind, if we
consider the position of those persons who set out to enforce God's law
on earth, it is but natural to say that they should be regarded as representatives of the Supreme Ruler. Islam has assigned precisely this very
position to them. Accordingly the Holy Qur'ān says:

> 'Allah has promised to those among you who believe and do
> righteous deeds that He will assuredly make them to succeed (the
> present rulers) and grant them vicegerency in the land just as He
> made those before them to succeed (others).'

The verse illustrates very clearly the Islamic theory of state. Two
fundamental points emerge from it.

1.   The first point is that Islam uses the term 'vicegerency' (*Khilāfah*) instead of sovereignty. Since, according to Islam, sovereignty
belongs to God alone, anyone who holds power and rules in accordance with the laws of God would undoubtedly be the vicegerent of the
Supreme Ruler and would not be authorised to exercise any powers
other than those delegated to him.

2.   The second point stated in the verse is that the power to rule over
the earth has been promised to *the whole community of believers;* it has not
been stated that any particular person or class among them will be
raised to that position. From this it follows that all believers are repo-
sitories of the Caliphate. The Caliphate granted by God to the faithful
is the popular vicegerency and not a limited one. There is no reservation in favour of any family, class or race. Every believer is a Caliph of
God in his individual capacity. By virtue of this position he is individually responsible to God. The Holy Prophet has said: 'Everyone of
you is a ruler and everyone is answerable for his subjects.' Thus one
Caliph is in no way inferior to another.

This is the real foundation of democracy in Islam. The following
points emerge from an analysis of this conception of popular vicegerency:

(a)   A society in which everyone is a caliph of God and an equal
participant in this caliphate, cannot tolerate any class divisions based

on distinctions of birth and social position. All men enjoy equal status and position in such a society. The only criterion of superiority in this social order is personal ability and character. This is what has been repeatedly and explicitly asserted by the Holy Prophet:

'No one is superior to another except in point of faith and piety. All men are descended from Adam and Adam was made of clay.'

'An Arab has no superiority over a non-Arab nor a non-Arab over an Arab; neither does a white man possess any superiority over a black man nor a black man over a white one, except in point of piety.'

After the conquest of Mekka, when the whole of Arabia came under the dominion of the Islamic state, the Holy Prophet addressing the members of his own clan, who in the days before Islam enjoyed the same status in Arabia as the Brahmins did in ancient India, said:

'O people of Quraysh! Allah has rooted out your haughtiness of the days of ignorance and the pride of ancestry. O men, all of you are descended from Adam and Adam was made of clay. There is no pride whatever in ancestry; there is no merit in an Arab as against a non-Arab nor in a non-Arab against an Arab. Verily the most meritorious among you in the eyes of God is he who is the most pious.'

(b)   In such a society no individual or group of individuals will suffer any disability on account of birth, social status, or profession that may in any way impede the growth of his faculties or hamper the development of his personality.

Every one would enjoy equal opportunities of progress. The way would be left open for him to make as much progress as possible according to his inborn capacity and personal merits without prejudice to similar rights of other people. Thus, unrestricted scope for personal achievement has always been the hallmark of Islamic society. Slaves and their descendants were appointed as military officers and governors of provinces, and noblemen belonging to the highest families did not feel ashamed to serve under them. Those who used to stitch and mend shoes rose in the social scale and became leaders of highest order (*imāms*); Weavers and cloth-sellers became judges (*muftīs*) and jurists and to this day they are reckoned as the heroes of Islam. The Holy Prophet has said:

31. al-Qur'ān, 24: 55.

'Listen and obey even if a negro is appointed as a ruler over you.'
(c)   There is no room in such a society for the dictatorship of any person or group of persons since everyone is a caliph of God herein. No person or group of persons is entitled to become an absolute ruler by depriving the rank and file of their inherent right of caliphate. The position of a man who is selected to conduct the affairs of the state is no more than this; that all Muslims (or, technically speaking, all caliphs of God) delegate their caliphate to him for administrative purposes. *He is answerable to God on the one hand and on the other to his fellow 'caliphs' who have delegated their authority to him.* Now, if he raises himself to the position of an irresponsible absolute ruler, that is to say a dictator, he assumes the character of a usurper rather than a Caliph, because dictatorship is the negation of popular vicegerency. No doubt the Islamic state is an all-embracing state and comprises within its sphere all departments of life, but this all-inclusiveness and universality are based upon the universality of Divine Law which an Islamic ruler has to observe and enforce. The guidance given by God about every aspect of life will certainly be enforced in its entirety. But an Islamic ruler cannot depart from these instructions and adopt a policy of regimentation on his own. He cannot force people to follow or not to follow a particular profession; to learn or not to learn a special art; to use or not to use a certain script; to wear or not to wear a certain dress and to educate or not to educate their children in a certain manner. The powers which the dictators of Russia, Germany and Italy have appropriated or which Ataturk has exercized in Turkey have not been granted by Islam to its *Amīr* (leader). Besides this, another important point is that in Islam *every individual is held personally answerable to God.* This personal responsibility cannot be shared by anyone else. Hence, an individual enjoys full liberty to choose whichever path he likes and to develop his faculties in any direction that suits his natural gifts. If the leader obstructs him or obstructs the growth of his personality, he will himself be punished by God for this tyranny. That is precisely the reason why there is not the slightest trace of regimentation in the rule of the Holy Prophet and of his Rightly-Guided Caliphs; and
(d)   In such a society every sane and adult Muslim, male or female, is entitled to express his or her opinion, for each one of them is the repository of the caliphate. God has made this caliphate conditional, not upon any particular standard of wealth or competence but only upon faith and good conduct. Therefore all Muslims have equal freedom to express their opinions.

EQUILIBRIUM BETWEEN INDIVIDUALISM AND COLLECTIVISM

Islam seeks to set up, on the one hand, this superlative democracy and on the other it has put an end to that individualism which militates against the health of the body politic. The relations between the individual and the society have been regulated in such a manner that neither the personality of the individual suffers any diminution, or corrosion as it does in the Communist and Fascist social system, nor is the individual allowed to exceed his bounds to such an extent as to become harmful to the community, as happens in the Western democracies. In Islam, the purpose of an individual's life is the same as that of the life of the community, namely, the execution and enforcement of Divine Law and the acquisition of God's pleasure. Moreover, Islam has, after safeguarding the rights of the individual, imposed upon him certain duties towards the community. In this way requirements of individualism and collectivism have been so well harmonized that the individual is afforded the fullest opportunity to develop his potentialities and is thus enabled to employ his developed faculties in the service of the community at large.

These are, briefly, the basic principles and essential features of the Islamic political theory.

11

Objectives of the Islamic Economic Order*

Muhammad Umar Chapra

ISLAM is not an ascetic religion[1] and does not aim at depriving Muslims of the 'good things that God has provided' (al-Qur'ān, 7: 32). It takes a positive view of life considering man not as a born sinner eternally condemned for his original sin, but as the vicegerent of God (al-Qur'ān, 2: 30) for whom has been created everything on earth (al-Qur'ān, 2: 29). Virtue therefore lies not in shunning the bounties of God, but in enjoying them within the framework of the values for 'righteous living' through which Islam seeks to promote human welfare.

The values for righteous living that Islam propagates permeate all

* This chapter is taken from Dr. Chapra's book *Economic System of Islam*, University of Karachi, 1971.

1. The Qur'ān says: 'And the monasticism which they have innovated, We did not prescribe it for them' (al-Qur'ān, 57: 27). Once after the Prophet had given a lecture on the certainty of the Day of Judgment and the accountability before God, a few of his Companions gathered in the house of 'Uthmān bin Maz'ūn and resolved to fast everyday, to pray every night, not to sleep on beds, not to eat meat or fat, not to have anything to do with women or perfume, to wear coarse clothes, and in general to reject the world. The Prophet heard of this and told them:
'I have not been directed by God to live in this manner. Your body certainly has rights over you; so fast but also abstain from fasting, and pray at night but also sleep. Look at me, I pray at night but I also sleep; I fast but I also abstain from fasting, I eat meat as well as fat, and I also marry. So whoever turns away from my way is not from me.' (See the commentary of verse 87 of *sūrah* 5 in *al-Kashshāf,* Beirut, 1947, v. 1, p. 67; and Ibn Kathir *Tafsīr al-Qur'ān al-'Azīm,* Cairo, n.d., v. 2, pp. 87-8. See also Bukhārī, Cairo, n.d. v. 3, pp. 49-50; Muslim, Cairo, 1955 v. 2, pp. 812-18; and Dārimī, Damascus, 1349 A.D., v. 2, p. 133).

sectors of human activity. There is no strictly mundane sector of life according to Islam. Action in every field of human activity, including the economic, is spiritual provided it is in harmony with the goals and values of Islam. It is really these goals and values that determine the nature of the economic system of Islam. A proper understanding of these is therefore essential for a better perspective of the economic system of Islam. These goals and values are:

(a)   Economic well-being within the framework of the moral norms of Islam;
(b)   Universal brotherhood and justice;
(c)   Equitable distribution of income; and
(d)   Freedom of the individual within the context of social welfare.

This list of goals is by no means complete but should provide a sufficient framework for discussing and elaborating the Islamic economic system and highlighting those characteristics which distinguish the Islamic system from the two prevalent systems, capitalism and socialism.

(a)   Economic well-being and the moral norms of Islam.

Eat and drink of that which God has provided and act not corruptly, making mischief in the world (al-Qur'ān 2: 60).

O mankind! Eat of what is lawful and good on earth and follow not the footsteps of the devil (al-Qur'ān 2: 168).

O you who believe! Forbid not the good things which God has made lawful for you and exceed not the limits. Surely, God loves not those who exceed the limits. And eat of the lawful and good that God has given you, and keep your duty to God in whom you believe (al-Qur'ān, 5: 87-88).

These verses of the Qur'ān, and there are many others like these,[2] strike the keynote of the Qur'ānic message in the economic field. Islam urges Muslims to enjoy the bounties provided by God and sets no quantitative limits to the extent of material growth of Muslim society. It even equates the struggle for material well-being with an act of virtue.

When the prayer is ended, then disperse in the land and seek of God's bounty ... (al-Qur'ān, 62: 10).

If God provides anyone of you with an opportunity for earning

2. See, al'Qur'ān, 2: 172; 6: 142; 7: 31 and 160; 16: 114; 20: 81; 23: 51; 34: 15; and 67: 15.

livelihood, let him not leave it unexploited until it is exhausted or becomes disagreeable to him.[3]

Any Muslim who plants a tree or cultivates a field such that a bird, or a human being, or an animal eats from it, this act will be counted as an act of charity.[4]

He who seeks the world lawfully to refrain from begging, to cater to his family, and to be kind to his neighbour, will meet God with his face shining like the full moon.[5]

Islam goes even further than this. It urges Muslims to gain mastery over nature because, according to the Qur'ān, all resources in the heavens and the earth have been created for the service of mankind,[6] and because, as the Prophet said, 'there is no malady for which God has not created a cure'.[7] From this, one cannot but infer that the goal of attaining a suitably high rate of economic growth should be among the economic goals of a Muslim society because this would be the manifestation of a continious effort to use, through research and improvements in technology, the resources provided by God for the service and betterment of mankind, thus helping in the fulfilment of the very object of their creation.

Islam has prohibited begging and urged Muslims to earn their livelihood.[8] From this premise one may infer that one of the economic goals of a Muslim society should be to create such an economic environment that those who are willing to and looking for work are able to find gainful employment in accordance with their abilities. If this is not accomplished then Muslim society cannot succeed even in its spiritual aims, because those unemployed would be subjected to a life of extreme hardship unless they depend on the dole, or resort to beg-

3. Ibn Mājah Cairo, 1952, v. 2, p. 727: 2148.
4. Bukhārī, v. 3, p. 128; Muslim, v. 3, p. 1189: 12; and Tirmidhī, v. 3, p. 666: 1382.
5. Cited on the authority of Bayhaqī's *Shu'b al-īmān* in *Mishkāt* Damascus, 1381, A.D., v. 2, p. 658: 5207.
6. Says the Qur'ān: 'God has made subservient to you whatever is in the heavens and whatever is in the earth and granted you his bounties both manifest and hidden' (31: 20). There are several verses of this meaning in the Qur'ān, for example, 14: 32-33; 16: 12-14; 22: 65 and 45: 12.
7. Bukhārī, v. 7, p. 158; and Ibn Mājah v. 2. p. 1138: 3439.
8. 'Beg not anything from the people' (Abū Dāwūd Cairo, 1952 v. 1, p. 382); 'The hand that is above is better than the hand that is below' (Bukhārī, v. 2, p. 133 and Nisā'ī, v. 5, p. 45-46); and 'A man has not earned better income than that which is from his own labour' (Ibn Mājah, v. 2, p. 723: 2138; and Nisā'ī, Cairo, 1964, v. 7, p. 212).

ging or immoral practices, all of which, particularly the last two, would be repugnant to the spirit of Islam.

This stress of Islam on economic well-being springs from the very nature of its message. Islam is designed to serve as a 'blessing' for mankind, and aims at making life richer and worth the living and not poorer, full of hardships. Says the Qur'ān:

> We sent you not but as a blessing for all mankind (al-Qur'ān, 21: 107);
>
> O mankind! There has come to you indeed an admonition from your Lord, and a healing for what is in your hearts, and for those who believe a guidance and a blessing (al-Qur'ān, 10: 57);
>
> God desires ease for you and desires not hardship for you (al'Qur'ān, 2: 185);
>
> God desires to alleviate your burdens, for man is created weak (al-Qur'ān, 4: 28); and
>
> God desires not to place a burden on you but He wishes to purify you and to complete His favour on you so that you may be grateful (al-Qur'ān, 5: 6).

On the basis of these verses of the Qur'ān Muslim Jurists have unanimously held that catering for the interests of the people and relieving them of hardships is the basic objective of the *Sharī'ah*.[9] Ghazālī, a great philosopher-reformer-sūfī contended that the very objective of the *Sharī'ah* is to promote the welfare of the people which lies in safeguarding their faith, their life, their intellect, their posterity and their property; and that therefore whatever ensures the safeguard of these five serves public interest and is desirable.[10] Ibn Qayyim emphasized that 'the basis of the *Sharī'ah* is wisdom and the welfare of the people in this world as well as the Hereafter. This welfare lies in complete justice, mercy, welfare and wisdom; anything that departs from justice to oppression, from mercy to harshness, from welfare to misery, and from wisdom to folly, has nothing to do with the *Sharī'ah*.'[11]

In this pursuit of an economically fuller and prosperous life it is possible for a Muslim to go to the extreme and to make material welfare an end in itself by ignoring spiritual values, acquiring wealth through unfair means, exploiting others, subjecting them to wrong and injustice, and by not promoting the good of others from what he

9. See Abū Zahrah *Uṣūl al-Fiqh,* Damascus, 1957, p. 355.
10. M. Ghazī al-Mustasfa Cairo, 1937, v. 1, pp. 139-40.
11. Ibn Qayyim *I'lām al-Muwaqqi'īn,* Cairo, 1955.

has earned or accumulated. Hence, since Islam also seeks to 'purify' life, the Qur'ān clearly warns Muslims against this danger: 'When the prayer is ended then disperse in the land and seek of God's bounty but remember God much so that you may be successful' (al-Qur'ān, 62: 10). It is generally understood by Muslim religious scholars that 're-membering God much' does not imply spending most of one's time in saying prayers or reciting the rosary, but that it implies living a mor-ally responsible life in accordance with the norms of Islam,[12] earning only by the right methods and abandoning all the wrong ones,[13] and is considering wealth as a stewardship for which account is to be render-ed by God (al-Qur'ān, 57: 7).

In this context it may be easier to understand those Qur'ānic verses and *aḥādīth* that emphasize the trifling nature of this world and its possessions.[14] These are trifling not in any absolute sense, but in rela-tion to spiritual values. If the worldly possessions can be acquired without sacrificing spiritual ideals, then there is no virtue in forsaking them, as the Prophet said: 'There is nothing wrong in wealth for him who fears God'.[15] But if there is a conflict then, one must be contented with whatever can be acquired rightfully even though it may be little, as the Qur'ān explains: 'Say the bad and the good are not equal, though the abundance of the bad may fascinate you; so keep your duty to God, O men of understanding, that you may succeed' (al-Qur'ān, 5: 100). One who cares more for the eternal values of Islam than for the worldly pleasures would not hesitate to make this sacrifice for he un-

---

12. Ibn Kathīr, while interpreting this verse, says: 'Remember God much' means that 'While selling or buying and taking or giving, you must remember God much so that these worldly pursuits do not cause you to lose sight of what benefits you in the Hereafter' *Tafsīr* v. 4, p. 367.

13. The Prophet exhorted: 'Fear God and be moderate in your pursuit of wealth; take only that which is allowed and leave that which is forbidden.' Ibn Mājah, v. 2, p. 725, 2144.

14. 'Say: The wordly possessions are but trifling, it is the Hereafter which is better for those who fear God' (al-Qur'ān, 4: 77; see also 29: 64 and 57: 20-21.) 'Live in this world as though you are a stranger or a wayfarer, and consider yourself among those in the grave' (Ibn Mājah, v. 2, p. 1378: 4114).
'What is this world compared to the Hereafter? Thrust your finger in the ocean and see what you get' *(Mishkāt,* v. 2, p. 648: 5156, on the authority of Muslim).
'Be detached from the world and God will love you, be detached from what the people have and they will love you' (Ibid., v. 2, p. 654: 5187, on the authority of Tirmidhī and Ibn Mājah).

15. Bukhārī, p. 113: 301.

derstands and appreciates what the Prophet meant by saying that
'The love of this world is the source of all evil'[16], and that 'He who loves
the world prejudices his Hereafter and he who loves the Hereafter
receives a setback in the world; so prefer that which is eternal to that
which is mortal'.[17]

This explains the manner in which Islam creates a harmony between the material and the moral by urging Muslims to strive for
material welfare but stressing simultaneously that they place this
material effort on a moral foundation thus providing a spiritual
orientation to material effort:

> And seek to attain by means of what God has given you the abode
> of the Hereafter, but neglect not your share in this world, and do
> good to others as God has done good to you, and seek not to make
> mischief in the world. Surely God loves not the mischief-makers
> (al'Qur'ān, 28: 77).

> The best of Muslims is he who is concerned about the affairs of
> this world as well as the affairs of the Hereafter.[18]

> He is not the best of you who renounces this world for the
> Hereafter nor is he who neglects the Hereafter for this world; the
> best of you is he who takes from this world as well as the Hereafter.[19]

This simultaneus stress on both the material and the spiritual aspects of life is a unique characteristic of the Islamic economic system.
The spiritual and the material have been so firmly dovetailed with
each other that they may serve as a source of mutual strength and
together contribute to real human welfare. The neglect of any one of
these two aspects of life cannot lead mankind to true welfare. If only
material well-being is catered for and there are accompanying moral
and cultural maladjustments, there would be increased manifestation
of the symptoms of *anomae,* such as frustration, crime, alcoholism,
extra-marital relations, divorce, mental illness and suicide, all indicating lack of inner happiness in the life of individuals. If only the
spiritual need of life is catered for, the mass of the people would find it
impractible and unrealistic, thus generating a dichotomy and conflict

16. Cited on the authority of Bayhaqī's *Shu'ab al-īmān* in *Mishkāt* v. 2, p. 659:
5213).
17. *Musnad* of Ahmad ibn Hanbal, cited in ibid., v. 2, p. 652: 5179.
18. Ibn Mājah, v. 2, p. 725: 2143.
19. *Hadīth* reported by Māīwardi, p. 117; also cited on the authority of Ibn
'Asakir, but with slightly different wording, by Suyūti in *al-Jāmi' al-Ṣaghīr,* v.
2, p. 135)

between material and spiritual values which may threaten to destroy all values in human society.

This synthesis of the material and the spiritual is what is missing in the other two systems, capitalism and socialism, as they are both basically secular and either amoral or morally neutral. No one can deny the achievements of the capitalist system in efficiency of the productive machinery and standards of living, nor can anyone deny the achievements of the socialist system in rates of economic growth. But both the capitalist and the socialist systems have neglected the spiritual needs of the human personality.

(b) Universal brotherhood and justice.

O mankind! We created you from a male and a female and made you into nations and tribes that you may know each other. Verily, the most honoured of you before God is the most righteous of you; surely God is Knowing, Aware (al-Qur'ān, 49: 13);

Your God is one, you are from Adam and Adam was from dust; an Arab has no superiority over a non-Arab nor a white over a black except by righteousness.[20]

Mankind is from Adam and Eve and all of you are alike in your descent from them. On the Day of Judgement, God will not ask you about your noble descent or your lineage; rather the most honoured of you before God on that Day will be the most righteous of you.[21]

Islam aims at establishing a social order where all individuals are united by bonds of brotherhood and affection like members of one single family created by One God from one couple. This brotherhood is universal and not parochial. It is not bound by any geographical boundaries and encompasses the whole of mankind and not any one familial group or tribe or race. The Qur'ān asserts, 'Say: O mankind! Surely I am a messenger of God to you all' (al-Qur'ān, 7: 158); and the Prophet stressed: 'I have been sent to all alike, the white or the black'.[22]

A natural corollary of this concept of universal brotherhood is mutual co-operation and help, particularly among Muslims who, beside being united to each other as to the rest of mankind by a common origin, are further united by bonds of common ideology, and have been characterized by the Qur'ān as 'brothers-in-faith' (al-Qur'ān, 9:

20. Prophet Muḥammad quoted on the authority of al-Ṭabarānī in *Majma' al-Zawā'id*, v. 8, p. 84; the quotation is the combination of two *hadīths*.
21. Ibn Kathīr, *Tafsīr*, v. 4, p. 218, see the commentary of verse 13 of *sūrah* 49.
22. Shāṭibī *al-Muwāfiqāt fī Uṣūl al-Sharī'ah*, Cairo, n.d., v. 2, p. 244, on the authority of Bukhārī, Muslim and Nisā'ī.

11)[23] and 'merciful among themselves' (al-Qur'ān, 48: 29). The Prophet stressed:

> Mankind is the family of God and the most beloved of them before Him is one who is the best of His Family.[24]
> Be kind to those on earth and He who is in the Heaven will be kind to you.[25]
> In mutual compassion, love, and kindness you will find the faithfuls like a body, so that if one part feels pain, the whole body responds with wakefulness and fever.[26]
> A Muslim is the brother of another Muslim; he neither wrongs him, nor leaves him without help, nor humiliates him.[27]

Closely linked to, and inseparable from, this concept of brotherhood is the emphasis of Islam on justice, the establishment of which on earth is unequivocally declared by the Qur'ān to be one of the principal objectives of the teachings of all the prophets of God including Muḥammad (al-Qur'ān, 57: 25). Faith that is mingled with injustice will not really be recognized by God as the Qur'ān proclaims: 'Those who have faith and mix not their faith with injustice, for them is peace and they are the ones rightly guided' (al-Qur'ān, 6: 83). Muslims are therefore not merely exhorted but persistently urged by the Qur'ān to establish justice: 'God commands justice and the doing of good' (al-Qur'ān, 16: 90), and 'when you judge between people, judge with justice' (al-Qur'ān, 3: 58).

Justice commands a place of such paramount importance in Islam that being just is considered to be a necessary condition for being pious and God-fearing, the basic characteristics of a Muslim. Says the Qur'ān:

> O you who believe! Be upright for God, bearers of witness with justice, and let not the hatred of others make you swerve from justice. Be just, this is nearer to piety, and fear God, for God is Aware of what you do (al-Qur'ān, 5: 8).

---

23. See also al-Qur'ān, 33: 5; and 49: 10.
24. *Mishkāt* v. 2, p. 613: 4998, the authority of Bayhaqī's *Shu'ab al-īmān*.
25. Ibid., 608: 4969, on the authority of Abū Dāwūd and Tirmidhī.
26. Bukhārī, v. 8, p. 12; and Muslim, v. 4, p. 1999: 66, see also *hadīth* numbers 65 and 67.
27. Muslim, v. 4, p. 1986: 32.

Moreover, the course of justice is to be followed even if this hurts one's own interest or the interests of one's near-ones. 'And when you speak, speak justly, even though it be (against) a relative' (al-Qur'ān, 6: 152), and 'Be the establishers of justice and witnesses to God, even if this be against yourselves, or your parents or your near-ones whether they be rich or poor, for God can best protect both. So follow not your low desires, lest you deviate. And if you swerve or decline to do justice then remember that God is aware of what you do' (al-Qur'ān, 4: 135).

The implications of justice in Islam would be clearer when discussed in the following sections on social and economic justice.

SOCIAL JUSTICE

Since Islam considers mankind as one family, all members of this family are alike in the eyes of God and before the Law revealed by Him. There is no difference between the rich and the poor, between the high and the low, or between the white and the black. There is to be no discrimination due to race or colour or position. The only criterion of a man's worth is character, ability and service to humanity. Said the Holy Prophet:

Certainly God looks not at your faces or your wealth; instead He looks at your heart and your deeds;[28]

The noblest of you are the best in character.[29]

To be even more emphatic the Prophet warned of the disastrous consequences of discrimination and inequality before Law for an individual or a nation:

Communities before you strayed because when the high committed theft they were set free, but when the low committed theft the Law was enforced on them. By God, even if Fāṭimah, daughter of Muhammad, committed theft, Muhammad would certainly cut her hand.[30]

Whoever humiliates or despises a Muslim, male or female for his poverty or paucity of resources, will be disgraced by God on the Day of Judgement.[31]

'Umar the second Caliph, wrote to Abū Mūsā al-Ash'arī, one of his governors, asking him to 'treat every-one before you alike in respect so

28. Muslim, v. 4, p. 1987: 34.
29. Bukhārī, v. 8, p. 15.
30. Ibid., p. 199; and Nisā'ī, v. 8, p. 65.
31. *Musnad* Imām Alī al-Rida, Beirut, 1966, p. 474.

that the weak does not despair of justice from you and that the high does not crave for an undue advantage'.[32] This spirit of social justice thoroughly permeated Muslim society during the period of the first four Caliphs and even in the later period though a little subdued, did not fail to find its full manifestation on several occasions. It may be pertinent to quote what the renowned jurist Abū Yūsuf wrote in a letter addressed to the Caliph Hārūn al-Rashīd: 'treat alike all individuals irrespective of whether they are near you or remote from you' and that 'the welfare of your subjects depends on establishing the Divine Law and eliminating injustice'.[33]

ECONOMIC JUSTICE

The concept of brotherhood and equal treatment of all individuals in society and before the Law is not meaningful unless accompanied by economic justice such that everyone gets his due for his contribution to society or to the social product and that there is no exploitation of one individual by another. The Qur'ān urges Muslims to 'Withold not things justly due to others' (al-Qur'ān, 26: 183),[34] implying thereby that every individual must get what is really due to him, and not by depriving others of their share. The Prophet aptly warned: 'Beware of injustice for injustice will be equivalent to darkness on the Day of Judgement.'[35] This warning against injustice and exploitation is designed to protect the rights of all individuals in society (whether consumers or producers and distributors, and whether employers or employees) and to promote general welfare, the ultimate goal of Islam.

Of special significance here is the relationship between the employer and the employee which Islam places in a proper setting and specifies norms for the mutual treatment of both so as to establish justice between them. An employee is intitled to a 'just' wage for his contribution to output and it is unlawful for a Muslim employer to exploit his employee'. The Prophet declared that three persons who will certainly face God's displeasure on the Day of Judgement are: one who dies without fulfiling his commitment to God; one who sells a free person

32. Abū Yūsuf, *Kitāb al-Kharāj,* Cairo, 1367 A.H.
33. Abū Yūsuf, pp. 4 and 6.
34. See also al-Qur'ān 83: 1-3, ('Woe to the cheaters; who when they take the measure (of their dues) from men, take it fully. And when they measure out to others or weigh out for them, they give less than is due').
35. Reported on the authority of *Musnad* of Aḥmad and Bayhaqi's *Shu'ab al-īmān* by Suyūṭī, v. 1, p. 8.

and enjoys the price; and one who engages a labourer, receives due work from him but does not pay him his wage.[36] This *hadīth*, by placing the exploitation of labour and the enslaving of a free person on an equal footing, suggests how averse Islam is to exploitation of labour.

What a 'just' wage is and what constitutes 'exploitation' of labour needs to be determined in the light of the teachings of the Qur'ān and the *Sunnah*.[37] Islam does not recognize the contribution to output made by factors of production other than labour and therefore the concept of exploitation of labour in Islam would have no relation with the concept of surplus value as propounded by Marx. It could be argued theoretically that 'just' wage should be equal to the value of the contribution to output made by the labourer. But this is difficult to determine and would have little practical value in regulating wages. There are however a number of *aḥādīth* from which may be inferred qualitatively the level of 'minimum' and 'ideal' wages. According to the Prophet, 'an employee (male or female) is entitled to at least moderately good food and clothing and to not being burdened with labour except what he (or she) can bear'.[38] From this *hadīth* it may be inferred that 'minimum' wage should be such that it resembles an employee to get a sufficient quantity of reasonably good food and clothing for himself and his family without overburdening himself. This was considered by the Prophet's Companions to be the minimum even to maintain the spiritual standard of Muslim society. 'Uthmān, the third Caliph, is reported to have said:

> Do not overburden your unskilled female employee in her pursuit of a living, because if you do so, she may resort to immorality; and do not overburden a male subordinate, for if you do so, he may resort to stealing. Be considerate with your employees and God will be considerate with you. It is incumbent upon you to provide them good and lawful food.[39]

The 'ideal' wage may likewise be inferred from the following *hadīth* to be a wage that would enable the employee to eat food and wear clothing just like the employer is himself capable of:-

36. Bukhārī, v. 3, p. 112.
37. Some of the quotations *(hadīth* or otherwise) used in the discussion, relate to slaves, but the term 'employees' is used in the translation. If a humane and just treatment is expected to be meted out to slaves, then employees are certainly entitled to an even better treatment.
38. *Mālik Muwaṭṭā* Cairo, 1951, Malik, v. 2, p. 980: 40.
39. Mālik, *Muwaṭṭā*, v. 2, p. 981: 42.

Your employees are your brothers whom God had made your subordinates. So he who has his brother under him, let him feed with what he feeds himself and clothe him with what he clothes himself . . .[40]

The 'just' wage cannot therefore be below the 'minumum' wage. Its desirable level would of course be closer to the 'ideal' wage so as to minimize the inequalities of income and to bridge the gulf between the living conditions of the employers and the employees which tends to create two distinct classes of the 'haves' and the 'have-nots', thus weakening the bonds of brotherhood which constitutes an essential feature of a truly Muslim society. Between the two limits, the actual level would be determined by the interaction of supply and demand, the extent of economic growth, the level of moral consciousness in Muslim society, and the extent to which the state plays its legitimate role.

Besides being paid at least 'minimum' wages and preferably 'ideal' wages, Islam requires that labourers should not be made to work so hard or in such miserable conditions that their health deteriorates or their ability to enjoy income or participate in family life gets impaired.[41] If they are made to perform a task which is beyond their capacity they should be provided with sufficient help to enable them to do the job without undue hardship. In the *ḥadīth* quoted above in which the prophet admonishes employers to consider the employees as their brothers, he said further:

. . . and do not burden them with what overpowers them. If you do so, then help them.[42]

From this *Ḥadīth* it may be inferred that fixation of maximum hours of work, creation of proper working conditions, and enforcement of precautionary measures against industrial hazards, would be fully in conformity with the spirit of Islamic teachings.

While this is the treatment expected of an employer for his employees, Islam, because of its commitment to justice, protects the employer by placing certain moral obligations on the employee as

40. Bukhārī, p. 15, and v. 3, p. 185; and Muslim, v. 3, p. 1283: 38.
41. 'I wish not to be hard on you. God willing you will find me among the righteous'. (al-Qur'ān, 28: 27). This statement of Shu'ayb while hiring Moses is an exhortation in the Qur'ān for all employers.
42. Bukharī, v. 1, p. 16, and v. 3, p. 185; and Muslim, v. 3, p. 1283: 38 and 40.

well. The first obligation is to do the job conscientiously and diligently with maximum possible degree of care and skill. The Prophet exhorted: 'God has made beneficence obligatory upon you'[43] and that 'God loves that when any one of you does a job, he does it perfectly.'[44] There can be no question that social and economic justice, which Islam stresses unambiguously, requires the efficient performance of the function for which one has been employed. On another occasion the Prophet said:

> An employee who excels in his devotion to God and also renders to his master what is due to him of duty, sincerity and obedience, for him there is double rewards (with God).[45]

A second obligation on the employee is to be honest and trustworthy. The Qur'ān says that the best person anyone can hire is the strong (able) and the honest(28: 26), and the Prophet has said:

> He whom we have appointed for a job and have provided with livelihood, then whatever he appropriates beyond this is ill-gotten.[46]

Thus if Islam has placed a number of obligations on the employer, the employee is also expected to do the job conscientiously and diligently, and be honest and trustworthy. The goal is justice to both employers and employees in all economic relationships. It is only by such a harmonious regulation of mutual responsibilities emphasizing co-operation and conscientious fulfilment of one's obligations, in an environment of brotherhood, justice, and supremacy of moral values, that there can be hope of eliminating labour-employer conflict and friction and establishing industrial peace.

(c) Equitable distribution of income

With the intense and unique commitment of Islam to human brotherhood and to social and economic justice, gross inequalities of income and wealth could not but be repugnant to its spirit. Such inequalities could only destroy rather than foster the feelings of brotherhood that Islam wishes to create. Besides, since all resources are, according to the Qur'ān, 'gifts of God to all human beings' (2: 29), there is no reason why they should remain concentrated in a few hands.

43. Muslim, v. 3, p. 1548: 57.
44. Cited on the authority of Bayhaqī's *Shu'ab al-īmān* by Suyūtī, v.1, p. 75.
45. Bukhārī, v. 3, p. 186.
46. Abū Dāwwūd, v. 2, p. 121.

Hence, Islam emphasizes distributive justice and incorporates in its system a programme for redistribution of income and wealth so that every individual is guaranteed a standard of living that is humane and respectable, and in harmony with the regard for the dignity of man inherent in the teachings of Islam (God's vicegerent on earth, al-Qur'ān, 2: 30). A Muslim society that fails to guarantee such a humane standard is really not worthy of the name as the Prophet declared: 'He is not a true Muslim who eats his fill when his next-door neighbour is hungry.'[47]

'Umar, the second Caliph, explaining the redistributive justice in Islam, emphasized in one of his public addresses that everyone had an equal right in the wealth of the community, that no one, not even he himself, enjoyed a greater right in it than any one else, and that if he were to live longer, he would see to it that even a shepherd on the Mount Ṣan'ā' received his share from his wealth.[48] The Caliph 'Alī is reported to have stressed that 'God has made it obligatory on the rich to provide the poor with what is adequately for them; if the poor are hungry or naked or troubled it is because the rich have deprived them (of their right), and it will be proper for God to account them for it and to punish them.'[49] The jurists have almost unanimously held the position that it is the duty of the whole Muslim society in general and of its rich in particular to take care of the basic needs of the poor and if the well-to-do do not fulfil this responsibility in spite of their ability to do so the state can and should compel them, to assume their responsibility.[50]

The Islamic programme for redistribution consists of three parts. One, as discussed earlier, Islamic teachings imply the rendering of assistance in finding gainful employment to those unemployed and those looking for work and a 'just' remuneration for those working; two, it emphasizes the payment of zakāt for redistributing income from the rich to the poor[51] who, because of personal disability or handicaps

---

47. Bukhārī, p. 52: 112.
48. Haykal, al-Fārūq 'Umar, Cairo, 1964, v. 2, p. 233.
49. Abū 'Ubayd Kitab al-Amwāl, Cairo, 1353 A.D., p. 595: 1909; for slightly different wording, see Nahj al-Balāghah Cairo n.d., v. 3, p. 231.
50. For some relevant details, see Siddiqi, Islām kā Naẓariyya-e Milkīyat, Lahore, 1968, pp. 272-79.
51. The Prophet, while appointing Mu'ādh as Governer of the Yemen, enumerated to him a list of duties, one of which was 'to educate people that God had made it obligatory upon them to pay the zakāt which is to be collected

(physical or mental or conditions external to them e.g. unemployment), are unable to attain a respectable standard of living by their own effort, 'so that', in the words of the Qur'ān; 'wealth does not circulate only among your rich' (59: 7); and three divisions of the estate of a deceased person, in accordance with a given formula, among a number of individuals so as to intensify and accelerate the distribution of wealth in society.

This Islamic concept of equity in the distribution of income and wealth and its concept of economic justice, does not however require that everyone be rewarded equally, irrespective of his contribution to society. Islam tolerates some inequalities of income because all men are not equal in their character, ability and service to society (al-Qur'ān, 6: 165; 16: 71 and 43: 32). Therefore, distributive justice in Islamic society, after guaranteeing a humane standard of living to all members through the institution of zakāt, allows such differentials in earnings as are in keeping with the differences in the value of the contributions or services rendered, each individual receiving an income corresponding to the social value of the services he contributes to society.

The Islamic stresses on distributive justice is so emphatic that there had been some Muslims who have been led to believe in absolute equality of wealth. Abū Dhar, a Companion of the Prophet, was of the opinion that it is unlawful for a Muslim to possess wealth beyond the essential needs of his family. However, most of the Prophet's Companions did not agree with him in this extreme view and tried to prevail upon him to change his position.[52] But even Abū Dhar was not a protagonist of equality of flows (income). He was in favour of equality of stocks (wealth accumulations). This, he asserted, could be attained if the entire surplus of income over 'genuine' expenses (al-'afw) was spent by the individual in improving the lot of his less fortunate brothers. The concensus of Muslim scholars, in spite of being intensely in favour of distributive justice, has however always been that if a Muslim earns by rightful means and from his own income and wealth fulfils his obligations toward the welfare of his society by paying zakāt and other required contributions, there is nothing wrong in his possessing more wealth than other fellow-Muslims.[53] In reality, however, if the

52. See the comments on verse 34 of sūrah 9 of the Qur'ān in the commentaries of Ibn Kathīr, v. 2, p. 352, and Jassās, Ahkām al-Qur'ān, Cairo, 1957, v. 3, p. 130.
53. See the commentary of Ibn Kathīr, v. 2, pp. 350-53.

from their rich and distributed to their poor' (Bukhārī, v. 2, p. 124; Tirmidhī, v. 3, p. 21: 625, and Nisā'ī, v. 5, pp. 3 and 41).

Islamic teachings of *Ḥalāl* and *Ḥarām* in the earning of wealth are followed, the norm of justice to employees and consumers is applied, provisions for redistribution of income and wealth are implemented and the Islamic law of inheritance is enforced, there cannot be any gross inequalities of income and wealth in Muslim society.

(d) Freedom of the individual within the context of social welfare

The most important pillar of Muslim faith is the belief that man has been created by God and is subservient to none but Him (al'Qur'ān, 13: 36 and 31: 22). This provides the essence of the Islamic charter of freedom from all bondage. Hence the Qur'ān says that one of the primary objectives of Muḥammad's Prophetic mission was to 'release them (mankind) from the burdens and chains upon them' (7: 157). It is this spirit of freedom which prompted 'Umar, the second Caliph, to declare: 'Since when have you enslaved people although their mothers had borne them free'.[54] Shāf'ī, the founder of the Shāf'ī school of Muslim jurisprudence, expressed the same spirit when he said: 'God has created you free and therefore be nothing but free.'[55]

Because man is born free, no one, not even the state, has the right to abrogate this freedom and to subject his life to regimentation. There is a consensus among Muslim jurists that restrictions cannot be imposed on a free, mature, and sane person. Abū Ḥanīfah, the founder of the Ḥanafī school of Muslim jurisprudence, goes further and feels that restrictions may not be imposed on a free, mature, and sane person even if he hurts his own interest by, to quote his own example, 'spending money aimlessly without any benefit.' The reason he gives for this is that depriving him of the freedom of choice is 'like degrading his humanity and treating him like an animal. The injury done by this would be greater than the injury done by his extravagance. A greater loss should not be inflicted to avoid a smaller loss.'[56]

This difference of opinion, however, exists only if an individual hurts his own interest, without, of course, over-stepping the moral bonds of Islam. But if the individual hurts the interests of others, then there is no difference of opinion that restrictions can and should be imposed on him. All jurists allow restrictions to be imposed if this

---

54. 'Alī al- Tantāwī and Nājī al- Tanṭāwī, *Akhbār 'Umar,* Damascus, 1959, p. 268.
55. Quoted without reference to the original source, by Yúsufuddin *Islām ke Ma'āshī Naẓariyye,* Hyderabad, India, v. 1, p. 140.
56. *al-Hidāyah,* Cairo, 1965, v. 3, p. 281; see also Jazīrī, *Kitāb al-Fiqh 'alā al-Madhāhīb al-Arba'ah,* Cairo, 1938, v. 2, p. 349.

prevents injury to others or safeguards public interest, as in Abū Hanīfah's words, 'controls on an untrained doctor, or a careless judge, or a bankrupt employer, because such controls remove a greater harm by inflicting a smaller harm.'[57] Social welfare has a place of absolute importance in Islam and individual freedom, though of primary significance, is not independent of its social implications.

To set into a proper perspective the rights of the individual vis-à-vis other individuals and society, the jurists have agreed upon the following basic principles:[58]

(1) The larger interest of society takes precedence over the interest of the individual.

(2) Although 'relieving hardship' and 'promoting benefit' are both among the prime objectives of the *Sharī'ah*, the former takes precedence over the latter.

(3) A bigger loss cannot be inflicted to relieve a smaller loss or a bigger benefit cannot be sacrificed for a smaller one. Conversely, a smaller harm can be inflicted to avoid a bigger harm or a smaller benefit can be sacrificed for a larger benefit.

Individual freedom, within the ethical limits of Islam, is therefore sacred only as long as it does not conflict with the larger social interest or as long as the individual does not transgress the rights of others.

II

NATURE OF THE ECONOMIC SYSTEM OF ISLAM.

The discussion of the goals of the Islamic economic system shows that material well-being based on the unshakable foundation of spiritual values constitutes an indispensable plank of the economic philosophy of Islam. The very foundation of the Islamic system being different from that of capitalism and socialism, which are both earthbound and not oriented to spiritual values, the superstructure must necessarily be different. Any attempt to show the similarity of Islam with either capitalism or socialism can only demonstrate a lack of understanding of the basic characteristics of the three systems.

The Islamic system is, besides, unflinchingly dedicated to human

57. *Al-Hidāyah*, v. 3, p. 281; and Jazīrī, v. 2, p. 349.
58. For a discussion of this subject, see Shātibī, v. 2, pp. 348-64; Abū Zahrah, pp. 350-64; and Dawālībī, *al-Madkhal ila 'Ilm Uṣūl al-Fiqh*, Beirut, 1965, pp. 447-49.

brotherhood accompanied by social and economic justice and equitable distribution of income, and to individual freedom within the
context of social welfare. This dedication is, it must be stressed, spiritually oriented and finely interwoven into the whole fabric of its social
and economic norms. In contrast with this, the orientation of modern
capitalism to social and economic justice and to equitable distribution
of income is only partial resulting from group pressures, is not the
outcome of a spiritual goal to establish human brotherhood, and does
not constitute an integral part of its overall philosophy; while the
orientation of socialism, though claimed to be the product of its basic
philosophy, is not really meaningful because of, on the one hand, the
absence of a dedication to human brotherhood and of spiritually-
based fair and impartial criteria for justice and equity, and on the
other hand, the loss of individual dignity and identity resulting from
the negation of the basic human need for freedom.

The commitment of Islam to individual freedom distinguishes it
sharply from socialism or any system which abolishes individual
freedom. Free mutual consent of the buyer and the seller is, according
to all schools of Muslim jurisprudence, a necessary condition for any
business transaction.[59] This condition springs from the verse of the
Qur'ān: 'O you who have faith! Devour not the property of anyone of
you wrongfully, except that it be trading by your mutual consent' (4:
29). The Prophet is also reported to have said: 'Leave people alone for
God gives them provision through each other.'[60] The only system that
would conform to this spirit of freedom in the Islamic way of life is one
where the conduct of a large part of the production and distribution of
goods and services is left to individuals or voluntarily constituted
groups, and where each individual is permitted to sell to or buy from
whom he wants at a price agreeable to both the buyer and the seller.
Freedom of enterprise, in contrast with socialism, offers such a possibility and it had been recognized by Islam along with its constituent
elements, the institution of private property.

The Qur'ān, the *Sunnah* and the *fiqh* literature have discussed in
significant detail the norms related to acquisition and disposal of
private and business property, and the purchase and sale of merchandise, as also the institutions of *zakāt* and inheritance, which would not
have been done in such detail if the institution of private ownership of
most productive resources had not been recognized by Islam. Besides,

59. Jazīrī, v. 2. pp. 153-168.
60. Cited by Ibn Rushd in *Bidāyat al- Mujtahid,* Cairo, 1960, v. 2, p. 167.

through-out the Muslim history, this principle has been universally upheld by Muslims with rare exceptions, and these exceptions have not been recognized to be within the mainstream of Islamic thought. A negation of this right of private ownership could not, therefore, be considered to be in conformity with the teachings of Islam.

The market mechanism may also be considered to be an integral part of the Islamic economic system because, on the one hand, the institution of private property is not workable without it; and, on the other, it offers the consumers a chance to express their desires for the production of goods of their liking by their willingness to pay the price, and also gives resource-owners an opportunity to sell their resources in accordance with their free will.

Profit motive, which is essential for the successful operation of any system incorporating freedom of enterprise, has also been recognized by Islam. Jazīrī, in his well-known work on the *fiqh* position of the four Sunnite schools of jurisprudence says:

> Buying and selling are allowed by the *Sharī'ah* so that people may profit mutually. There is no doubt that this can also be a source of injustice, because both the buyer and the seller desire more profit and the Lawgiver has not prohibited profit nor has He set limits to it. He has, however, prohibited fraud and cheating and ascribing to a commodity attributes it does not possess.[61]

This is because profit provides the necessary incentive for efficiency in the use of resources which God has given to mankind. This efficiency in the allocation of resources is a necessary element in the life of any sane and vigorous society. But since it is possible to convert profit from an instrument into a primary goal thus leading to many social and economic ills, Islam places certain moral restraints on this motive so that it fosters individual self-interest within a social context and does not violate the Islamic goals of social and economic justice and equitable distribution of income and wealth.

Recognition by Islam of the freedom of enterprise along with the institution of private property and the profit motive, does not make the Islamic system akin to capitalism which is based on freedom of enterprise. The difference is significant and is due to two important reasons. Firstly, in the Islamic system, even though property is allowed to be privately owned it is to be considered as a trust from God, because everything in the heavens and earth really belongs to God and, man

61. Jazīrī, v. 2, pp. 283-84.

being the vicegerent of God, enjoys the right of ownership only as a trust. Says the Qur'ān:

> To God belongs whatever is in the heavens and whatever is in the earth (2: 284);
>
> Say: To whom belong the earth and whoever is therein, if you know? They will say: To God. Say: Will you not then mind? (23: 84-5).;
>
> And give them of the wealth of God which He has given you (24: 33).

Secondly, because man is the vicegerent of God and the wealth he owns is a trust from Him, he is therefore bound by the conditions of the trust, or more specifically, the moral values of Islam, particularly the values of *ḥalāl* and *ḥarām,* brother-hood, social and economic justice, equitable distribution of income and wealth, and fostering the common good. The wealth he owns should be acquired in accordance with the teachings of Islam and should be used for the objectives for which it has been created. Said the Holy Prophet: 'This wealth is certainly green and sweet (enticing); but he who acquires it rightfully, for him it is an excellent assistant, while he who acquires it without his right, is like one who eats but never satiates.'[62]

What difference do the two factors – holding property as a trust from God, and the commitment to spiritual values – make, will become apparent if some of the limitations of the market system, in the capitalist frame of reference, are discussed.

First, the market system represents a plebiscite where each unit of currency spent by an individual represents a ballot and where national resources get automatically allocated among different wants on the basis of total ballots cast by all individuals. If more money is being spent on liquor than on milk, it is because the desire for liquor is more urgent and so more of the national resources get allocated to the production of liquor. This, according to the price system, brings about an optimum allocation of national resources. The market system is therefore a judge who is morally neutral and makes decisions only on the basis of the results of this plebiscite. However, the Islamic economic system cannot be morally neutral. In Islam, the allocation of resources is optimum if it is first in conformity with the norms of Islam and then in accordance with consumers' preferences. In a truly Islamic society there is no likelihood of any divergence between the two. But, if there is

62. Muslim, v. 2, p. 728: 122.

any divergence, then the state cannot be a passive observer. It must educate public opinion in accordance with the teachings of Islam and guide and regulate the machinery of production and distribution so as to bring about an allocation of resources which is in conformity with the goals of Islam. There arises the question of who will decide whether the allocation of resources is or is not in conformity with the teachings of Islam. This would not be done by the hierarchy of any organized church, which Islam has not established, but by the democratic process of decision making inherent in the political teachings of Islam.

Second the market system assumes that the wants of different individuals can be compared with respect to their urgency by the use of prices because each unit of currency represents a ballot. The willingness on the part of two individuals to spend an equal amount of money is assumed to indicate wants of equal urgency. Even if such an inter-personal comparison of the urgency of wants is possible, the free-play of the market forces for a desired allocation of resources would require that there exist an equitable distribution of income in the economy. In the absence of such an equitable distribution of income in the economy, allocation of resources produced by the market system may not be in comformity with the wishes of the majority of consumers. It would allow the upper strata of income groups, getting a share of national income significantly more than in proportion to their numerical size, to divert scarce national resources, by the sheer weight of their votes, into products considered socially less desirable. Therefore, the resultant allocation of resources would also be socially less desirable. Of itself the price system is not concerned with how many votes an individual has; it is concerned with the aggregate of votes in favour of any one good or service relative to some other good or service. Therefore, an equitable distribution of income, which is one of the goals of the Islamic system is a prerequisite to the attainment of a desirable allocation of resources through the functioning of the price system.

Third, there may be imperfections in the efficient operation of the market forces introduced by monopolies or monopsonies, or conditions in which prices may not reflect real costs or benefits. Not only that prices of goods or services may be far above opportunity costs or that payments to resource owners may be far above or below the value of their contribution to real output, but also because social costs and benefits may be disregarded by individuals in their accounting although these costs or benefits may be very important from the point of view of social welfare which carries a significant weight in the Islamic system. The self-correcting tendencies in the price system which tends to eliminate the divergence between private and social interests may take an intolerable long time because of the imperfections usually found in the operation of the market, and the limited horizon of individuals and firms. In the face of such imperfections, the market system alone, without some guidance, regulation, and control from a welfare-oriented government, may not be able to achieve an optimum allocation of resources.

Fourth, in the capitalist market system, since the individual is the primary owner of his own goods, he may do what he pleases with them. Hence there is no moral sanction against destruction of output by, say burning or dumping into the ocean, in order to raise prices or to maintain them at a higher level. But in the Islamic system, since all wealth is a trust from God, it would be a grave moral crime to do so. Destroying both life and property has been declared by the Qur'ān to be equivalent to spreading mischief and corruption in the world (2: 205). It was this teaching of the Qur'ān, which prompted Abū Bakr, the first Caliph, to instruct his general, Yazīd ibn Abī Sufyān, going on a war assignment, not to kill indiscriminately, or to destroy vegetable or animal life even in enemy territory.[63] If this is not allowed in war, there is no question of its being allowed in peace, and that too for raising prices! The social cost of such an act is much too high and the Islamic state just cannot allow it. Fifth, by itself the market system, even under conditions of healthy competition which is a prerequisite for its efficient operation, has manifested no inherent tendency to solve the economic problems of unemployment, economic fluctuations and stagnation, or to bring about an equitable distribution of the social product. There has, therefore, to be some direction and regulation by a goal-oriented government.

Sixth, success in the competitive struggle may be possible through means which are morally questionable, and which conflict with the goals of social and economic justice and equitable distribution of income. Therefore, unless there are moral checks on individuals accompanied by effective regulations by a morally-oriented government, competition may not necessarily eliminate the inefficient, reward socially useful behaviour, enforce social and economic justice and foster an equitable distribution of income.

63. (p. 26) Mālik *Muwaṭṭā*, v. 2, p. 448: 10. See also Māwardī *al-Aḥkām al-Sulṭānīyah*, Cairo, 1960, p. 34

Therefore, although the market system has been recognised by Islam because of the freedom it offers to individuals it is not to be considered sacred and inalterable. It is the goals of Muslim society which are more important. The market system is only one of the means to attain these goals, particularly the goal of individual feeedom. The market system must therefore be modified as necessary to make it conform to the ideals of Islam as much as possible. An active role of the government has been recognized by Islam for the purpose of achieving the desired modifications in the operation of the market. But government intervention alone cannot create a healthy market economy oriented to justice and social welfare even though it can remove some of the limitations of the market system. Other shortcomings of the market system can be removed only by the emergence of social health at a deeper level to be attained by dovetailing the economic system with a moral philosophy that also incorporates norms of social and economic justice, equitable distribution of income and wealth and social welfare. Hence the sharp distinction between Islam and capitalism which, in spite of its present recognition of the role of the government in the economy, is nevertheless essentially secular and lacks a morally-based philosophy for social and economic justice and public welfare.

Part IV
Islam and the World

12

What Islam Gave to Humanity*

Abdul Hamid Siddiqui

ISLAM, as it has been declared by the Holy Qur'ān, is the perfect religion and in fact the completion of the Lord's favour upon man so far as the regulation of his life is concerned.

'This day I have perfected your religion for you, completed My favours upon you and have chosen for you *Al-Islām* as your religion. (al-Qur'ān, 5 : 4).

This verse eloquently speaks of the fact that the favours of Allah in the form of *Dīn* (Code of life) have been perfected in *Al-Islām* and nothing that is not rooted in it, whether in the form of belief or in the form of individual and social behaviour, is acceptable to Allah. A religion as self-contained and realistic as Islam is, must provide answers to all spiritual and secular questions and should offer to humanity not only a new metaphysical outlook, but a comprehensive programme of revolution in human life — both in its individual and social aspects.

Let us start with the very basic concept of religion. To a non-Muslim nurtured on a traditional concept of religion, it is only a private relationship between man and his Creator. But for a Muslim religion comprehends the whole of life — its pattern of thought and behaviour. It posits the ideal of a life in which, from the cradle to the grave, not a single moment is spent out of tune with or merely unprovided for by a

* This article was published in *The Criterion,* Journal of the Islamic Research Academy, Karachi, Vol. 3, No. 3, May-June, 1968. Reproduced with the permission of the editor.

religious ruling. No sphere is left in which the thoughts and deeds of a Muslim — both in his personal and public life — are inconsequential for his fate in the hereafter. In short in Islam, one cannot find a no man's land to which religion does not lay a claim. That is the reason why Allah exhorts people to accept Islam in its entirety:

'O you who believe! come all of you
into submission (to Him);
follow not the footsteps of the devil.
He is an open enemy for you.' (al-Qur'ān, 2: 208).

Islam is the only religion of the world which knows no distinction betwen the religious and secular, but views in one sweep the entire life of man. The philosophy of ethics, law and morals, manners and mores, arts and sciences, forms of social, political and economic organization — including the nature of family and marriage — side by side with the problems of worship and theology — have their legitimate place in the all-inclusive system of Islam. The Qur'ān calls upon Muslims to say:

'Verily my prayers and my sacrifices and my life and death are all for Allah.' (al-Qur'ān, 6: 163).

It means that the whole life of man in all its spheres should be an expression of complete submission to Allah, the Creator of this Universe and the Rightful Master.

The word 'Ibādah does not signify worship only. It stands for submission and prayer, and worship is only a symbol of submission.

'Follow that which is sent down towards you from your Lord; and follow not any patrons beside Him.' (al-Qur'ān, 7: 3).

It implies that only by obeying the commands of Allah vouchsafed to humanity through the Holy Prophet, one proves one's fidelity and loyalty to God.

Then the Qur'ān also explains that Allah out of His boundless favours and infinite mercy has revealed everything that a man needs in following the path of righteousness.

'Shall I then seek a judge other than Allah when He it is who has sent down to you the Book fully explained.' (al-Qur'ān, 6: 115).

The people who cast aside the teachings of Allah and those of the Apostle and follow the other paths deviating from the one shown by God Almighty are in fact the wrongdoers:

'Or have they associates who have prescribed for them any religion that Allah does not sanction? And were it not, for the word of judgement, it would have been decided between them. And surely for the wrongdoers is a painful chastisement.' (al-Qur'ān, 42: 21).

The Qur'ān emphatically asserts that only Islam is to be followed in every sphere of life and those who take a course of action other than the one sanctioned by Allah are wrongdoers since they, besides God, look to some other deities for help and guidance.

The basic concept of religion in Islam is that it is as vital a necessity as the sunshine and air. Just as the Sustainer and the Nourisher of the world has made provision of all those things which a man needs for his physical development, in the same way, He has vouchsafed to him the Divine knowledge not only for the satisfaction of his religious yearnings, but for the fullest growth of his spiritual and moral self.

'His is the creation and the Command.' (al-Qur'ān, 7: 54).

The Lord who has created this world and all that exists in it and has created resources to maintain it and lead it to perfection, has also given al-Islām, a Code of life by following which man can find peace and happiness in this world and the world to come. The man who does not follow it in letter and spirit and takes man-made laws for guidance is described by the Qur'ān as one who has taken others as his Lords in derogation of Allah.

'They take their priests and their anchorites to be their Lords in derogation of Allah.' (al-Qur'ān, 9: 31).

Most of the commentators agree that it does not mean they took them actually for gods and worshipped them; the meaning is that they looked upon them as the main source of guidance and showed unconditional obedience to them. They did whatever they were commanded to do by their priests and did not see whether these commands were based on the Holy Book. It is related in a *Ḥadīth* that when this verse was revealed, 'Adī Ibn Ḥātim, a convert from Christianity, asked the Holy Prophet as to the significance of this verse, for he said, 'We did not worship our priests and monks.' The Holy Prophet's reply was: 'Was it not that the people considered lawful what their priests declared to be lawful, though it was forbidden by God.' Ḥātim replied in the affirmative, what the Prophet said, was what the verse meant.[2]

The exposition of the Holy Prophet is clearly indicative of the fact

2. Tirmidhī *Sahīh: Kitāb Tafsīr al-Qur'ān.* Delhi, 1353 H. p. 117.

that if a man takes the findings of any person or institution which are not substantiated by the revelations, as final and accepts them as gospel truths he is committing the grave offence of associating other gods with Allah. The Lordship of Allah is unrivalled and it necessitates the complete submission of man to Him in all walks and spheres of life and the rejection of everything which is not supported by the *Sharī'ah*.

The Islamic concept of religion as a complete Code of Life has in fact spiritualized all aspects of human existence. It was hitherto thought that the spirit and matter are entities essentially opposed to each other. Religion is concerned only with the soul and has nothing to do with the mundane activities of human life which are nothing but evil. The highest good, in the eyes of non-Muslim theologians, was therefore to spurn the worldly affairs of man and spend one's life in a convent or cave, seeking one's redemption by freeing one's spirit from the entanglements of matter and restoring it to its ideal state from which it has lapsed by an incomprehensible act of perversity called the 'Original Sin'. It was due to this notion that self-torture remained for some centuries the chief measure of human excellence in Medieval Europe and tens of thousands of the most devoted men fled to the wilderness to induce godliness by laceration. All human relations were rent asunder and the religious man took his abode in the ghostly gloom of the sepulchre, amid mouldering corpses, when the desert wind sobbed round his lonely cell, and the cries of wild beasts were borne upon his ears.

A new concept of piety based on self-denial came into being. The depravity of human nature, especially the supposed essential evil of the body, led to the absolute suppression of the whole sensual side of man. The chief form of virtue which entitled man to salvation, was a perpetual struggle against all carnal impulses. Religion thus assumed a very sombre hue in which there was no hope, no joy. The pious man dissatisfied with the world and its glory felt himself a stranger on the earth and led his life on the belief that he was dreadfully fettered by his body and saw in it a wretched prison and grave. The thought of the ancient orphic play on the Greek word for 'body' (Soma-Seima) body prison, which Plato appropriated, runs through the religious literature of all Christian countries. The fettered soul, it was believed, must yearn for freedom from the bounds of physical organism in order to soar to heavenly heights. This could be achieved only if a man tore himself forcibly from all the ensnaring charms of the outer world and in fact the whole world of senses, including all types of human relations.

The idea of a religious man was that of an extremely individualistic, un-social being. To flee from the social order, and take up the solitary life is the presupposition of salvation. It is in absolute loneliness, isolated from all other human beings that the religious and pious man stands face to face with himself and with God. The urges of the flesh and the human relations obstruct the elevation of the soul. Lecky writes:

'To break by ingratitude the heart of the mother who had borne him, to persuade the wife who adored him that it was her duty to separate from him for ever, to abandon his children, uncared for and beggars to the mercies of the world, was regarded by the true hermit as the most acceptable offering he could make to his God.'[3]

This type of religious concept implies religion, as an esoteric life fit only for a few gifted persons who journey to God aside from the broad high-way on solitary paths of their own. They have no concern with society. Their business is only to save their own souls. The severity of their devotion should in no way be impaired by the discharge of the simpler duties to humanity. The exhortation of a Kempis' 'imitation of Jesus' is 'This is sovereign wisdom to strive after the kingdom of Heaven by dispensing with the world.'

We may conclude that the fundamental psychic experience in all other religions except Islam is that of denial of the impulse of life, a denial born out of the weariness of life. The case of Islam is however different. It teaches man to live with assertion and will. This religion in contrast to the passive, quietest, resigned attitude towards everything that is going on in the world, exhorts a man to be an active participant in the struggle of life. Here the world of matter or that of the senses is not to be despised or hated, but shaped according to the will of the Lord. The world according to Islam is not a torture cell where an elementally wicked humanity is to live for the purgation of its soul. This world with all its resources is a sacred trust from the Lord by means of which man can show his true worth. It must not therefore be spurned, but properly used. This body is not a prison but an effective instrument for the spirit to achieve its goal. Islam stands in striking contrast to most religions of the world in this aspect. In other religions piety is synonymous with the denial of life, on the contrary according to Islam piety stands for belief in life and its assertion and throwing oneself joyfully and resolutely in its arms. On the one hand there is an

3. Lecky, *History of European Morals*, Longman, 1910, Vol. II, p. 125.

uncompromising denial, on the other there is an incomparable hope and will.

The first thing that Islam impresses on the minds of the people is that this world and all that exists in it have been created not for mere trifling but have been brought into existence with definite aims and purposes.

'And we created not the heaven and the earth and what is between them for sport. Had we wished to take a pastime, we would have it from before Ourselves, but by no means would we do (so).' (al-Qur'ān, 21: 16. 17).

Then in the Sūrah al Dukhān, the Holy Qur'ān emphatically says that this world is created with a Divine purpose.

'We created not the heavens, the earth and all between them merely in (idle sport). We created them not except for just ends; but most of them do not understand.' (al-Qur'ān, 44: 38, 39).

Then addressing the human beings the Holy Qur'ān observes:

'Do you then think that We have created you in vain?' (al-Qur'ān, 23: 115).

Everything that has been created by the Lord has not only a divine purpose to serve, but it has been shaped into perfect form. There is no flaw or defect in it. The wonderful beauty of creation from the tiny atom to the brilliant star in the realm of matter, and from the smallest and to the most developed form of life all speak to the Lord's perfect wisdom.

'Such is the Knower of the unseen and the seen, the Mighty, Merciful, who made beautiful everything that He created.' (al-Qur'ān, 32: 6, 7).

All these verses clearly speak of the fact that there is nothing evil in the creation of the world and that of man. It is beautiful, in proper proportion and adapted for the functions it has to perform.

Man, according to Islam, is made of the goodliest fabric,[4] he whom even the Malā'ik (angels) were made to offer obeisance, and for whom whatsoever is in the earth is made to do service.[5]

According to Islam there is no stigma attached to any individual and he shall not suffer for any sin committed by any of his ancestors.

4. al-Qur'ān, 95: 4.
5. Ibid., 2: 29, 34.

'Every soul earns only to its own account: no bearer of burdens can bear the burden of another.' (al-Qur'ān, 6: 164).

Elsewhere we have:

'That no bearer of burdens heaves the burden of another, and that man shall have nothing but what he strives for.' (al-Qur'ān, 53: 38, 39).

These verses categorically repudiate the Christian doctrine of atonement and the inborn indignity of earthly life. Man is responsible for his own actions and his status in piety is determined by his own deeds and misdeeds. He is neither born sinful according to Christian idea nor is he originally low and impure and has painfully to stagger through a long chain of incarnations towards the ultimate goal of perfection.

There is no conflict between the body and soul of man in Islam. Physical urges are an integral part of man's nature: not the result of the original sin, and therefore they are positive, God-given forces to be accepted and sensibly used for the spiritual growth of man. Piety in Islam does not consist in suppressing the demands of the body, it aims at co-ordinating them with the demands of the spirit in such a way that life might become full and righteous. The Muslims have been asked not to forbid themselves the use of the bounties of the Lord.

'Say: Who has forbidden the beautiful gifts of God, which he has brought forth for His servants? And the things, clean and pure, which He has provided for sustenance. My Lord forbids only indecencies such of them as are apparent and such as are concealed and sin and highhandedness without justice, and that ye associate with Allah that for which He has not sent down any authority and that you say of Allah what you know not.' (al-Qur'ān, 7: 32, 33).

It means that demands of the body are the integral parts of human personality and man's spiritual growth is intimately linked up with all other aspects of his nature, including urges of the flesh. The denial of the bounties of the Lord in the form of the material world is no virtue in Islam, but the real virtue lies in avoiding and rejecting everything that the Lord has forbidden. Islam does not condemn outright the appetites of man; it justifies them to the extent where a man can put a restraint upon them and control them according to the moral consciousness and thus use them for spiritual development.

'O you apostles! Eat of things that are good and do what is right; of your good things I am cognizant.' (al-Qur'ān, 23: 51).

A Muslim has been asked to beg from his Lord the good of this world and the world to come[6] because his salvation depends upon his right and proper behaviour in this material world and the way in which he exploits the material resources for the advancement of his spiritual self. The attitude of Islam towards the physical needs of a man can be well judged from the following *Hadīth*. It is narrated on the authority of 'Abd Allah b. 'Amr b. al-'Ās that he was once asked by the Holy Prophet whether it was correct that he observed fasts during the days and spend nights standing in prayer. 'Abd Allāh affirmed that. The Holy Prophet observed: 'Don't do that. Keep fast at times and break it at times, offer prayer and go to bed also. Your body has a right upon you.'[7]

This *Hadīth* speaks in unequivocal terms of the fact that Islam is emphatically opposed to those pseudo-mystics, other worldly idealists and self-centred ascetics who completely ignore the urges of the flesh. It boldly says 'yes' to the world of matter and accepts it with all its limitations and risks, but it teaches us, nonetheless, not to attribute to earthly life that exaggerated value which modern civilization attributes to it.

'Monasticism', the cult of retirement from the world into solitude, only to lead a life of prayer and meditation, is alien to the spirit of Islam.

'But the monasticism which they innovated for themselves, We did not prescribe for them. (We commanded) only the seeking for the pleasure of God, but that they did not foster, as they should have done.' (al-Qur'ān, 57: 27).

God certainly says that man should renounce the idle pleasures of life and keep his urges and impulses under full control. But that does not mean gloomy life, nor perpetual and formal prayers in isolation. God's service is done through pure lives in the turmoil of this world. 'No *rahbāniyya* in Islam' is the oft quoted saying of the Holy Prophet. It is narrated on the authority of Sa'd bin Abī Waqqāṣ that when the wife of 'Uthmān bin Maz'ūn complained of being neglected by her husband, Muḥammad (peace be upon him) advised him, saying, 'Monasticism was not prescribed to us. Do you detest the norm given to

6. al-Qur'ān, 2: 201.
7. Bukhārī, *Saḥīḥ: Kitāb al-Ṣawm.*

you by me.' He replied in the negative. Upon this the Holy Prophet remarked: 'My practice is that I offer prayer and enjoy sleep, I observe fast and relish food, I marry and *divorce;* he who deviates from the path shown by me has nothing to do with me. O, 'Uthmān, your family has a right upon you. Your own self has a right upon you.'[8]

The very chapter from which the above mentioned *Ḥadīth* is quoted stresses the point that the Holy Prophet forbade people to retire from the world and devote themselves exclusively to prayer and meditation and to deny all worldly pleasures for themselves.

Islam is not a religion of self-denial, but that of self-assertion up to the limit prescribed by Allah. It inspires confidence in man and persuades him to lead his life in a creative manner, and thus strengthen his individuality through active contact with his material and cultural environment. This strong, active personality is however to be dedicated to the service of the Lord.

'While the Christian outlook,' says Muhammad Asad, 'implies that earthly life is a bad business, the modern West — as distinct from Christianity — adores life in exactly the same way as the glutton adores his food: he devours it, but has no respect for it. Islam, on the other hand, looks upon earthly life with respect. It does not worship it, but regards it as an organic stage on our way to a higher existence. But just because it is a stage, and a necessary stage, man has no right to despise or even to underrate the value of his earthly life. Our travel through this world is a necessary, positive part in God's plan. Human life, therefore, is of tremendous value; but we must never forget that it is purely of instrumental value. In Islam there is no room for the material optimism of the modern West which says: 'My Kingdom is of this world alone,' nor for the life contempt of the Christian saying, 'My Kingdom is not of this world.' Islam goes the middle way. The Qur'ān teaches us to pray:

'Our Lord, give us the good in this World and the good in the Hereafter.' (al-Qur'ān, 2: 201).

An ideal prayer, favourite of the Holy Prophet, succintly sums up the ideal of a Muslim. The blessings of this world and those of the world to come are begged for.

It should, however, be noted that the object desired and sought for is not the 'world' at all but 'good' and good only wheresoever it may be found — whether in this world or in the next.

8. Dārimī, *Sunnan, Kitāb-un-Nikāh.*

This removes the puzzling paradox that most of the hostile critics of Islam find in it. As to recognizing, using and enjoying this world, Islam is a most practical religion. But on its doctrine of salvation it is absolutely and entirely other-worldly.[9] To a non-Muslim it is indeed strange that both material benefits and spiritual salvation should be desired in one breath. The fact is that for a Muslim 'good' is the main objective of his life and it is achieved by performing righteous deeds in the material world. The aim before a Muslim is spiritual through and through but according to Islam, it is not by bidding goodbye to the world of matter, but by using it in accordance with the Divine Commands that one can attain spiritual heights. Thus this world and its pleasures are not an end in themselves but these provide opportunities to the people to train their moral consciousness and thus resist the well-nigh irresistible temptations of the flesh in face of the Lord's commands. The material world should not therefore be despised and condemned but must be used as a training ground for higher ends.

> Surely we have made whatsoever is on the earth as an adornment for it, that we may test them which of them is best in conduct. (al-Qur'ān, 18: 7).

> And strain not your eyes towards that with which We have provided different classes of them (of) the splendour of this world's life, that We may thereby try them. But the provision of your Lord is better and more enduring. (al-Qur'ān, 20: 131).

Thus adornment and the splendour of this worldly life — worldly riches, glory, power, wealth, position and all that the worshippers of the world scramble for — are not an end in themselves for the Muslims. The possession or want of them does not betoken a man's real value or position in the spiritual world, the world which is to endure. Yet they have their uses. They measure the true worth of man. He who makes use of them according to the commands of Allah and does not become a slave to them is successful in the eyes of Allah and he who yields before these worldly allurements miserably fails in this test. This is how Islam harmonizes the conflicting demands of matter and spirit and makes the entire life of a man a spiritual whole. It is indeed one of the marvellous contributions of Islam that it has spiritualized all the sectors of human life and has thus brought harmony and coherence amongst the apparently conflicting spheres of life. Islam inculcates an

9. Vide Duncan Black Macdonald: *The Religious Attitude and Life in Islam*, Khayyat, Beirut, 1965, p. 43.

intense good consciousness, not by the renunciation of external forces but by a proper adjustment of man's relations to these forces in view of the light received by them from Islam. Here the spirituality is not something divorced from social responsibilities but it rests on man's undertaking them properly. 'Islam,' observes Wilfred Cantwell Smith, 'is by tradition and by central genius a practical religion of ethics including social ethics, and organized, legalized ethics. The practical and the social aspect of Islam can be well realized from the prayer which is the most effective means to develop God consciousness.'

Unlike other religions, Islam has not confined its prayer only to inner meditation. It has enjoined along with meditation the movements of the body and that too under the Command of an Imam in the company of his fellow-brothers. The point that Islam stresses is that when God has created both soul and body together, both should submit before Him in unison for their salvation.

Secondly, it is in social environment and not in a convent or a cave that one can attain true piety. Islam not only determines the relation with God, but on the basis of this relation it determines man's relation with man and man's relation with the universe.

'The main purpose of the Qur'ān, is to awaken in man the higher consciousness of his manifold relations with God and the universe. It is in view of this essential aspect of Qur'ānic teaching that Goethe, while making a general review of Islam as an educational force, said to Eckerman: 'You see this teaching never fails; with all its system, we cannot go, and generally speaking no man can go, further than that. The problem of Islam was really suggested by the mutual conflict, and at the same time mutual attraction, presented by two forces of religion and civilization. The same problem confronted early Christianity. The great power in Christianity is the search for an independent content for spiritual life, which according to the insight of its founder, could be elevated, not by the forces of a world external to the soul of man, but by the revelation of a new world within his soul. Islam fully agrees with this insight and supplements it by the further insight that the illumination of the new world thus revealed is not something foreign to the world of matter but permeates it through and through.'[10]

God consciousness in Islam does not develop in a total breach with the real life and its diverse problems, but is animated and intensified by grappling with that in the way in which God has directed his men to do. It is in this manner that the organic whole of human life has been

10. Wilfred C. Smith, *Pakistan as an Islamic State*, Lahore, p. 24.

eminently preserved by the Muslims. 'The whole of this earth has been made a mosque for me' is a well-known saying of the Holy Prophet and it gives us an idea of sanctity that is attached both to the physical world and the social relations. Mosque is a sacred place of worship where all Muslims without any distinction of caste, creed and colour meet and bow together before their Lord. It means that all temporal activities which are carried on in this world have the sanctity of worship if these are pursued in this spirit.

Islam, like all other religions, affirms Reality, not divorced from the external world, but by active and intimate contact with that. The Muslim is exhorted by the Qur'ān to see the signs of Reality in the physical world, in the process of history and in his own inner self because it is the same Reality which is articulated in all these spheres. God reveals His signs in the inner (*Anfus*) and outer (*Āfāq*) experience and we should try to understand the will of that Greater Reality which is reflected in all these phenomena.

'Verily in the creation of the heavens and of the earth, and in the succession of the night and of the day, are signs for men of understanding, who, standing and sitting and reclining, bear God in mind and reflect on the creation of the heavens and of the earth; and say: O Our Lord! Thou hast not created this in vain.' (al-Qur'ān, 3: 190-191).

Here the Muslim has been asked to see the magnificent signs of Reality in nature and not to pass by them as if he is deaf and blind and affirm the truth that the whole of nature as revealed to the sense perception of man is a challenging testimony of the Mighty Lord Who has created this universe. The Muslims have, therefore, conferred on science, something of the sanctity of worship. No wonder that many of the outstanding theologians, whose names are now household words all over the world, were at the same time the great pioneers of scientific knowledge and they worked in their laboratories with the same zeal and fervour as in the religious centres. Rom Landau, author of the well-known book, *Islam and the Arabs,* while discussing the mainsprings of the Arab's scientific achievements, observes, 'They might be summarized as the ardent desire to gain a deeper understanding of the world as created by Allah; an acceptance of the physical universe, as not inferior to the spiritual but co-valid with it; a strong realism that faithfully reflects the unsentimental nature of the Arab mind; and finally their insatiable curiosity. Everything that was in the universe was Allah's, from the mystic ecstasy and a mother's love to the flight of arrows, the plague that destroys an entire country and the sting of a mosquito. Each one of these manifests the power of God and thus each is worthy of study. In Islam religion and science do not go their separate ways. In fact the former provided one of the main incentives for the latter.'

'The Muslim history thus furnishes no instance of the persecution of scientists. We, on the other hand, find as many men of genius in the middle ages as now. The list is too long to be presented in this article. It will suffice here to evoke a few glorious names without contemporary equivalents in the West: Jābir Ibn Ḥayyān, al-Kindī, al-Khawārizmī, al-Farghānī, al-Rāzī, Thābit Ibn Qurrā, al-Battānī, Ḥunayn Ibn Isḥāq, al-Fārābī, Ibrāhīm Ibn Sinān, al-Mas'ūdī, al-Ṭabarī, Abū'l-Wafā', 'Alī Ibn 'Abbās, Abū'l-Qāsim, Ibn al-Jazzār, al-Bīrūnī, Ibn Sīnā, Ibn Yūnus, Al-Karkhī, Ibn al-Haytham, 'Alī Ibn 'Īsā, al-Ghazzālī, al-Zarqab, 'Umar Khayyām! A magnificent array of names which it would not be difficult to extend.' [11] But this does not come within the scope of my subject. I am concerned only with the fact that Islam is not opposed to science; it rather inculcates in its followers the greatest respect for learning and learning includes every type of knowledge provided it is acquired with sincerity and devotion and for the service and welfare of humanity. It is therefore quite natural that the progress of Muslims in the realm of science was not lop-sided, as is the case in the West today. Since a Muslim is concerned with achieving a complete view of Reality, he cannot remain content with the partial one-sided, intellectualistic approach which gives only a snapshot of force in Reality and misses its kindness and spirituality. The Muslims controlled science by ethical principles of Islam and it did not prove to be a sheer drive for power. Science was subordinated to Law in order to ensure that the tremendous power which it is capable of releasing is used for human and constructive purposes. To put it differently, it can be said that the Muslims humanized science and the spirit of God was breathed into it, to use the phrase of the Qur'ān.

This all-inclusive and synthetic attitude of Islam, towards life and its problems was also articulated in a political system fundamentally different from both that of theocracy and Western Democracy. The state in Islam is not a condemnable organization and its founding is not the service of the devil. Islam is a single unanalyzable Reality

11. George Sarton: *Introduction to the History of Science*, Washington, 1950, Vol. 1, p. 17. See also pp. 165-66.

which loses much of its force and beauty when it is fragmented into water-tight compartments. Thus in Islam it is the same Reality which appears as the Church, looked at from one point of view and the state from another' . . . The state from the Islamic standpoint, is an endeavour to transform those ideal principles into space-time forces, an inspiration to realize them in a definite human organization.'[12]

It is admitted that the primary or immediate concern of Islam is to develop the personality of the individual as a God fearing man and equip him with the talent to live in peace with himself and peace with the external world of relations. Jesus rightly said: 'The kingdom of heaven is within you.' The idea is perfectly correct and Islam fully subscribes to this view, since no just kingdom can be founded on the earth by unjust men, who have not first created the kingdom of heaven in the realm of their heart. But Islam says, 'This is not enough; the kingdom of heaven must be externalized so that the healthy political and social structure may help men and women to develop their personalities according to Islam. The State is an agency whereby the ethical and spiritual values of Islam find expression in corporate life. The Holy Qur'ān says:

> 'Those who, if we establish them in the land, will keep up prayer and pay the poor-rate and enjoin good and forbid evil. And Allah's is the end of affairs.' (al-Qur'ān, 22: 41).

This verse clearly speaks of the fact that the state is not the creation of the devil's mind. It has some very noble function to perform; the organizing of a community on such moral and spiritual bases that piety and goodliness thrive and wickedness in all its forms is weeded out.

This attempt to externalize the goodliness and piety is very significant in Islam. It means that the religious piety serves its true end when it is calculated to transform the human world. To flee from the social order, and take up the solitary life is not virtue in Islam. To be sure a Muslim stands in the presence of God as an individual, but he is never isolated from other men. The distress which vexes is not his own only; it is that of his brethren as well; the salvation for which he longs can be attained when he paves the way for the salvation of his fellow believers, nay, that of entire humanity; the values, standards, and tasks which he, in his religious devotion, learns to recognize as an inescapable necessity, are seen to be duties not for him only but for all

12. Iqbal: *Reconstruction of Religious Thought in Islam*, p. 154.

men. Hence the self consciousness of the Muslim has an active and social quality. This means that whatever a Muslim does in life has its value in history and its worth can be judged from the type of manhood that it has created and the good that it has brought to the maximum number of people.

This is the reason why so much stress has been laid to reflect on the past and present experience of mankind and to see for themselves the moral and social outlook which led to their rise and the ethical disintegration which brought about their ruin.

> Already before your time have precedents been made. Traverse the earth then, and see what has been the end of those who falsify the signs of God. (al-Qur'ān, 3: 136).

> See they not how many a generation we destroyed before them, whom we had established on the earth in strength such as we have not given to you — for whom we poured out rain from the skies in abundance, and gave streams flowing beneath their feet, yet for their sins we destroyed them, and raised in their wake fresh generations (to succeed them). (al-Qur'ān, 6: 6).

> And how many a generation have we destroyed before them, who had better possession and appearance; say as for him who is in error, the Beneficient will prolong his length of day, until they see what they were threatened with, either the punishment or the Hour. Then they will know who is worse in position and weaker in force. (al-Qur'ān, 19: 74, 75).

These verses make clear the role of observation and reasoning in Islam. It is through observation that we can see the forces which are working in elevating and degrading the different human groups in history.

But mere observation is not enough. That which is great and vital, the drama of the human soul is completely hidden from direct observation. The Muslim's task in Islam is not to see the outward manifestations of the different events of human life but to study the inner life of the actors in events and give an account of their motives and aims. It implies that knowledge of history, unlike that of nature and her laws is not a biological necessity; it is a psychological and, above all, a sociological need.

The historical references and the accounts of the past are given in the Qur'ān not so much to fill in the many gaps in our factual knowledge as to make sense out of the vast deal that we do know. For a historical fact is not an isolated phenomenon. It has so many causal relationships that their significance can be determined.

The Holy Qur'ān treats the events of the past not only to revive them in our memory, but to make them meaningful for us. It selects the significant events, interprets them in the light of moral law and then evaluates them according to ethical judgements and in the whole process of selecting, interpreting, and evaluating the facts it answers the unavoidable questions, how, why and what of it and this reveals the nature of man and the world, his possible or proper destiny.

This attitude of Islam towards historical knowledge is of great significance in human understanding. The Muslim historians not only kept the high ideal of objectivity and exactitude in surveying the whole course of human development but sought to determine its origin, course and goal.

This can be illustrated from the fact that the famous world history of Ibn Khaldūn is entitled *Kitāb-al-'Ibar*. The word *'Ibr* here stands as a prominent key word which reveals the underlying idea for which the history was studied by the Muslims.

'Ibar is the plural of *'Ibrah*, a noun derived from the root *'i-b-r* which means to travel, to cross, to go beyond the borders of the city or a land. It also means to pass from the outside to the inside of a thing. Arabic dictionaries elaborate extensively on the idea of expressing, explaining and interpreting the meaning of something; and of wondering about, enquiring into, contemplating and penetrating to the innermost significance of an object.

Imām Rāghib in his famous book *Mufradāt* says it is the state under which a man on the basis of concrete facts deduces unseen conclusions. It also means to learn a lesson, to take warning or to take an example.

The Holy Qur'ān and the *Ḥadīth* on various occasions have urged us to view past events, both reported and experienced, as indications that should awaken in us moral sense and enhance its ability to act according to the demands of God: to penetrate behind the apparently meaningless succession of events and discern the ever-present design of the Creator.

According to the Qur'ān God does not unfold Himself in history, as Hegel believed, but there is no denying the fact that it is not without a purpose that the Lord gives dominance to certain peoples at one time and deprives them of this privileged position at another occasion. This ebb and rise of the fortune or misfortune of peoples has a divine purpose to serve. The Holy Qur'ān observes:

If a wound has afflicted you, a wound like it has also afflicted the (disbelieving) people. And we bring these days to men by turn, that Allah may know those who believe and take witnesses from among you. And Allah loves not the wrong-doers. (al-Qur'ān, 3: 139).

The use of historical events as a warning against certain patterns of action, and exhortation to adopt a certain course of life, is not an absolutely new concept. All the revealed books have clear indications of this. There is enough in the historical narratives and literature of the pre-Islamic period which embody this trend, but the way in which along with the objectivity and exactitude of events the moral aspect is deepened is a purely post-Islamic development.

It were the Muslims only who taught the world to preserve the historical events with perfect accuracy and then to study them for *'ibrah,* i.e. for spiritual training and preparation for the final accounting. The famous history of Ibn Khaldūn is a testimony of this attitude. He not only narrated facts, but linked them in the chain of cause and effect, interpreted them and formulated general laws that lay behind them. His famous *Muqaddimah* is an illuminating discussion of his interpretations of historical narratives.

The foregoing discussion makes it abundantly clear that the interest of the Holy Qur'ān and the *Sunnah* in history, regarded as a source of Human knowledge, extends further than mere indication of historical facts. This has manifested itself in various aspects of human culture. It has given us one of the most fundamental principles of historical criticism. Since accuracy in recording facts which constitute material of history is an indispensable condition of history as a science and an accurate knowledge of facts ultimately depends on those who report them, the very first principle of historical criticism is that the reporters' personal character is an important factor, in judging his testimony.

'O believers! if any bad man comes to you with a report, verify it' (al-Qur'ān, 49: 6).

It was the application of the principle embodied in this verse to reporters of the Prophet's traditions out of which were gradually evolved the canons of historical criticism.

This is one aspect of the achievements of Muslims in history. The second aspect, i.e. the treatment of historical knowledge as an *'ibrah* in which the events crossed from historical events to their nature and causes and an effort to grasp the unseen reality of which these events were mere manifestations, is far more important. This is an area in which the Muslims made unique contributions. They interpreted facts, comprehended the forces that worked behind them and interpreted them and thus made them meaningful and purposive.

The growth of the historical sense in Islam is a fascinating subject and it leads to an important point: the role and place of intellect in Islam. The observation of the signs of God in nature and history and on the bases of these observations the perception of ultimate Reality requires along with seeing (*nazr*), the reasoning and understanding (*fahm*).

Have you not seen how God makes the clouds move gently, then joins them together, then makes them into a heap? then you see the rain pouring forth from their midst. And He sends down from heaven mountain masses (of clouds) wherein is hail. He strikes with it whom He pleases and turns it away from whom He pleases and the vivid flash of His lightning wellnigh blinds the sight. It is God who alternates the night and the day. Surely in these things is an instructive example for those who have vision. (al-Qur'ān, 24: 43, 44).

13

The Western World and its Challenges to Islam*

Seyyed Hossein Nasr

NOWADAYS it is in the nature of things that if one wishes to discuss the challenges presented to Islam by the West and, in fact, by modern civilization in general, one must begin by using the sword of discrimination and by embarking on a kind of 'intellectual iconoclasm'. Modern civilization takes pride in having developed the critical mind and the power of objective criticism, whereas in reality it is in fundamental sense the least critical of all known civilizations for it does not possess the objective criteria to judge and criticize its own activities. It is a civilization which fails in every kind of basic reform because it cannot begin with the reform of itself. In fact, one of the characteristic features of the modern world is the singular lack of intellectual discernment and of the sharp edge of criticism in its true sense.

There is a traditional saying according to which Satan hates sharp points and edges. This old adage is a most profound truth which applies directly to the present-day situation. Being everywhere, the Devil manifests his influence by dulling all sharp points and edges which are accessible to him so that sharp distinctions disappear. The edges of clearly defined doctrines undergo a corrosive process and their sharpness of definition gradually fades. Truth and error become ever more intermingled, and even sacred rites and doctrines which are the

* This essay is based on a lecture delivered to a predominantly Muslim audience in the Islamic Cultural Centre, London, during the first Festival of Islam held in that city in November, 1971. The text was originally published in *The Muslim,* London, and later in a revised form in *The Islamic Quarterly,* London, (Vol. XVII, Nos. 1 and 2, January to June, 1973.)

most precious of God's gifts to man, become hazy and indefinite as a result of this corrosive influence which makes everything wishy-washy and ambiguous. To discuss the challenge of the modern world to Islam requires, therefore, a rigorous application of intellectual discernment based ultimately upon the *shahādah*, the first letter of which, when written in Arabic, is in fact in the form of a sword. This sword must be used to break the false idols of the new age of ignorance (*jāhiliyyah*), idols which so many Muslims accept without even troubling to question their nature. It must be used to cut away and remove all the false ideas and 'isms' that clutter the mind of modernized Muslims. It must help to chisel the soul of the contemporary Muslim from an amorphous mass into a sharp crystal that glows in the Divine Light. It must never be forgotten that a crystal glows precisely because of its sharply defined edges.

One must always remember that in the present situation any form of criticism of the modern world based upon metaphysical and religious principles is a form of charity and in accordance with the most central virtues of Islam. Also, one should never forget that the Prophet of Islam – upon whom be peace – not only possessed *adab* in its most perfect form, but also asserted the truth in the most frank and straightforward manner. There were moments of his life when he was extremely categorical, and he never sacrificed the truth for the sake of *adab*. Islam has never taught that one should accept that two and two is five in order to display *adab*. In fact *adab* has always been the complement to the perception and assertion of the truth in every situation and circumstance. Once an eminent spiritual authority from North Africa said, 'Do you know what *adab* is? It is to sharpen your sword so that when you have to cut a limb it does not hurt.' It is this type of attitude that is needed by Muslims in their discussion of the West and its challenges to Islam. The truth not only has a right to our lives and our beings; it also has the prerogative of asking us to make sense to others and to express and expound it whenever and wherever possible. Today we need to be critical even to the degree of stringency, precisely because such an attitude is so rare and so much in demand.

What is lacking in the Islamic world today is a thorough examination and careful criticism of all that is happening in the modern world. Without such criticism nothing serious can ever be done in the business of confronting the West. All statements of modernized Muslims which begin with the assertion, 'The way to harmonize Islam . . .' and concluded with whatever follows the 'and', are bound to end in failure unless what follows is another divinely revealed and inspired world-view. Attempts to harmonize Islam and Western socialism or Marxism or existentialism or evolution or anything else of the kind are doomed from the start simply because they begin without exposing the system or 'ism' in question to a thorough criticism in the light of Islamic criteria, and also because they consider Islam as a partial view of things to be complemented by some form of modern ideology rather than a complete system and perspective in itself whose very totality excludes the possibility of its becoming a mere adjective to modify some other noun which is taken almost unconsciously as central in place of Islam. The rapid change in fashions of the day which make Islamic socialism popular one day and liberalism or some other Western 'ism' the next is itself proof of the absurdity and shallowness of such an approach. He who understands the structure of Islam in its totality knows that Islam can never allow itself to be reduced to the status of a mere modifier, or contingency, vis-à-vis a system of thought which remains independent of it.

The defensive and apologetic attitude adopted by so many modernized Muslims towards various fashionable modes of thought that issue from the West almost with the rapidity of seasonal changes is closely allied to their lack of a critical sense and a discerning spirit. Usually, obvious shortcomings and what is easy to criticize are criticized, but few have the courage to stand up and criticize the basic fallacies of our times. It is easy to point out that the life of students in traditional madrasahs is not hygienic, but it is much more difficult to take a firm stand and assert the fact that much of what is taught in the modern educational institutions is far more deadly for the soul of the students than the physically unhealthy surroundings of some of the old madrasah buildings. There are too few people in the Islamic world today who can confront the West, criticize, and, with the sword of the intellect and the spirit, answer at its very foundations the challenge with which the West confronts Islam. Such is the case today; but it does not have to be so. There is no logical reason why a new intellectual élite could not develop in the Islamic world with the capacity to provide an objective criticism of the modern world from the point of view of the eternal verities contained within the message of the Islamic revelation.

Today in the Islamic world there are essentially two main classes of people concerned with religious, intellectual, and philosophical questions: the 'ulamā' and other religious authorities in general (including the Sufis) and the modernists. It is only recently that a third group has gradually begun to emerge, namely, a group which, like the 'ulamā' is traditional, but which knows the modern world. But the number of this third class is still very small indeed. As far as the 'ulamā' and other traditional spiritual authorities are concerned, they usually do not possess a profound knowledge of the modern world and its problems and complexities. But they are the custodians of the Islamic tradition and its protectors, without whom the very continuity of the tradition would be endangered. They are usually criticized by the modernists for not knowing European philosophy and science or the intricacies of modern economics and the like. But this criticism, which is again of the facile kind so easily levelled by the modernists, is for the most part misplaced. Those who possessed the financial and political power in the Islamic world during the past century rarely allowed the *madrasahs* to develop in a direction which would permit them to give the 'ulamā' class the opportunity of gaining a better knowledge of the modern world without becoming corrupted by it. In the few places where attempts were made to modify the *madrasah* curriculum the hidden intention was more often to do away with the traditional educational system by deforming it beyond hope of redemption than to extend its programme in any real sense to embrace courses which would acquaint the students with the modern world as seen in the light of Islamic teachings. Furthermore, few attempts have ever been made to create institutions which would provide a bridge between the traditional *madrasahs* and modern educational institutions. At all events, the modernists have no right to criticize the 'ulamā' for a lack of knowledge of things for the mastery of which they never received the opportunity.

In the second of our three classes we have the product of either Western universities or universities in the Islamic world which more or less ape the West. Now, the universities in the Islamic world are themselves in a state of crisis — a crisis of identity, for an educational system is organically related to the culture within whose matrix it functions. A jet plane can be made to land in the airport of any country in Asia or Africa, no matter where it may be, and be identified as part of that country. But an educational system cannot be simply imported, and the fact that modern universities are facing a crisis in the Islamic world of a different nature from that which is found in the West is itself proof of this assertion. The crisis could not but exist, because the indigenous Islamic culture is still alive. Moreover, this crisis affects deeply those who are educated in these universities and who are usually called 'the intelligentsia'. This expression, like the term 'intellectual' is one that is most unfortunate in that those to whom it is applied are often the furthest removed from the domain of the intellect in its true sense. But by whatever name they are called, most members of this class, who are products of Western-oriented universities, have for the most part one feature in common, and that is the predilection for all things Western and a sense of alienation *vis-à-vis* things Islamic. This inferiority complex *vis-à-vis* the West among so many modernized Muslims — a complex which is, moreover, shared by modernized Hindus, Buddhists, and other Orientals who are affected by the psychosis of modern forms of idolatry — is the greatest malady facing the Islamic world, and it afflicts the very group which one would expect to face the challenge of the West. The encounter of Islam with the West cannot therefore be discussed without taking into consideration the type of mentality which is often the product of modern university education[1] and which, during the past century, has produced most of the apologetic Islamic writings which try to concern themselves with the encounter of Islam and the West.[1a]

This apologetic, modernized type of approach has attempted to answer the challenge of the West by bending backwards in a servile attitude to show in one way or another that this or that element of Islam is just what is fashionable in the West today while other elements, for which there could not be found a Western equivalence by even the greatest stretch of the imagination, have been simply brushed aside as unimportant or even extraneous later 'accretions'.[2] Endless arguments have been presented for the hygienic nature of the Islamic rites of the 'egalitarian' character of the message of Islam, not because

1. It must be said, however, that because of the very rapid decadence into which Western society has lapsed during the past two decades, some of the younger Muslims who have experienced the Western world on an 'intellectual' level are far less infatuated with it than before and have in fact begun to criticize it. But of these, the number that think within the Islamic framework are very limited. The various works of Maryam Jameelah contain many thoughtful pages both on this theme and the whole general problem of the confrontation between Islam and Western civilization. See especially her *Islam versus the West,* Lahore, 1968.

1a. A few of the modernized *'ulamā'* must also be placed in this category. See W. C. Smith, *Islam in Modern History* (P.U.P., 1957), where the style and approach of such an apologetic attitude as it concerns Egypt is analysed.

2. It is here that 'fundamentalist' puritanical movements such as that of the *Salafiyya* and the modernist trends meet.

such things are true if seen in the larger context of the total Islamic message, but because hygiene and egalitarianism are the currently accepted ideas in the West or at least they were before the 'hippie' movement. By affirming such obvious and too easily defended characteristics, the apologists have evaded the whole challenge of the West, which threatens the heart of Islam and which no amount of attempts to placate the enemy can avert. When surgery is needed there must be a knife with which to remove the infected zone. Also when error threatens religious truth nothing can replace the sword of criticism and discernment. One cannot remove the negative effect of error by making peace with it and pretending to be its friend.

The apologetic attitude is even more pathetic when it concerns itself with philosophical and intellectual questions. When one reads some items in this category of apologetic literature, which issued mostly from Egypt and the Indian sub-continent at the beginning of this century and which tried to emulate already very stale and defunct debates that went on between theology and science in Victorian England or France of the same period, the weakness of such works, which were supposed to answer the challenge of the West, becomes most apparent, and even more so against the background of the decades that have since gone by. Of course, at that time one could hear the strong voice of the traditional authorities, who, basing themselves on the immutable principles of the Islamic revelation, tried to answer these challenges on a religious level, even if they were not aware of the more abstruse and hidden philosophical and scientific ideas that were involved. But this type of voice gradually diminished, without, of course, ceasing to exist altogether, while the other, that of the modernists, became ever more audible and invasive.

This phenomenon has led to the rather odd situation today in which, among the educated, practically the most ardent defenders of Western civilization in the world are Westernized Orientals. The most intelligent students at Oxford or Harvard have far less confidence in the West than those modernized Orientals who for some time have sacrificed everything on the altar of modernism and are now suddenly faced with the possibility of the total decomposition of this idol. Therefore, they try all the more desperately to cling to it. For the modernized Muslims, especially the more extreme among them, the 'true meaning' of Islam has been for some time now what the West has dictated. If evolution has been in vogue 'true Islam' is evolutionary. If it is socialism that is the fashion of the day, the 'real teachings' of Islam are based on socialism. Those acquainted with this type of mentality and the works it has produced are most aware of its docile, servile and passive nature. Even in the field of law how often have completely non-Islamic and even un-Islamic tenets been adopted with a *bismillāh* added at the beginning and a *bihī nasta'īn* at the end?

Now suddenly this group, which was willing to sell its soul to emulate the West, sees before its eyes the unbelievable sign of the floundering of Western civilization itself. How painful a sight it must be for such men! Therefore they try in the face of all evidence to defend the Western 'value system' and become ferociously angry with those Westerners who have themselves begun to criticize the modern world. Probably, if the obvious decomposition of modern civilization, which became gradually evident after the Second World War, had become manifest after the First World War when the traditions of Asia were much more intact, a great deal more of these traditional civilizations could have been saved. But the hands of destiny had chartered another course for mankind. Nevertheless, even in the present situation there is a great deal that can be done, for as the Persian proverb says, 'As long as the root of the plant is in the water there is still hope.' On the plane of true activity according to traditional principles the possibility of doing something positive always exists, including the most obvious and central act of stating the truth, and acting accordingly.[3] Despair has no meaning where there is faith (īmān). Even today if in the Islamic world there comes to be formed a true intelligentsia at once traditional and fully conversant with the modern world, the challenge of the West can be answered and the core of the Islamic tradition preserved from the paralysis which now threatens its limbs and body.

To realize exactly how much can still be saved in the Islamic world it is sufficient to remember that for the vast majority of Muslims Islamic culture is still a living reality in which they live, breathe and die. From Indonesia to Morocco for the overwhelming majority, Islamic culture must be referred to in the present tense and not as something of the past. Those who refer to it the past tense belong to that very small but vocal minority which has ceased to live within the world of tradition and which mistakes its own loss of centre for the dislocation of the whole of Islamic society.

The tragedy of the situation resides, however, in the fact that it is precisely such a view of Islam as a thing of the past that is held by most

3. See F. Schoun, 'No activity without Truth', *Studies in Comparative Religion*, iii (1969), 194-203.

of those who control the mass media in the Islamic world and who therefore exercise an influence upon the minds and souls of men far beyond what their number would justify. In most places those who hold in their hands such means as radio, television, and magazines live in a world in which Islamic culture appears as a thing of the past precisely because they are so infatuated with the West that no other way of seeing things seems to have any reality for them even if the other way be a still living reality existing at their very doorsteps.

Strangely enough, this Westernized minority in the Islamic world has gained a position of ascendancy at the very moment when the West has lost its own mooring completely and does know what it is doing or where it is going. If a simple Persian or Arab peasant were to be brought to one of the big Middle Eastern airports and asked to observe the Europeans entering the country, the contrast in nothing more than the dress, which varies from that of a nun to near nudity, would be sufficient to impress upon his simple mind the lack of homogeneity and harmony of the products of Western civilization. But even this elementary observation usually escapes the thoroughly Westernized Muslim who, though well-wishing, if nothing else, does not want to face the overt contradictions in the civilization he is trying to emulate so avidly.

Of course the situation has changed somewhat during the past three decades. Muslims who went to Europe between the two world wars thought of the trees along the Seine or the Thames rivers practically as *Shajarāt al-ṭūbā* and these rivers as the streams of paradise. Whether consciously or unconsciously, most members of this generation of modernized Muslims almost completely transferred their image of paradise and its perfections to Western civilization but today this homogeneity of reaction and blind acceptance of the West as an idol is no longer to be observed. The inner contradictions of the West that have become even more manifest during the past three decades no longer permit such an attitude. The present-day generation of modernized Muslims are much less confident about the absolute value of Western civilization than their fathers and uncles who went to the West before them. This in itself can be a positive tendency if it becomes the prelude to a positive and objective evaluation of modernism. But so far it has only sown additional confusion in the ranks of modernized Muslims, and only here and there has it resulted in the appearance of a handful of Muslim scholars who have awakened to the reality of the situation and have ceased to emulate the West blindly. But alas! The main problem, which is the lack of a profound knowledge based upon the criteria of Islamic culture, still remains. There are still too few 'occidentalists' in the Islamic world who could perform the positive aspect of the function 'orientalists' have been performing for the West since the eighteenth century.[4]

Despite the weakening of confidence in the West on the part of modernized Muslims, Muslims are still on the receiving-end of the realm of both ideas and material objects. Lacking confidence in their own intellectual tradition, most modernized Muslims are, like a *tabula rasa,* waiting to receive some kind of impression from the West. Moreover, each part of the Islamic world receives a package of ideas that differs in kind according to the part of the Western world to which it has become closely attached. For example, in the domain of sociology and philosophy the Subcontinent has for the past century closely followed English schools and Persia French.[5] But everywhere the modernized circles are sitting and waiting to adopt whatever comes along. One day it is positivism and the next structuralism. Rarely does anyone bother to adopt a truly Islamic intellectual attitude which would operate in an active sense and function with discernment towards all that the wind blows our way. It is almost the same as in the field of fashion where in many Islamic lands women remain completely passive as obedient consumers and emulate blindly whatever a few Western fashion makers decide for them. In dress fashion as in philosophical and artistic fashion modernized Muslims have no role to play at the source where decisions are made.

It is of course true that even Western people themselves are hardly aware of the deeper roots of the movements that sweep the West one after another and that twenty years ago no one foresaw that such an extensive movement as that of the hippies would become widespread in the West. But modernized Muslims are even further removed from the current in that they are unaware not only of the roots but even of the stages of incubation and growth of such movements and wait until

4. We do not mean that Muslim 'occidentalists' should emulate the prejudices and limitations of the orientalists but that they should know the West as much as possible from the Islamic point of view in the same way that the best among the orientalists have sought to know the East well albeit within the frame of reference of the West. Of course, because the anti-traditional nature of the modern West, such a frame of reference has not been adequate when dealing with the religious and metaphysical teachings of Oriental traditions, but that is another question which does not enter our present discussion.
5. See S. H. Nasr, *Islamic Studies,* (Beirut 1967) ch. viii.

they occupy the centre of the stage, at which time they then react either with surprise or again in a state of blind surrender. The ecological crisis is a perfect example of this state of affairs. The Muslims have waited until the crisis has become the central concern of a vast number of Western peoples before even becoming aware of the existence of the problem. And even now, how many people in the Islamic world are thinking of this crucial problem in the light of the extremely rich tradition of Islam concerning nature which in fact could provide a key for the possible solution of this major crisis were men to accept to use this key? [6]

To study in a more concrete fashion the challenges of the West to Islam, it is necessary to take as example some of the 'isms' which are fashionable in the modern world today and which have affected the cultural and even religious life of the Islamic world. Let us start with Marxism or, more generally speaking, socialism. [7] Today in many parts of the Islamic world there is a great deal of talk about Marxism which, although not concerned with religion directly, has an important indirect effect upon religious life, not to speak of economic and social activity. Many who speak of Marxism or socialism in general in the Islamic world do so with certain existing problems of society in mind for which they are seeking solutions. But very few of them actually know Marxism or theoretical socialism in a serious sense. When one hears numerous young Muslim students speaking about Marxism in so many university circles, one wonders how many have actually read *Das Kapital* or even important secondary sources, or would defend the Marxist position seriously on a purely rational plane. The Marxist fad has become an excuse for many young Muslims to refuse to think seriously about the problems of Islamic society from the Islamic point of view: to accept the label of the black-box with its unknown interior is all that is required to inflate the ego and inveigle the mind into entertaining the illusion that one has become an 'intellectual' or a member of the liberated 'intelligentsia' and that by following the already established Marxist solutions to all kinds of problems as thought out in a completely different socio-cultural context in other lands, one no longer has any responsibility to think in a fresh manner about the

6. See S. H. Nasr, *The Encounter of Man and Nature* (London, 1968), pp. 93 ff.
7. As regards socialism, which is at this very time enjoying great popularity in the form of 'Islamic socialism', Arab socialism etc., the term is usually a misnomer for social justice and is adopted in many circles without an analysis of its real meaning for political expediency or simply to appear modern or progressive.

problems of Islamic society as an Islamic society. It is precisely this blind adherence to Marxism as a package whose content is never analysed or as an aspirin to soothe every kind of pain that prepares the ground for the worst kind of demagogy. Instead of discussing problems in a reasonable and meaningful manner, those who have fallen under the influence of what is loosely called Marxism develop a blind and unintelligent obedience to it, which leads to a senseless confrontation and finally a mental sclerosis resulting in untold harm to the youth of Islamic society, to say nothing of its obvious harm to the life of faith.

Unfortunately, the response given by Islamic authorities to the challenge of dialectical materialism has for the most part hitherto consisted in the presentation of arguments drawn from the transmitted *(naqlī)* or religious sciences rather than from the rich intellectual tradition of Islam contained in the traditional intellectual *('aqlī)* sciences.[8] Now, religious arguments can be presented only to those who already possess faith. Of what use is it to cite a particular chapter of the Qur'ān to refute an idea held by someone who does not accept the authority of the Qur'ān to start with? Many of the works written by the *'ulamā'* in this field can be criticized precisely because they address themselves to deaf ears and present arguments that are of no efficacy in the context in question. This is especially saddening when we consider that the Islamic tradition possesses such a richness and depth that it is perfectly capable of answering, on the intellectual level, any arguments drawn from the modern European philosophy. What, in reality, is all modern philosophy before traditional wisdom but a noise that would seek, in its self-delusion, to conquer the heavens? So many of the so-called problems of today are based on ill-posed questions and on ignorance of truths which traditional wisdom alone can cure, a traditional wisdom found from ancient Babylonia to medieval China in one of its most universal and certainly most diversified forms in Islam and the vast intellectual tradition which Islam has brought into being during its fourteen centuries of historical existence.

The danger of Marxism for Islam has recently become all the more serious with the appearance, in certain countries, of a Marxism with an

8. A major exception to this is the five-volume *Uṣūl'i falsafa* of 'Allāma Sayyid Muhammad Husayn Tabātabā'ī, one of the most venerable masters of traditional Islamic philosophy in Persia today, with the commentary of Murtaḍā Mutahharī (Qum, 1392 (A. H. solar)). As far as we know, this is the only work of an Islamic character which has tried to answer dialectical materialism from a philosophical point of view drawing from traditional Islamic philosophy, especially the school of Mullā Sadrā.

Islamic veneer, creating a most tempting trap for some simple souls. This insidious use of religion, often with direct political aims in mind, is in fact more dangerous than the anti-religious and at least 'honest' Marxism and corresponds to the thought and attitude of that class of persons whom the Qur'ān calls the *Munāfiqun* (hypocrites). In this case there is no way of giving an Islamic response except by answering such pseudo-syntheses intellectually and by clearly demonstrating that Islam is not any thing that might come along prefaced with a bismillah, but, rather, a total vision of reality which cannot compromise with any half-truths whatsoever.

Another 'ism' of greater danger to Islam with a longer history of protrusion into the Islamic world than Marxism is Darwinism or evolutionism in general, whose effect is particularly perceptible among the Muslims of the Indian subcontinent, obviously because of the strong influence of British education there. There is not time here to point out the arguments presented by many outstanding European biologists against evolution[9] or to marshall all the proofs brought forth by contemporary anthropologists to show that whatever may have occurred before, man himself has not evolved one iota since he set foot upon the stage of terrestrial history.[10]

Alas, practically no contemporary Muslim thinker has taken note of these sources and made use of their arguments to support the traditional Islamic view of man. For a notable segment of modernized Muslims evolution remains practically like a religious article of faith whose overt contradiction of the teachings of the Qur'ān they fail to realize.

In fact, the Darwinian theory of evolution, which is meta-physically impossible and logically absurd, has been subtly woven in certain quarters into some aspects of Islam to produce a most unfortunate and sometimes dangerous blend. We do not mean only the shallow

9. See Nasr, *Encounter of Man and Nature,* pp. 124 ff., where these arguments as well as references to works on biology in which they have been set forth are presented. See also G. Berthault, *L'évolution, fruit d'une illusion scientifique,* Paris, 1972.

10. See, for example, Leroi'Gourhan, *Le Geste et la parole,* 2 vols. (Paris 1964-5); J. Servier, *L'homme et l'invisible* (Paris, 1964); E. Zolla (ed.) *Eternità e storia. I valori permanenti nel divenire storico* (Florence 1970); and G. Durand, 'Defiguration philosophique et figure traditionelle de l'homme en Occident', *Eranos-Jahrbuch* (xxxviii (1969), Zurich 1971), pp. 45-93. Even an academic authority like Levi-Strauss, the founder of structuralism, has said, 'les hommes ont toujours pensé aussi bien'.

Qur'ānic commentators around the turn of the century, but even a thinker of the stature of Iqbal, who was influenced by both the Victorian concept of evolution and the idea of the superman of Nietzsche. Iqbal is an important contemporary figure of Islam, but with all due respect to him he should be studied in the light of the *ijtihād* which he himself preached so often and not be put on a pedestal. If we analyse his thought carefully we see that he had an ambivalent love-hate relationship vis-à-vis Sufism. He admired Rūmī yet expressed dislike for a figure like Ḥāfiz. This is due to the fact that he was drawn, on the one hand, by the Sufi and, more generally speaking, Islamic idea of the perfect man *(al-insān al-kāmil)* and, on the other, by the Nietzschian idea of the superman which are in fact at the very antipodes of each other. Iqbal made the great mistake of seeking to identify the two. He made this fatal error, despite his deep understanding of many aspects of Islam, he had come to take the prevalent idea of evolution too seriously. He demonstrates on a more literate and explicit level a tendency to be found among many modern Muslim writers who instead of answering the fallacies of evolution have tried to bend over backwards in an apologetic manner to accept it and even to interpret Islamic teachings according to it.[11]

The general tendency among Muslims affected by the evolutionist mentality is to forget the whole Islamic conception of the march of time.[12] The Qur'ānic chapters about eschatological events and the latter days are forgotten. All the *hadīths* pertaining to the last days and the appearance of the Mahdī are laid aside or misconstrued, either through ignorance or malevolence. Just one *hadīth* of the Prophet asserting that the best generation of Muslims were those who were the contemporaries of the Prophet, then the generation after, then the following generation until the end of time is sufficient to nullify, from the Islamic point of view, the idea of linear evolution and progress in history. Those who think they are rendering a service to Islam by incorporating evolutionary ideas into Islamic thought are in fact

11. It must be said, however, that fortunately in Islam there have not as yet appeared any figures representing 'evolutionary religion' possessing the same degree of influence as can be seen in Hinduism and Christianity where such men as Sri Aurobindo and Teilhard de Chardin have rallied numerous suppoters around themselves. The metaphysical teachings of Islam based upon the immutibility of the Divine Principle has until now been too powerful to permit the widespread influence of any such deviation.

12. See Abu Bakr Siraj-ud-Din, 'The Islamic and Christian Conceptions of the March of Time', *The Islamic Quarterly*, i (1954), 229-35.

falling into a most dangerous pit and are surrendering Islam to one of the most insidious pseudo-dogmas of modern man, created in the eighteenth and nineteenth centuries to enable men to forget God.

Moreover, the acceptance of the evolutionary thesis brings into being overt paradoxes in daily life which cannot be easily removed. If things are going to evolve for the better, then why bother to expend one's efforts on betterment? Things will improve by themselves anyway. The very dynamism preached by modernists is against the usually accepted idea of evolution. Or, seen from another view, it can be argued that if the effort, work, movement and so on that are preached in the modern world are effective, then man can influence his future and destiny. And if he can affect his future, then he can also affect if for the worse, and there is no guarantee of an automatic progress and evolution. All of these and many other paradoxes are brushed aside in certain quarters because of the enfeebled intellectual attitude which has as yet to produce a serious and also widely known Islamic response of a metaphysical and intellectual nature to the hypothesis of evolution. The challenge of evolutionary thought has been answered in contemporary Islam in almost the same way as has the case of Marxism. There have been some religious replies based upon the Holy Book but not an intellectual response which could also persuade the young Muslims whose faith in the Qur'ān itself has been in part shaken by the very arguments of the evolutionary school. Meanwhile, works of evolutionary writers of even the nineteenth century such as Spencer, who are no longer taught as living philosophical influences in their homeland, continue to be taught in universities far and wide in the Islamic world, especially in the Subcontinent, as if they represented the latest proven scientific knowledge or the latest philosophical school of the West. Few bother even to study the recent anti-evolutionary developments in biology itself as well as the reassertion of the pre-evolutionary conception of man – movements which are gaining even greater adherence in many circles in the West today. And what is worse, there are too few efforts on the part of the Muslim Intellectual élite to formulate from Islamic sources the genuine doctrine of man and his relation to the universe which would act as a criterion for the judgement of any would-be theory of man and the cosmos, evolutionary or otherwise, and which would also provide the light necessary to distinguish scientific facts from mere hypotheses and scientific evidence from crass philosophical materialism parading in the garb of a pseudo-religious belief.[13]

Another important 'philosophical' challenge to the Islamic world is connected with the Freudian and Jungian interpretation of the psyche. The modern psychological and psychoanalytical approach tries to reduce all the higher elements of man's being to the level of the psyche and, moreover, to reduce the psyche itself to nothing more than that which can be studied through modern psychological and psychoanalytical methods. Until now, this way of thinking has not affected the Islamic world as directly as has evolutionism, and I do not know of any important Muslim writers who are Freudian or Jungian; but its effect is certain to increase soon. It must therefore be remembered that Freudianism as well as other modern Western schools of psychology and psychotherapy are the by-products of a particular society very different from the Islamic. It needs to be recalled also that Freud was a Viennese Jew who unfortunately turned away from Orthodox Judaism. Few people know that he was connected to a messianic movement which was opposed by the Orthodox Jewish community of central Europe itself and that therefore he was opposed to the main-stream of Jewish life, not to speak of Christianity. Many study Freudianism, but few delve into its deeper origins which reveal its real nature.[14]

Recently one of the outstanding figures of Sufism from the East wrote a series of articles on Sufism and psychoanalysis in French, making a comparison between the two. With all due respect to him it must be said that he has been too polite and lenient towards psychoanalysis, which is truly a parody of the initiatory methods of Sufism. Fortunately for Muslims, until now the influence of psychoanalysis has not penetrated deeply among them, and they have not felt the need for it. This is due most of all to the continuation of the practice of religious rites such as the daily prayers and pilgrimage. The

13. See Lord Northbourne, *Looking Back on Progress* (London, 1971); M. Lings, *Ancient Beliefs and Modern Superstitions* (London, 1955); and F. Schuon, *Light on the Ancient Worlds*, trans. Lord Northbourne (London, 1965).

14. See W. N. Perry, 'The Revolt against Moses', *Studies in Comparative Religion*, i (1967), 103-19; F. Schuon, 'The Psychological Imposture', ibid., pp. 98-10s; and R. Guenon, *'The Reign of Quantity and the Signs of the Times'*, trans. Lord Northbourne (Baltimore 1972), chs. xxiv ff. As far as Jung is concerned, his influence can be even more dangerous than that of Freud precisely because he deals more with traditional symbols but from a psychological rather than spiritual point of view. See Burckhardt, 'Cosmology and Modern Science III', *Tomorrow*, xiii (1965), 19-31; id., *Scienza mordernae saggezza tradizionale*, (Torino, 1968), ch. iv.

supreme centre for pilgrimage in Islam is, of course, Makka, but there are other sacred localities throughout the Muslim world which are reflections on this centre. The supplications, 'discourses', and forms of pleading that are carried out in such centres by men, women and children open their souls to the influx of divine grace and are a most powerful means of curing the ailments, and untying the knots, of the soul. They achieve a goal which the psychoanalyst seeks to accomplish without success but often with dangerous results because he lacks the power which comes from the Spirit and which alone can dominate and control the soul.

But psychoanalytical thought, which is agnostic or even in certain cases demonic, is bound to penetrate gradually into the Islamic world, mostly perhaps through the translation of Western literature into Arabic, Persian, Turkish, Urdu and other Islamic languages. The effect of such translations will be to bring into being, and in fact it is already bringing into being, a so-called 'psychological literature' opposed to the very nature and genius of Islam. Islam is a religion which stands opposed to individualistic subjectivism. The most intelligible material symbol of Islam, the mosque, is a building with a space in which all elements of subjectivism have been eliminated. It is an objective determination of the Truth, a crystal through which the light of the Spirit radiates. The spiritual ideal of Islam itself is to transform the soul of the Muslim, like a mosque, into a crystal reflecting the Divine Light.

Truly Islamic literature is very different from the kind of subjectivistic literature we find in the writings of Franz Kafka or at best in Dostoevsky. These and similar figures are of course among the most important in modern Western literature, but they, along with most other Western literary figures, nevertheless present a point of view that is very different from, and often totally opposed to, that of Islam. Among older Western literary figures who are close to the Islamic perspective one might mention first of all Dante and Goethe who, although profoundly Christian, are in many ways like Muslim writers. In modern times one could mention, but on another level, of course, T. S. Eliot who, unlike most modern writers, was a devout Christian and possessed, for this very reason, a vision of the world not completely removed from that of Islam.

In contrast to the works of such men, however, the psychological novel, through its very form and its attempt to penetrate into the psyche of men without a criterion for Truth as an objective reality, is an element that is foreign to Islam. Marcel Proust was without doubt a master of the French language and his 'In Search of Time Past' is of much interest to those devoted to modern French literature, but this type or writing cannot become the model for a genuinely Muslim literature. Yet it is this very type of psychological literature that is now beginning to serve as a 'source of inspiration' for a number of writers in Arabic and Persian. It is of interest to note that the most famous modern literary figure of Persia, Sadeq Hedayat, who was deeply influenced by Kafka, committed suicide from psychological despair and that, although certainly a person of great literary talent, he was divorced from the Islamic current of life and is today opposed by Islamic elements within Persian society. Nevertheless, such writers, who often deal with psychological problems found in Western society, problems which the Muslims have not experienced until now, are becoming popular among the Muslim youth who thereby become acquainted and even afflicted by these new maladies.

One of the worst tragedies today is that there has appeared recently in the Muslim world a new type of person who tries consciously to imitate the obvious maladies of the West. Such people are not, for example, really in a state of depression but try to put themsleves into such in order to look modern. They compose poetry that is supposed to issue from a tormented and depressed soul whereas they are not depressed at all. There is nothing worse than a state of nihilism except the imitation of the state of nihilism by someone who is not nihilistic but tries to produce nihilistic literature or art only to imitate the decadence of Western art. The influence of psychology and psychoanalysis combined with an atheistic and nihilistic point of view and disseminated within the Islamic world through literature and art presents a major challenge to Islam which can be answered only through recourse to traditional Islamic psychology and psychotherapy contained mostly within Sufism and also through the creation of Islamic – in the true sense of the term – literary criticism which would be able to provide an objective evaluation of so much that passes for literature today.

The degree of penetration of anti-Islamic psychological and also philosophical Western ideas through literature can be best gauged by just walking through the streets near universities in different Middle Eastern cities. Among the books spread on the ground or on stands everywhere one still observes traditional religious books, and especially, of course the Qur'ān. But one observes also the presence of a large number of works in Islamic languages dealing with subjects ranging all the way from Marxism and existentialism to pornography presented most often as 'literature'. Naturally, there are rebuttals and answers as well, for Islam and its spirituality are still alive, but the very presence of all this type of writing itself reveals the dimension of the challenge involved.

As far as nihilism is concerned, the Islamic answer is particularly strong, and the Muslims, even modernized ones, have not experienced nihilism in the same way as have Westerners. The main reason for this is that in Christianity the Spirit has been almost always presented in a positive form, as an affirmation, as the sacred art of Christianity reveals so clearly. The void or the 'nihil' has not usually been given a spiritual significance in Christian art such as we observe, for example, in Islamic and also Far Eastern art.[15] Therefore, as a result of the rebellion against Christianity, modern man has experienced the nihil only in its negative and terrifying aspect while some have been attracted to Oriental doctrines especially because of the latter's emphasis upon the void.

In contrast to Christianity where the manifestation of the Spirit is always identified with an affirmation and a positive form, Islamic art makes use of the 'negative' or the 'void' itself in a spiritual and positive sense in the same way that metaphysically the first part of the *Shahāda* begins with a negation to affirm the vacuity of the things vis-à-vis Allah. The space of Islamic architecture and city-planning is not the space around an object or determined by that object. Rather, it is the negative space cut out from material forms as, for example, in traditional bazaars. When one walks through a bazaar one walks through a continuous space determined by the inner surface of the wall surrounding it and not by some object in the middle of it. That is why what is now happening architecturally in many Middle Eastern cities such as the building of some huge monument in the middle of a square to emulate its counterpart in the West is the negation of the very principles of Islamic art and is based on a lack of understanding of the positive role of negative space and the 'nihil' is Islamic architecture. The void or negative space has always possessed a positive spiritual role in Islam and its art, and it is precisely this positive aspect of the void in

15. On the significance of the void in Islamic art see T. Burckhardt, 'The Void in Islamic Art', *Studies in Comparative Religion*, iv (1970), 96-9; S. H. Nasr, 'The Significance of the Void in the Art and Architecture of Islamic Persia', *Journal of the Regional Cultural Institute* (Tehran), v. (1972), 128-8; id., 'The Significance of the Void in the Art and Architecture of Islam', *The Islamic Quarterly*, xvi (1972), 115-20.

Islamic spirituality that has prevented Muslims from experiencing nihilism and nothingness in their purely negative sense and in the manner that nihilism has manifested itself as practically the central experience of modern man.

To return to the question of psychology and psychoanalysis, it must be added that the presence of this perspective in so much art criticism in the West has permitted this type of thought to seep into the mind of a small but significant portion of Islamic society through art – significant because it wields influence and often forms the taste of the psychologically passive masses of traditional Muslims. Traditional Islamic literary criticism and literary tastes are thereby being influenced by the completely anti-traditional ideas emanating from Jungian and Freudian circles and threatening one of the most central and accessible channels of Islamic norms and values. It might, furthermore, be added that Jungian psychology is more dangerous than the Freudian in this respect, in that it seems to be dealing with the sacred and the noumenal world whereas in reality it is deforming the image of the sacred by confusing the spiritual and psychological domains and subversively relegating the luminous and transcendent source of archetypes to a collective unconscious, which is no more than the dumping-ground for the collective psyche of various peoples and their cultures. Islamic metaphysics, as all true metaphysics, stands totally opposed to this blasphemous subversion as well as to the methods of profane psychoanalysis which are, as already stated, no more than a parody of Sufi techniques. But how many contemporary Muslims are willing to stand up and assert their basic differences rather than trying to glide over them in order to placate the modern world with all its essential errors and subsequent evils?

Another challenge to Islam, which has come to the fore only since the Second World War, is the whole series of movements of thought and attitudes loosely bound together under the title of existentialism, which is the latest wave of Western thought to reach the Muslims following various forms of positivism. There are, of course, many branches of existentialism, ranging from the *Existenz Philosophie* of the German philosophers to the theistic philosophy of Gabriel Marcel and finally to the agnostic and atheistic ideas of Sartre and his followers. This type of philosophy, which developed on the European continent early in this century, still holds the centre of the stage in many continental countries. Although it has not as yet had a serious effect upon the Muslim world, during the past few years its influence, which can certainly be characterized as negative, is beginning to make itself felt again through art and more directly through properly so called philosophical works, which are starting to influence some of those Muslims who are concerned with philosophy and the intellectual life. Because of the anti-metaphysical attitude of much of what is taught in this school and its forgetting of the meaning of being in its traditional sense, which lies at the heart of all Islamic philosophy, the spread of existentialism especially in its agnostic vein is a most insidious danger for the future of Islamic intellectual life.

Furthermore, there is the tendency in certain quarters to interpret Islamic philosophy itself in the light of Western modes of thought, the latest being the existential school. Muslim 'intellectuals' are directly to blame for this dangerous innovation *(bid'ah)*, which strangely enough is also the most blind and unintelligent type of imitation *(taqlīd)*.[16] If this type of interpretation continues, it will cost the new generation of Muslims very dearly. Today one sees everywhere in different Muslim countries Muslims learning about their own intellectual and philosophical past from Western sources, many of which may contain useful information and be of value from the point of view of scholarship, but all of which are of necessity from a non-Muslim point of view.

In the field of thought and philosophy in the widest sense the countries that have suffered most are those which use English or French as the medium of instruction in their universities — countries such as Pakistan, the Muslim sectors of India, Malaysia and Nigeria, or, in the Maghrib, countries such as Morocco and Tunisia. It is high time, with all their talk of anti-colonialism, for Muslims to overcome the worst possible type of colonialism, namely colonialism of the mind, and to seek to view and study their own culture, especially its intellectual and spiritual heart, from their own point of view. Even if, God forbid, there are certain Muslims who want to reject some aspect of their intellectual heritage, they would first of all need to know that heritage. Both acceptance and rejection must be based upon knowledge, and there is no excuse for ignorance, no matter what direction one wishes to follow. One cannot reject what one does not know any more than one can accept something in depth without true knowledge. Nor can one throw away what one does not possess. This is a very simple truth, but one that is too often forgotten today.

16. See S. H. Nasr, *Islamic Studies,* chs. viii, ix.

This point recalls an incident that occurred some years ago when a famous Zen master visited a leading Western university. After his lecture on Zen a graduate student asked, 'Don't the Zen masters believe that one should burn the Buddhist scrolls and throw away the Buddha images?' The master smiled and answered, 'Yes, but you can only burn a scroll which you possess and throw away an image which you have.' This was a most profound answer. The master meant that you can only transcend the exoteric dimension of religion if you practise that exotericism and subsequently penetrate into its inner meaning and transcend its forms. He who does not practice exotericism cannot ever hope to go beyond it; he merely falls below it and mistakes this fall for a transcending of forms. The same applies on another level to man's traditional intellectual heritage. One cannot go 'beyond' the formulations of the sages of old when one does not even understand them. He who tries to do so mistakes his pitiful ignorance and 'expansion' and apparent 'freedom' from traditional norms of thought – an ignorance which is in reality the worst kind of imprisonment by the limitations of one's own nature – for the true freedom which comes from the illimitable horizons of the world of the Spirit alone and which can be reached only through the vehicle provided by religion and its sapiential doctrines.

Contemporary Muslims should be realists enough to understand that they must begin their journey, in whatever direction they wish to go, from where they are. A famous Chinese proverb asserts that 'the journey of a thousand miles begins with a single step . Now this first step must of necessity be from one's location, and that is as much true culturally and spiritually as it is physically. Wherever the Islamic world wants to go, it must begin from the reality of the Islamic tradition and from its own real and not imagined situation. Those who lose sight of this fact actually do not travel effectively at all. They just imagine that they are journeying. A Pakistani or a Persian or an Arab 'intellectual' who wants to be a leader of thought for the Muslim people must remember who he is if he wishes to be effective and not be cut off from the rest of Islamic society. No matter how hard he tries to make a corner of Lahore or Tehran or Cairo belong to the setting of Oxford or the Sorbonne, he will not succeed. The so-called Muslim intellectuals of the Westernized kind who complain that they are not understood and appreciated by Islamic society forget that it is they who have refused to appreciate and understand their own culture and society and are therefore subsequently rejected by their own community. This rejection is in fact a sign of life, an indication that Islamic culture still possesses life.

As far as philosophy is concerned, the countries where Muslim languages are used for university instruction are in a somewhat better position, especially in Persia, where Islamic philosophy still continues as a living tradition and where it is not easy to say no matter what in the name of philosophy without being seriously challenged by the traditional intellectual elite. Of course, even this part of the Muslim world has not been completely spared from condescending and apologetic studies of Islamic thought from the point of view of Western philosophy, but, relatively speaking, there is less of a Western philosophic influence because of the two reasons alluded to above: namely the language barrier and a still living tradition of Islamic philosophy. The effect of Iqbal's two philosophical works in English, *The Development of Metaphysics in Persia* and *The Reconstruction of Religious Thought in Islam,* in Pakistan, and of their fairly recent translations into Persian in Persia presents an interesting case worthy of study.

Yet, even in lands using Muslim languages, books do appear in such languages as Persian, and particularly Arabic, on philosophy from a perspective totally alien to that of Islam and bearing such titles as *Falsafatunā* (Our Philosophy), as if philosophy as a vision of the truth or quest after wisdom or *sophia* could ever be 'mine' or 'ours'. No Arab or Persian traditional philosopher ever used such an expression. For Muslims who cultivated Islamic philosophy, philosophy was always *al-falsafah* or *al-hikmah,* 'the philosophy', a vision of the truth transcending the individualistic order and derived from the Truth (*al-Ḥaqq*) itself. The very appearance of such concepts and terms as 'our philosophy' or 'my thought' in the Muslim languages itself reveals the degree of departure from the Islamic norm. It is against such errors that the weapon of the traditional doctrines contained in the vast treasury of Islamic thought must be used and answers drawn from these sources be provided before any further erosion of Islamic intellectual life takes place.

Returning to the question of existentialism and traditional Islamic philosophy in Persia, it must be mentioned that because of the type of traditional philosophy surviving there, based on the principality of being *(aṣālat al-wujūd)* and itself called *falsafat al-wujūd* (which some have mistakenly translated as existentialism), existentialism of the European kind has encountered strong resistance from traditional circles. Actually, anyone who has studied traditional Islamic philosophy from Ibn Sīnā and Suhrawardī to the great exponent of the metaphysics of being, Ṣadr al-Dīn Shīrāzī (Mullā Ṣadrā), will readily understand the profound chasm which separates traditional Islamic 'philosophy' of being from modern existentialism, which even in its apparently most profound aspects can only reach, in a fragmentary fashion, some of the rudimentary teachings contained in their fullness in traditional metaphysics. Henry Corbin, the only Western scholar who has expounded to any extent this later phase of Islamic philosophy in the West, has shown the divergence of views between Islamic philosophy and existentialism as well as the correctives which the former provides for the latter in the long French introduction to his edition and translation of Ṣadr al-Dīn Shīrāzī's *Kitāb al-Mashāʿir* (rendered into French as *Le Livre des pénétrations métaphysiques*).[17] It is, incidentally, interesting to note that it was through Corbin's translation of Heidegger's *Sein und Zeit* that Sartre was first attracted to existentialism, while Corbin himself completely turned away from this form of thought to the ocean of the 'Orient of Light' of Suhrawardī and the luminous philosophy of being of Ṣadr al- Dīn Shīrāzī.

To conclude this discussion, one last basic point must be mentioned, and that is the ecological crisis which was brought into being by modern civilization but which is now a challenge to the very life of men everywhere, including, of course, Muslims in the Islamic world. Anyone who is aware of what is going on today knows that the most immediate problem, at least of a material order, which faces the world is the ecological crisis, the destruction or the loss of equilibrium between man and his natural environment. Islam and its sciences have a particularly urgent and timely message which, as mentioned above, can help to solve, to the extent possible, this major challenge to the world as a whole. However, this message unfortunately received the least amount of attention from modernized Muslims themselves.

We know that Muslims cultivated the different sciences of nature such as astronomy, physics and medicine avidly and made great contributions to them without losing their equilibrium and harmony with nature. Their sciences of nature were always cultivated within the matrix of a 'philosophy of nature' which was in harmony with the total

17. See Mullā Ṣadrā, *Kitāb al-Mashāʿir* (*Le livres des penetrations metaphysiques*) (Tehran-Paris 1964), ch. iv of the introduction; see also T. Izutsu, *The Concept and Reality of Existence* (Tokyo 1971), where a profound analysis of Islamic ontology is to be found, even if in chapter ii certain comparisons are made with Western existentialism which appear to us difficult to accept.

structure of the universe as seen from the Islamic perspective. There lies in the background of Islamic science a true philosophy of nature which if brought to light and presented in a contemporary language can be substituted for the present false natural philosophy, which, combined with a lack of true metaphysical understanding of first principles, is largely responsible for the present crisis in man's relation with nature.[18]

Unfortunately, the Islamic scientific heritage has only too rarely been studied by Muslims themselves, and, if such a study is made, it is usually based on an inferiority complex which tries to prove that Muslims preceded the West in scientific discoveries and therefore are not below the West in their cultural attainment. Rarely is this precious Muslim scientific heritage seen as an alternative path to a science of the natural order which could and did avoid the catastrophic impasse modern science and its applications through technology have created for men. Muslims with vision should be only too happy that it was not they who brought about the seventeenth-century scientific revolution whose logical outcome we observe today. Muslim scholars and thinkers must be trained with the goal of revitalizing the philosophy of nature contained in the Islamic sciences and of studying these sciences themselves.

The end thus proposed is very different from the goal espoused by so many modernized Muslims who pride themselves that Islam paved the way for the Renaissance. They reason that since the Renaissance was a great event in history and since Islamic culture helped create the Renaissance, therefore Islamic culture must be of value. This is an absurd way of reasoning which remains completely unaware of the fact that what the modern world suffers from today is the result of steps taken by the West mostly during the Renaissance when Western man rebelled to a large extent against his God-given religion. Muslims should be grateful that they did not rebel against heaven and had no share in that anti-spiritual humanism which has now resulted in an infra-human world. What Islam in fact did was to prevent the individualistic rebellion against heaven, the Promethean and Titanesque spirit which is so clearly shown in much of Renaissance art and which stands diametrically opposed to the spirit of Islam based on submission to God. It is true that Islamic science and culture were a factor in the rise of the Renaissance in the West but Islamic elements were

18. See S. H. Nasr, *Science and Civilization in Islam* (Cambridge, 1968); and S. H. Nasr, *An Introduction to Islamic Cosmological Doctrines* (Cambridge, 1964).

employed only after they were divorced from their Islamic character and torn away from the total order in which alone they possess their full meaning and significance.

Muslims should cultivate the study of the Islamic sciences, firstly to show young Muslims (so many of whom have the tendency to stop praying upon learning the first formulas of algebra) that for many centuries Muslims cultivated the sciences, including most of the mathematics taught in secondary schools today, and yet remained devout Muslims; and, secondly, to bring out the underlying harmony of the Islamic sciences with Islamic philosophy, theology and metaphysics, a harmony that is closely related to the philosophy of nature alluded to above. The great masterpieces of Islamic science such as the works of Ibn Sīnā, al-Bīrunī, Khayyām, and Naṣīr al-Dīn Ṭūsī can all be employed with both ends in view.

Finally, it must be asserted categorically once again that to preserve Islam and Islamic civilization, a conscious and intellectual defence must be made of the Islamic tradition. Moreover, a thorough intellectual criticism must be made of the modern world and its shortcomings. Muslims cannot hope to follow the same path as the West without reaching the same, or even worse, impasse because of the rapidity of the tempo of change today. The Muslim intelligentsia must face all the challenges here mentioned and many others with confidence in themselves. They must cease to live in the state of a psychological and cultural inferiority complex. They must close ranks among themselves and also join forces with the other great traditions of Asia not only to cease to be on the defensive but also to take the offensive and provide from their God-given treasury of wisdom the medicine which alone can cure the modern world of its most dangerous malady, provided of course the patient is willing to undergo the cure. But even if we take the dimmest point of view with a consideration of the present-day situation and realize that all cannot be saved, the assertion of the truth itself is the most valuable of all acts, and its effect goes far beyond what can usually be envisaged. The truth must therefore be asserted and the intellectual defence of Islam made on every front in which it is challenged. The result is in God's Hands. As the Qur'ān asserts, 'Truth hath come and falsehood hath vanished away. Lo! falsehood is ever bound to vanish' (XVII, 81, Pickthall translation).

14

Islam and the Crisis of the Modern World*

Muhammad Qutb

DAZZLED by the achievements of science during the 18th and 19th centuries, many westerners thought that religion had exhausted all its usefulness and surrendered to science once for all. Almost all the eminent western psychologists and sociologists expressed themselves in similar terms. Freud, the renowned psychologist, for instance, while demonstrating the futility of religion in modern times, says that the human life passes through three distinct psychological phases: superstition, religion and science. This being the era of science, so all religion was pronounced out of date.

There is no denying that there were certain causes which led the men of science in Europe to adopt a view of life antagonistic to religion. It was mainly due to the great controversy, that raged between men of science and the Christian church, which made them think — quite justifiably of course — that whatever the church stood for was reactionary, retrogressive, backward and superstitious, and that therefore it must vacate its seat for science so as to enable humanity to move ahead on the path of civilization.

RELIGION AND SCIENCE

Without appreciating the difference between the peculiar conditions of life obtaining in Europe at the time of this unhappy conflict and

* This chapter is excerpted from the author's book *Islam: The Misunderstood Religion*, Kuwait: Dārul Bayān Bookshop which is an English translation of his *Shubuhāt Hawl al-Islām*. The translation has been thoroughly revised by the editor.

those in the Islamic world, a section of people has been demanding the renunciation of religion and of the sacred traditions that have come to us from our earlier generations. This move has been strengthened by the puerile imitation of the West that is gaining currency in the Muslim lands. Many a naïve people fancy that the only way to progress is to follow the dominant nations of Europe, intellectually and culturally. To achieve this they have to discard their religion just as Europe had done failing which they fear they would be trapped in an abyss of reactionism, backwardness and humbug.

But such people overlook the fact that even in the West, not all the outstanding scholars were antagonistic towards religion; nor do their works exhibit anything of this sort. On the other hand we find some of these eminent intellectuals who were never under the spell of Europe's Godless materialism and who affirmed that religion is a psychological as well as an intellectual necessity for mankind.

The most noted figure among them is the astronomer Sir James Jeans, who started his intellectual career as a Godless sceptic but was led finally by his scientific explorations to the conclusion that the greatest problems of science could not be resolved without believing in God. The famous sociologist Jeans Bridge went so far as to eulogize Islam for achieving a successful amalgam of the temporal with the spiritual into a harmonious system of thought blended with a practical code of life. The well-known English writer Somerset Maugham epitomized the whole attitude of modern Europe towards religion when he remarked that Europe had in the present era discovered a new god — Science, in place of the old one.

The god of science has, however, turned out to be extremely fickle, everchanging and constantly shifting positions, upholding one thing as a fact and reality today and rejecting it the other day as false and spurious. Consequently its 'worshippers' are doomed to a perpetual state of restlessness and anxiety, for how can they find rest and peace of mind under such a capricious god? That the modern west is afflicted with this uncertainty and restlessness is borne out by the large number of psychological and nervous disorders that are so common in modern society today.

Yet another result of this deification of modern science is that the world we live in had become devoid of all meaning and purpose with no higher order or power to guide it. Tension and conflict between different forces have become the order of the day. As a result everything in this world suffers change: economic and political systems change; relations between states and individuals alter; even scientific 'facts' change. What can man expect save misery and perpetual restlessness in a world with such a sombre setting where no Higher Power exists whom he should turn to for support, strength and comfort in this ruthless struggle of life.

It is religion and religion alone that can bring peace and tranquillity to the world. It instils in man love for goodness and the courage to stand up to the forces of evil and tyranny was a necessary condition of obtaining God's pleasure and to make His will predominant on this earth awaiting with patience for his reward in the Hereafter. Doesn't mankind really need peace, tranquillity and comfort, in a word, religion?

MAN WITHOUT RELIGION

What will become of man if his life is devoid of belief in an eternal life in the hereafter? Belief in the continuity of life in the next world is a revolutionary concept. Under its impact, man's life upon earth assumes new dimensions opening higher horizons of progress before him, in the absence of which he is inevitably oppressed by a torturous sense of nothingness, as it means a virtual cutting short of man's total lifespan, making him a mere plaything in the hands of his whims and caprices which teach him nothing but to derive the maximum possible amount of pleasure during this short sojourn upon the earth. Mutual rivalries, savage battles and conflicts over the possession of material gains follow, as there is no Higher Power to control and restrain one's desires. Blinded by greed and lust, man tries to gain whatever he can in the shortest span of time. His total perspective of life and its mission is lost altogether. This degrades man to lower planes of feelings and thought. His imagination sinks low and so do his ideals and the means to achieve them. Mankind is doomed to a perpetual life of hideous internecine wars that scarcely permit it to pursue higher and nobler ends in life. In such a world there is hardly any room for love or sympathy, as men are obsessed with carnal pleasures, and spurred by uncontrolled passions. In such a context, how can they strive for lofty aspirations or even appreciate genuine human feelings?

In such a world men do gain some material profits. But of what use are these when their fellowmen are constantly wrangling over them, each ready to cut his brother's throat only to enhance his own material welfare? Materialism so spoils life that even man's material achievements are rendered useless and senseless. Men are enslaved by greed, lust and avarice. Blind appetites gain control over them. They lose their grip on them and become their slaves. This results in the dehumanization of man.

The predicament of the nations is not different. They, for similar reasons, get entangled in devastating wars which spoil all harmony in life. And science, with all its dreadful weapons, is employed for the extermination of the human race rather than to contribute towards man's well-being and his moral advancement.

Viewed in this context religion means broadening the mental horizon of mankind, for life is not confined to this world alone but continues even beyond it — towards eternity. This inspires hope in man's heart, encourages him to live and strive for the achievement of higher ideals and to remain steadfast against evil and oppression. Religion teaches love, sympathy and universal brotherhood and is thus the only way to peace, prosperity and progress. It equips man in the best possible way for the hard struggle of life.

Furthermore it is faith and faith alone that can inspire man to rise above his self and suffer for noble and lofty ideals. Deprived of faith, he is left with nothing else to look up to outside his own self. He is torn away from the total reality of the creation and is rendered into an isolated being. This reduces him to an unsocial animal, a brute.

Many a man fell fighting in the noble cause of truth spending the whole of their lives in the struggle yet achieving nothing in the materialistic sense of the word. What inspired these noble souls to engage in a battle that brought them no material rewards, that caused them the loss of whatever little they happened to possess? This has been one of the products of faith. Such behaviour can never be produced in pursuit of selfish motives. Avarice, greed, lust, etc., can never make a man achieve anything really good and noble. That is why the material triumphs won by selfish avarice are self-centred, short-lived and temporary. The incentive of immediate gain cannot equip a man with a noble character, nor can it give him the courage to stand fast suffering patiently for long for a lofty ideal.

There are some so-called reformers who seek inspiration from hatred rather than love. The hatred may be personal in character or it may be based on class, or region or nation. Such rancour-inspired people may realize some of their objectives, may even muster courage to sacrifice for such ends, but a doctrine based on malevolence and hatred can never lead humanity to anything good. They may remove certain evils and put an end to the existing state of injustice but would generate new evils and injustices and fail to remedy the ailments of mankind.

On the other hand a creed that does not aim at the immediate gains of this world, nor derives inspiration from malevolence but fosters in men noble passions of love, fraternity and the determination to lay down their lives serving their fellowmen can heal the festering sores of humanity and pave the way for future progress and prosperity. The essence of such a creed is faith in God and His love. This produces a virtuous mode of living that helps man get nearer to his Creator, and become a true servant of humanity. Belief in the Hereafter gives man a firm sense of security, banishing from his heart the fear of extinction with his physical death and promising him an eternal life. This in other words means that his efforts shall not be wasted but shall be crowned with fullest reward in the life to come, even if he is unable to achieve anything in this world. This is a natural corollary of belief in God and the Hereafter. It is true of religion as such. But as far as Islam is concerned it does not stop here, it goes a long way ahead: it has a far more fascinating story to tell.

IS ISLAM OUT OF DATE

Those who may imagine that Islam has become outmoded and is no longer needed, do not know as to what it stands for, nor do they seem to understand its real mission in human life. The image of Islam that emerges from books on Islam and Islamic history written mostly by Western orientalists and their disciples and taught ever since the colonial period is something like this: Islam was revealed merely to put an end to idolatry and guide man to the worship of God alone; that the Arabs were torn into antagonistic tribes, Islam came and united them and made them a strong and unified nation; that they were addicted to drinking and gambling and led depraved lives; Islam stopped them from these depravities and abolished other evil customs prevalent among them such as burying alive their daughters and wasting away their strength in acts of revenge; and that Islam called upon Muslims to disseminate its message, which they did, this in turn leading to the battles that ultimately determined the boundaries of the Islamic world as we know it today. This, according to these people, was the sole purpose of Islam in human life! This being its historical mission, it has long since been fulfilled: there is no idol-worship in the Islamic world; the once antagonistic tribes have been more or less subject to a process of absorption losing their identity in the larger nationalities or communities. As far as gambling and drinking are concerned let us bear in mind that human civilization has advanced to such an extent now that it is useless to declare such pastimes unlawful as we see that despite all religious taboos they still persist. It is no use insisting on their abolition. Thus they conclude that Islam has served its purpose in this world; it has had its day but is no longer needed. It has nothing new to offer. We must, therefore, turn towards the modern civilization and seek progress through it.

One listens to this prattle from all quarters. Even some educated and otherwise enlightened persons repeat these assertions like a parrot. This case against Islam is, however, a product of sheer ignorance and prejudice. We must not judge Islam on hearsay. Let us try to understand what Islam is and what it stands for.

Islam, in a word, means liberation from all sorts of slavery such as may inhibit the progress of humanity or may not allow it to follow the path of virtue and goodness. It means man's freedom from dictators who enslave him by force or fear, make him do what is wrong and deprive him of his dignity, honour, property or life. Islam liberates man from such tyranny by telling him that all authority vests in God and God alone; He alone is the Real Sovereign. All men are His subjects and as such He alone controls their destinies, none of them having the power to cause any benefit or avert any distress from his ownself independent of the Divine Will. All men shall be presented before Him on the Day of Judgement to account for their performance in this life. Thus Islam brings to man freedom from fear or oppression inflicted on him by men like himself and who, in reality, are as helpless as he is and who are no less subject to the Will of God Almighty than he himself is.

Islam also means freedom from lust, including the lust for life, as it is this very weakness of man which is exploited by tyrants and dictators intentionally or otherwise in enslaving their fellowmen. But for it no man would silently accept subservience to men like himself or sit idle to watch tyranny on the rampage and dare not challenge it. It is a great blessing of Islam that it taught man to fight tyranny and oppression bravely rather than cringe before them in abject servitude. Says the Qur'ān: 'Say: If it be that your fathers, your sons, your brothers, your mates, or your kindred, the wealth that you have gained, the commerce in which you fear a decline, or the dwellings in which you delight — are dearer to you than God, or His Apostle, or the striving in His cause — then wait until God brings about His Decision: and God guides not the rebellious.' (al-Qur'ān, 9: 24).

As against blind passions and appetites, the love of God generates in life the values of love, virtue, truth, and striving hard in His way, the way of all that is good and lofty in life. Islam subjects human passions in the service of these noble goals of life. The love of God becomes the dominant and real directing force in man's life. Without this no man can claim to be a true Muslim.

A man steeped in sensual pleasures may entertain the mistaken belief that he enjoys life more than others do. But soon he has to realize his mistake, for he is gradually reduced to a mere slave to his blind passions. He is doomed to a perpetual life of deprivation and restlessness, for animal desires once run rampant become insatiable: the appetite increases with every effort to satisfy it. The result is a craze for the maximization of sensual pleasure. Such an attitude towards life is not conducive to progress, material or spiritual. Humanity cannot approach higher realms of nobility unless it is freed from the dominance of the blind animal appetites. It is only through control of the animal self that man is freed to make progress — in the fields of science, arts or religion.

It is for this very reason that Islam attaches such a great importance to the freeing of man from his animal passions. For this purpose it neither favours monasticism nor gives man unbridled freedom to serve the demands of the flesh. It aims at the attainment of a balance between these two extremes. Whatever is there in the world is for man. It is there to serve him and not to dominate or rule over him. He should not allow himself to be made a slave to these, rather he should use them as means to a higher end, i.e. his spiritual perfection by disseminating the word of God amongst his fellowmen. Thus Islam has a twofold objective in view:

(a) in the individual life it aims at providing to each and every individual a just and adequate share so as to enable him to lead a decent and clean life; and

(b) in the collective sphere it arranges things in such a way that all the social forces of a society are directed towards the enhancement of progress and civilization in accordance with its basic outlook upon life and in such a way that the balance between the constituent units and the whole, between the individuals and the community, is established.

Islam has had a most liberalizing effect on human intellect as it is diametrically opposed to all sorts of superstition. Humanity has, in the course of history, fell a prey to a number of absurdities, in theory and practice. Some of these were even described to have some divine origin. All these acted as shackles for the human minds, which groped about in the dark before the advent of Islam. With Islam it attained maturity and freedom from this hotch-potch of nonsense, symbolized in the so-called gods, distorted Jewish traditions, and the imbecilities of the Christian Church. Islam freed man from all superstitions and brought him back to God and established direct relation between man and his Creator.

Islam uses a very simple terminology. Its teachings are very easy to understand, perceive and believe in. It invites man to make use of the faculties given to him and to seek the fullest possible understanding of the world around him. It does not admit of any inborn hostility between reason and religion or for that matter between science and religion. Islam impresses upon man in clear and unequivocal terms that it is God and God alone who has in His immense mercy subjected all the things on this earth to man, and that all the facts that are discovered by scientific investigation and the material benefits that flow from that to man, are in fact blessings from God, for which man should offer his thanks to God, and strive hard so as to become a worthy servant of so Merciful and Beneficent a Master. Thus Islam holds knowledge and science as a part of faith rather than regard them as an evil intrinsically opposed to genuine belief in God.

What is the state of the world today. Has man freed himself from all superstition, imbecilities and absurd beliefs? Has he discovered the man within himself? Has he liberalized himself from the yoke of worldly tyrants indulging in the exploitation of man by man? If such a millenium has not been achieved despite all developments in science and technology, then Islam has still a great and glorious part to play.

THE CHALLENGE FROM SCIENCE

Half of the inhabitants of the world today remain idol-worshippers. India, China, Japan and a great many other parts of the world are instances in view. The other half is engaged in the worship of a new found deity whose corrupting influence on man's thoughts and feelings is no less significant. This deity is styled as Modern Science.

Science is a powerful instrument to help us increase our knowledge of the world around us. As such it has an impressive record of achievements to its credit. All these brilliant achievements were, however, vitiated by one fatal mistake of the westerners: they installed science as supreme God, declaring that it alone had the right to claim the adoration and submission of man to it. Thus they denied themselves all means of acquiring knowledge save that recognized by empirical science which let humanity wander further away rather than bring it nearer to its real destination. Consequently the otherwise vastly immense range of human endeavour and progress was shrunk and made co-extensive with the limitations of empirical sciences. The total dimensions of the human situation are not taken care of within the scope of science whose domain is limited. It is of immense help in discovering the knowledge of the means of life, but fails to guide us in the realm of objectives of life, its values and norms, and the nature of the ultimate reality.

Some protagonists of science claim that science alone can introduce man to the secrets of this universe and life, and conclude that only that which is upheld by science is true; the rest is all trash! But while making such a statement they overlook the fact that science with all its brilliant and impressive record is still in its infancy and ever hesitant to commit itself as regards the veracity or otherwise of many things, for the simple reason that it cannot penetrate deep into the heart of reality beyond attempting a mere superfluous survey of it. Yet its votaries assert in the authoritative way that there is no such thing as human soul. They deny that man, confined as he is within the limitations of his sensory organs, can ever have any contact with the Unknown — not even a glimpse of it through telepathy[1] or dreams. They repudiate all these not because they have proved them to be mere illusions but simply because the experimental science with its inadequate instruments has not yet been able to fathom their mystery. That they belong to a higher order of things not subject to man's observation was however sufficient to make these gentlemen turn their backs on them and pronounce their non-existence. Non-existence is one thing, non-susceptible to one instru-

---

1. Telepathy is defined as the communication of impressions from one mind to another without the aid of the senses. The most notable example of this is the incident when the Caliph 'Umar called out to Sāriyah, a Muslim commander, saying: 'Sāriyah! To the Mountain! To the mountain!' Sāriyah heard this warning coming from hundreds of miles away. So he led his contingent to the mountain, escaped the enemy lying in ambush and won a victory over them. Although telepathy is now recognized as a scientific fact yet the modern scientist is so biased that its having anything to do with 'soul' is denied outright. It is explained as a manifestation of a sixth but yet not fully explained faculty of the human mind.

ment of investigation a very different matter. But they fail to see the difference between the two.

Such then is the 'enlightened ignorance' man suffers from today, which shows how desperately he stands in need of Islam to blow away these allegedly scientific cobwebs of knowledge. Idol-worship was the older form wherein human folly found expression; the cult of science-worship is its latest version. To liberate human reason and spirit, both of these yokes must be shaken off. It is in this perspective that Islam emerges as the only hope for humanity, for it alone can restore peace between religion and science, bring back once more the tranquillity and concord to our distressed world and enable man to satisfy his both cravings, the desire for knowledge and the search for tru†h, the need to control the forces of nature, and to integrate with the Ultimate: God.

WHAT ISLAM STANDS FOR

Islam establishes not only peace and harmony but also rids mankind of tyranny and oppression. The contemporary world presents in this respect no better view than it did fourteen hundred years ago, when Islam freed it from all false gods. Tyranny still on the rampage in the guise of haughty kings, insolent demagogues and heartless capitalists who are busy in sucking the blood of the millions, subjugating them and making capital out of their helplessness and misery. There is still another class of dictators who rule with sword, usurp peoples' liberties and claim that they are merely instruments in enforcing the people's or the proletariat's will.

Islam brings to an end man's rule over man. It makes the rulers as much subject to the Divine Law as are all other men and women. Islam does not allow any man to subjugate others or impose upon them his will. Only God's commands are to be obeyed and only the Prophet's examples are to be followed. The ruler, in such a community, shall, as a part of his obligations towards men and God, be required to enforce Divine Law failing which he may no longer have any lawful claim to the people's obedience. They may in such a situation quite lawfully disregard his orders. This was explicitly stated by the first Caliph Abū Bakr (May God be pleased with him) when he said that 'Obey me only so long as I obey God with respect to you; and if I should happen to deviate from God's obedience, then in that case my obedience shall no longer be incumbent upon you.' As such the ruler in Islam has no priviliged right to use the Public Exchequer or to formulate state legislation in defiance of the *Sharī'ah*. Moreover, it is only the trust-worthy people who have any right to rule, who are elected to a post of authority through a free, just and impartial election with no checks on voters save those of justice, virtue and decency.

Such an Islamic State will not only liberate its citizens from all tyrants at home but shall safeguard their freedom against any outside aggression as well. This is so because Islam itself is a religion of glory and power and as such it cannot tolerate that men should degrade themselves by prostrating at the feet of the false god of imperialism. Islam prescribes a very simple code of life for man. It exhorts him to strive hard to gain the pleasure of his Creator, surrender his will to that of his Lord, follow His commandments and come forward with all the sources at his disposal to fight against the spectre of imperialism and tyranny.

Let Man therefore turn towards Islam for this is the time for all human beings to flock together under its banner so as to wipe out from the face of the earth all the vestiges of imperialism and exploitation of man by man. Here is the way to real freedom, one which allows no serfdom, promises all men freedom in thought, action, property and religion, jealously safeguarding their integrity as well as honour. For only thus can we become Muslims worthy of our God, the object of our adoration — in Whose path we tread, the path He chose for us: 'This day I have perfected for you religion and completed my favour on you and chosen for you Islam as religion.' (al-Qur'ān, 5: 3).

Such a radical reformation effected by Islam is by no means a paro-chial one confined to the Muslim community alone, but is, on the other hand, by its very nature universal in character. It is nothing less than a blessing for the world of today afflicted as it is with internecine wars, with a still another and far more terrible world war looming large on the horizon.

Islam is the only future hope of humanity; and its victorious emerg-ence out of the present ideological warfare is the only guarantee of man's salvation. But important as the triumph of Islam is for the future of mankind, its realization is not easy to come by. It can be effected only if the people who are already in its folds and profess loyalty to it should pledge themselves for its glory and triumph. Islam freed man-kind from the tyranny of animal appetites fourteen hundred years ago; now it can once again shake off the shackles of lust and free man to direct all his faculties to reach a higher spiritual plane and establish virtue and goodness in life.

ISLAMIC REVIVAL

The revival of Islam is a practical and realizable undertaking. The history of Islam proves beyond any doubt that it is quite capable of raising man above a purely animal level. What was possible in the past is quite possible in the present and what is possible in the case of individuals is equally realizable in the case of nations. Mankind has not undergone any temperamental change ever since. The human society in the sixth century was at as low a level and was as much taken up with sensual pleasures as it is today. There is no difference in the nature of the basic human ailment, although some of the symptoms, the outwardly forms or names of the vices indulged in, are dissimilar. Ancient Rome was no less rotten morally than its modern counterparts. Similarly in ancient Persia, moral anarchy was as widespread as is in the present day world. Dictators of today are not very different from the dictators of the past. It was in this historical perspective that Islam was revealed to the world. It brought about a complete change, lifted mankind from the abyss of moral degradation, gave human life a lofty purpose, dynamism, movement and infused into it a spirit to strive hard in the way of truth and goodness. Humanity under Islam flourished, prospered and there was set afoot a dynamic intellectual and spiritual movement that encompassed the East as well as the West. The world of Islam became the mainspring of light, excellence and progress in the world for a long time to come. During this long period of its dominance never did the Islamic world find itself lagging behind materially, intellectually or spiritually. Its followers were looked upon as symbols of goodness and excellence in all spheres of human activity till they ceased to reflect in their lives the noble and exalted ideals of Islam and became mere slaves to their whims and animal desires. It was then that all their glory and power came to an end in accordance with the immutable law of God.

The modern Islamic movement that is still gathering momentum derives its strength from the past and makes use of all the modern available resources with its gaze fixed on the future. It has great potentialities and as such has a bright future ahead, for it is fully capable of performing that great miracle which has once changed the face of history.

This does not, however, mean that Islam is a mere spiritual creed, or a plea for morality, or just a scheme of intellectual research in the kingdom of heavens and earth. It is a practical code of life that fully embraces worldly affairs. Nothing escapes its penetrating eyes. It takes notice of all the diverse patterns of relationships binding men together irrespective of the fact that such relationships fall under the economic, political and social categories. It regulates them by prescribing suitable laws and norms of behaviour and enforces them in human life. Its most outstanding characteristic is that it establishes a unique harmony between the individual and society, between reason and intuition, between work and worship, between this world and the Hereafter.

WHY THE WORLD NEEDS ISLAM TODAY

We have tried to examine briefly the threats that confront man today and to show how relevant in fact how necessary Islam is to mankind in our own times. Let us conclude by summing up some of the distinct features of Islam which make it all the more necessary for the modern man to seek his salvation through this ideology.

Firstly, it must be well understood that Islam is not a mere ideological vision. It is a practical system of life that fully appreciates all the genuine needs of mankind and tries to realize them.

Secondly, in trying to meet the genuine requirements of man Islam effects a perfect balance between all areas of life and activity. It starts with the individual maintaining a balance between his requirements of body and soul, reason and spirit and in no case allows one side to predominate the other. It does not suppress the animal instincts in order to make the soul ascend the higher planes, nor does it allow man, in his efforts to fulfil his bodily desires, to stoop down to the low level of animalism and hedonism. On the contrary, it makes them both meet on a single higher plane doing away with all the internal psychological conflicts that threaten the human soul or set a part of it against the other parts. In the social sphere, it proceeds to achieve an equilibrium between the needs of the individual and those of the community. It does not allow an individual to transgress against other individuals, or against the community. Nor does it allow the community to commit transgression against the individual. It also does not approve of one class or group of people to enslave another class or group of people. Islam exercizes a beneficient constraint on all these mutually opposed forces, prevents them from coming into collision with one another, and harnesses them all to co-operate for the general good of mankind as a whole.

Thus Islam strikes a balance between different sectors of society and between different aspects of existence, spiritual as well as material. Unlike communism, it does not believe that economic factors, i.e. the material aspect alone, dominate the human existence. Nor does it contribute to what the pure spiritualists or idealists say claiming that spiritual factors or high ideals alone are sufficient to organize human life. Islam rather holds that all these diverse elements put together form what is called human society; and that the best code of life is that which takes note of all these, making full allowance for body as well as reason and spirit and arranging them all in the framework of a harmonious whole. Thirdly, it must always be kept in mind that Islam has an altogether independent existence of its own as a social philosophy as well as an economic system. Some of its outward manifestations may on the surface appear to resemble those of capitalism or socialism, but in fact it is far from being the one or the other. It retains all the good characteristics of these systems, yet is free from their shortcomings and perversions. It does not extol individualism to that loathful extent which is the characteristic of the modern West. It was from this germ that modern capitalism sprang and institutionalized that concept of individual's freedom where man is allowed to exploit other individuals and the community only to serve his personal gain. Islam guarantees personal freedom and provides opportunities for individual enterprise but not at the cost of society or ideals of social justice. The reaction to capitalism has appeared in the form of socialism. It idolizes the social basis to an extent that the individual is reduced to an insignificant cog of the social machine, with no existence whatever of its own outside and independent of the herd. Therefore, the community alone enjoys freedom as well as power; the individual has no right to question its authority or demand his rights. The tragedy of socialism and its variants is that they assign to the state absolute powers to shape the lives of the individuals.

Islam strikes a balance between the two extremes of capitalism and socialism. Being appreciative of their role Islam harmonizes the individual and the state in such a way that individuals have the freedom necessary to develop their potentialities and not to encroach upon the rights of their fellowmen. It also gives the community and the state adequate powers to regulate and control the socio-economic relationships so as to guard and maintain this harmony in human life. The basis of this whole structure as envisaged by Islam is the reciprocity of love between individuals and groups; it is not erected on the basis of hatred and class conflict as is the case with socialism.

It may also be pointed out here that this unique system of life as envisaged by Islam, did not originate as a result of any economic pressure, nor was it an outcome of some mutually conflicting interests of antagonistic groups of people. NO. It was revealed to the world as the ordained system of life at a time when men attached no particular importance to the economic factors, nor did they know anything about social justice in the sense we know it in modern times. Both socialism and capitalism are much later developments. Islam presented its scheme of social reform much before any of the social movements of our times. It guaranteed the basic needs of man — food, housing, and sexual satisfaction — more than thirteen hundred years ago. The Holy Prophet (peace be upon him) said that: 'Whosoever acts as a public officer for us (i.e. the Islamic State) and has no wife, he shall have a wife; if he has no house, he shall be given a house to live in; if he has no servant, he shall have one; and if he has no animal (a conveyance), he shall be provided with one.' This historical announcement of fundamental human rights not only contains those rights voiced by many a revolutionary in our times, it adds to them some more as well, without, however, necessitating any inter-class hatred, bloody revolutions, and without of course rejecting all those human elements in life that do not fall under the above three heads: food, housing and family.

These are some of the salient features of the Islamic code of life. They are sufficient to show that a religion with such laws and principles, and so comprehensive as to include the whole of the human existence, emotions, thoughts, actions, worship, economic dealings, social relationships, instructive urges and spiritual aspirations — all arranged in the framework of a single harmonious but unique system of life, can never lose its usefulness for mankind. Nor can such a religion ever become obsolete, as its objectives are the same as those of life itself and therefore destined to live on so long as there is life on this planet.

Considering the existing state of affairs in the contemporary world, mankind cannot reasonably afford to turn its back upon Islam or reject its system of life. Mankind is still afflicted with the most savage and odious forms of racial prejudices. America and South Africa may offer a case in point in this respect. Surely the twentieth century world has yet a great deal to learn from Islam. Long ago Islam freed humanity from all racial prejudices. It did not content iself with the presentation of a beautiful vision of equality alone but it achieved in practice an unprecedented state of equality between all people, black, white or yellow, declaring that none enjoyed any superiority over the others except in virtue and piety. It not only freed the black from slavery but also fully recognized their rights to aspire even to the highest seat of authority in the Islamic State. They could become the heads of the Islamic State. The Holy Prophet (peace be upon him) said: 'Listen and obey even if a negro slave be appointed as your superior so long as he should enforce amongst you the Law of God.'

How can also the world of today ignore the message of Islam stricken as it is with the evils of imperialism and tyranny with all their barbarous attributes, for Islam alone can help mankind shake off these chains. It is opposed to imperialism and all forms of exploitation. The way Islam treated the peoples of the countries it conquered was so generous, just and sublime that the eyes of the 'Civilized' Europe can hardly penetrate those heights. We may in this regard cite the famous decision of the Caliph 'Umar to whip the son of 'Amr ibn al-'As, the victorious general and honoured governor of Egypt as he had beaten an Egyptian Copt without any legal justification, while the renowned father himself had a very narrow escape from the whip of the Caliph. This shows what social liberty and human rights were enjoyed by the subjects of the Islamic State.

Then there is the evil of capitalism that has poisoned all life. Its abolition and the need to rid humanity of its evil consequences again calls for Islam. For, Islam prohibits usury and hoarding which taken together form the mainstay of the capitalist economy. This in other words means that Islam alone can effectively check the evils of capitalism as it did check them fourteen hundred years ago.

Similarly the world dominated by the materialistic, godless communism stands in need of Islam, which achieves and maintains social justice of the highest order without destroying the spiritual mainsprings of human life. Nor does it confine man's afforts to the narrow world of the senses. Above all, it neither endeavours nor aims at the imposition of its own creed on mankind forcibly with the iron rod of a proletarian dictatorship, for, 'There is no compulsion in religion; indeed the righteousness has been differentiated from the wickedness.' (al-Qur'ān, 2: 256).

Finally, the world with the shadows of war still hanging over it cannot but turn towards Islam — the only way to establish and maintain real peace on this earth.

The era of Islam has in a way just started, not ended; it is not a spent force, but a living dynamic force. Its future is as bright as its great historical past is glorious when it illumined the face of earth at the time when Europe was still groping its way in the dark recesses of medievalism.

A SHORT BIBLIOGRAPHY ON ISLAM

ISLAMIC OUTLOOK ON LIFE

HAMIDULLAH, M., *Introduction to Islam*, Paris: Centre Cultural Islamique, 1980.

A simple and generally authentic introduction to Islam: Its beliefs, doctrines and practices. Good for beginners. The book also contains essential information about prayers, direction of the *Qiblah* from different parts of the world and a thumb-nail sketch of Islamic history.

MAWDŪDĪ, Abū'l A'lā, *Towards Understanding Islam*. Translated and edited by Khurshid Ahmad, Leicester: The Islamic Foundation, 1981.

A clear, concise and authoritative introduction to Islam, expounding its beliefs and doctrines and their *rationale*. The book provides a comprehensive and all-embracing view of Islam as a way of life and constitutes a standard text-book on Islam. This book has been translated in twenty-five languages of the world.

'AZZĀM, 'Abdur-Rahmān, *The Eternal Message of Muhammad*, New York: Devin Adsir Co., 1964. Also in Mentor Books, London and New York, The New English Library, 1964.

An introduction to the life and message of the Prophet Muhammad focusing attention on their practical and spiritual significance and their impact on human history in general and Islamic history in particular.

JAMĀLĪ, Mohammad Fādhil, *Letters on Islam*, London: Oxford University Press, 1965.

Written in the form of letters of a father to his teenage son, the book expounds the essential beliefs and practices of Islam.

QUTB, Muhammad, *Islam: The Misunderstood Religion*, Kuwait: Darul Bayan Books, 1967.

An exposition of the basic concepts of Islam and a forthright unapologetic defence of Islamic values and principles. The book deals with most of the misunderstandings which have been systematically implanted in the minds of modern-educated people, Muslims and others.

NASR, Seyyed Hossein, *Ideals and Realities of Islam*, London: Allen & Unwin, 1966, Boston, U.S.A., 1972.

A balanced and intellectually sophisticated exposition of the basic teachings of Islam. The book tackles with clarity and conviction a number of questions on which orientalists and modernist writings try to create confusion in the mind of the common reader. The author also exposes the fallacy of superimposing the secular western model over Muslim society and demonstrates how the *Sharī'ah* is capable of leading Muslims to a more respectable future.

NASR, Seyyed Hossein, *Encounter of Man and Nature*, London: Allen & Unwin, 1968.

A thought-provoking study of the intellectual crisis of modern man. The author examines and contrasts the materialistic and the Islamic approaches to life and reality, and shows how the Islamic approach alone achieves harmony between man and nature. The Darwinian theory of evolution is also critically examined.

ASAD, Muhammad, *Islam at the Crossroads*, Lahore: Arafat Publications, 1969 (first edition 1934).

A thought-provoking treatise emphasizing the original revolutionary spirit of Islam and challenging the intellectual spell of the contemporary west. The discussion on the place and role of the *Sunnah* is particularly useful.

PICKTHALL, Muhammad Marmaduke, *Cultural Side of Islam*, Lahore: Shaikh Muhammad Ashraf, 1927.

A systematic exposition of some major social values of Islam and their actualization in history. Issues dealt with include relation between the sexes, the position of non-Muslims in the Islamic state, tolerance and Muslim contribution to the arts and sciences.

JAMEELAH, Maryam, *Islam in Theory and Practice*, Islamic Publications, Lahore, 1967.

A collection of thirty essays on different aspects of Islamic religion and culture and on the revivalist trends in the world of Islam.

AHSAN, M. M., *Islam: Faith and Practice*, Leicester: The Islamic Foundation, Revised edition 1991.

This small book briefly explains what a Muslim must believe and comprehend to live Islamically. One of the most widely used reference works on Muslim beliefs and life-manners.

ABDALATI, Hammudah, *Islam in Focus*, Riyadh: International Islamic Federation of Student Organizations, 1986.

This book deals with the ideological foundations of Islam. It gives an overview of the main concepts of Islam, including Islamic values and etiquettes: piety, righteousness, sanctity of life, freedom, equity and purification from sin. The book also covers Islamic articles of faith and different aspects of individual and social life in Islam.

MAWDŪDĪ, Abū'l A'lā, *Let Us Be Muslims*, Leicester: The Islamic Foundation, 1985. Edited by Khurram Murad.

Based on brief but lucid Friday congregational addresses, this is the most intellectually satisfying and spiritually enlightening exposition of different aspects of *Īmān*, *Islām*, Prayers, Fasting, *Zakāt*, Pilgrimage (*Hajj*) and *Jihād*.

HAMID, Abdul Wahid, *Islam: The Natural Way*, Leicester: MELS, 1989.

Seeks to show that Islam is the natural way for all creation. This book presents an interesting discussion on livelihood, family, neighbourhood, community, Ummah, inter-faith interaction, global vision and the Hereafter.

THE QUR'ĀN AND THE PROPHET

PICKTHALL, Muhammad Marmaduke, *The Meaning of the Glorious Qur'ān*, New York: New American Library, 1953 (with Arabic text, Karachi: Taj Company). .

One of the best English translations of the Qur'ān available today.

'ALĪ, 'Abdullāh Yūsuf, *The Holy Qur'ān*, Lahore: Shaikh Muhammad Ashraf, 1934; Beirut: Darul Arabia, 1973.

A generally good and dependable translation although the same cannot be said about the explanatory notes. Very useful index.

MAWDŪDĪ, Abū'l A'lā, *Towards Understanding the Qur'ān*, translated by Zafar Ishaq Ansari, The Islamic Foundation, Vols. I-VI, 1988-98.

This is an English rendering of Mawdūdī's *magnum opus: Tafhīm al-Qur'ān*. These six volumes contain the *tafsīr* of the first twenty-four *Sūrahs* of the Qur'ān (*al-Fātihah* to *al-Nūr*), covering the first two and a half volumes of the six-volume Urdu *tafsīr*. It is expected that the whole *tafsīr* will be completed in twelve or thirteen volumes.

Saḥīḥ Muslim, translated by A. H. Siddiqui, Lahore: Shaikh Muhammad Ashraf, 1972 (3 volumes).

A careful and dependable translation of *Jāmi' as-Saḥīḥ* of Imām Muslim, one of the two most authentic collections of the *hadīth*. Although the Arabic text has not been given, the translation is good and the explanatory notes are useful.

HAMIDULLAH, M., *Saḥīfah Hammām ibn Munabbih*, Paris: Centre Cultural Islamique, 1961.

Text and translation of one of the earliest collections of the *hadīth* with a scholarly introduction on the history of *hadīth*-collection and compilation.

SIDDIQUI, A. H., *Prayers of the Prophet*, Lahore: Shaikh Muhammad Ashraf, 1968.

A collection of some of the prayers of the Prophet with their English translation. Truly captures the spirit of the Islamic prayer.

SIDDIQUI, A. H., *The Life of Muḥammad*, Lahore: Islamic Publications Ltd., 1969.

One of the best available biographies of the Prophet. The author also examines most of the points raised by the orientalist and Christian missionary critiques of the life of the Prophet.

ISMAIL, Vehbi, *Muḥammad, the Last Prophet*, Cedar Rapids, Iowa, 1962.

Vehbi Ismail, an Albanian American, has written this short biography of the Prophet for American-born Muslim children. Useful but somewhat apologetic.

WAHEEDUDDIN, Faqir, *The Benefactor*, Karachi: Lions Press, 1967, Washington: Crescent Publications, 1973.

. This short, beautifully produced study on the life of the Prophet and the four Rightly-Guided Caliphs presents the essential spirit and message of the *sīrah*. Very useful for students, beginners and non-Muslims.

SIDDIQUI, Naeem, *Muḥammad: The Benefactor of Humanity*, translated and abridged by R. A. Hashmi, Delhi: Board of Islamic Publications, 1972.

This life of the Prophet is unique in the sense that it presents the Prophet in his role as a *Dā'iyyah* (caller towards Islam) and also shows how, under his leadership, the Islamic movement evolved during his life-time. The English translation is unfortunately poor and defective.

ASAD, Muhammad, *The Message of the Qur'ān*, Gibraltar: Dar al-Andalus, 1980.

Muhammad Asad's monumental exegesis of the Qur'ān in clear and purposeful language. The work is based on classical commentaries and addresses modern concerns.

QUṬB, Syed, *In the Shade of the Qur'ān* (Vol. 30), London: MWH Publishers, 1979. Vol. 1 (*Sūrahs* 1–2), Leicester: The Islamic Foundation, 1999.

Translation by M. A. Salahi and A. A. Shamis, the first book covers translation of the last 30th *Juz'* (chapter) of Syed Quṭb's *magnum opus, Fī Ẓilāl al-Qur'ān*. The Vol.1 covers *sūrahs al-Fātiḥah* and *al-Baqarah*. A modern exegesis in classical tradition.

MURAD, Khurram, *Way to the Qur'ān*, Leicester: The Islamic Foundation, 1985.

This short book aims to provide the reader with the necessary guidelines to understand the Qur'ān. It contains chapters on what the Qur'ān means to us, what rules of reading should be observed and why we should strive to understand it more fully.

DENFFER, Ahmad von, *'Ulūm al-Qur'ān: An Introduction to the Sciences of the Qur'ān*, Leicester: The Islamic Foundation, revised edition 1994.

Branches of knowledge related to understanding the Qur'ān are called *'Ulūm Al-Qur'ān*. This book deals with traditional subjects, for example, history and transmission of the text as well as recent issues such as orientalists' views and recordings of the Qur'ān. It deals with the technical aspects of the topic of Qur'ānic study and is the first book of its kind in English.

LINGS, Martin, *Muhammad: His Life Based on the Earliest Sources*, Cambridge: Islamic Texts Society, 1983.

An authentic biography of the Prophet (peace be upon him). While remaining close to the Arabic sources the book renders the Arabic original sources into comprehensible and idiomatic English. Reflects both the simplicity and grandeur of the story.

BASHIER, Zakaria, *The Makkan Crucible*, Leicester: The Islamic Foundation, 1991.

BASHIER, Zakaria, *Hijra: Story and Significance*, Leicester: The Islamic Foundation, 1983.

BASHIER, Zakaria, *Sunshine at Madinah: Studies in the Life of the Prophet Muhammad*, Leicester: The Islamic Foundation, 1990.

Trilogy dedicated to a penetrating study of the life and mission of the Prophet Muhammad (Allah's blessings and peace be upon him). Based on original sources and modern writings on the *Sīrah*, the series covers major aspects of the life of the Prophet at Makkah and Madinah with focus on the revolution in the lives of the people living in the Muslim state. An effort to study the *Sīrah* that is authentic, original and thoroughly contemporary.

HAYKAL, Muhammad Husayn, *The Life of Muhammad*, translated by Ismail Raji al-Faruqi: American Trust Publications, U.S.A., 1976.

This book aims to reveal the character of the Prophet in the light of historic reality, and also to bring out the essence of Islam as exemplified in the life of the greatest Muslim.

THE ISLAMIC SYSTEM

MAWDŪDĪ, Abū'l A'lā, *The Islamic Way of Life*. Translated and edited by Khurshid Ahmad and Khurram Murad, The Islamic Foundation, 1986.

A brief, to-the-point introduction to the Islamic social order. After introducing the Islamic concept of life, the author presents brief discourses on the moral, spiritual, social, economic and political systems of Islam.

MAWDŪDĪ, Abū'l A'lā, *Islamic Law and Constitution*, translated and edited by Khurshid Ahmad, Lahore: Islamic Publications, 1960.

A collection of Mawdūdī's writings dealing with the nature and scope of Islamic law and the principles of state and government in Islam. A path-breaking study which has influenced the course of constitution-making and law-reform in Pakistan and a number of other Muslim countries.

MAWDŪDĪ, Abū'l A'lā, *Purdah and the Status of Woman in Islam*, translated by al-Asha'arī, Lahore: Islamic Publications Ltd., 1972.

A Muslim critique of the contemporary Western concept of woman's emancipation and an exposition of the Islamic social order with emphasis on relations between the sexes, at personal and institutional levels.

MAWDŪDĪ, Abū'l A'lā, *Birth Control*. Translated and edited by Khurshid Ahmad and Misbahul Islam Faruqi, Lahore: Islamic Publications, 1968.

A thorough examination of the moral, social, political and economic aspects of birth control as a national policy and their impact on society and history.

ASAD, Muhammad, *The Principles of State and Government in Islam*, Berkeley: University of California Press, 1962.

A brief introduction to the nature of the Islamic state and its principles of state policy. The essentials of an Islamic constitution can be derived from this study.

PĀSHA, Prince Said Halīm, *The Reform of Muslim Society*, translated by M. M. Pickthall, Lahore, 1947.

A thought-provoking essay on the necessity of Islamic state and the need for the re-establishment of the *Sharī'ah*.

HAMIDULLAH, M., *The Muslim Conduct of State*, Lahore: Shaikh Muhammad Ashraf, 1953.

A scholarly study of the origins and development of Islamic international law.

SIDDIQUI, M. Mazharuddin, *Women in Islam*, Lahore: Institute of Islamic Culture, 1952.

An inquiry into the role of woman in Muslim society and in what respects this is different from the western model. The author's approach is generally balanced but unfortunately becomes somewhat apologetic on issues like polygamy and birth control.

AHMAD, Khurshid (ed.), *Studies in the Family Law of Islam*, Karachi: Chirāgh e-rāh Publications, 1961.

A collection of studies presenting an exposition of the Family Law of Islam and a critique of the modernist attempts to deform it.

RAMADĀN, Said, *Islamic Law: Its Scope and Equity*, London: Macmillan, 1970.

An introduction to the nature of Islamic Law, its basic values and principles, its relevance in contemporary times and an examination of the rights of non-Muslims in an Islamic State.

CHAPRA, M. 'Umar, *Economic System of Islam*, London: Islamic Cultural Centre, 1970; Karachi: University of Karachi, 1971.

A clear and lucid statement of the socio-economic objectives of Islam and how they would affect the working of a modern economy. The integration of the material and moral aspects and the role of the state in an Islamic economy are thoroughly discussed.

CHAPRA, M. 'Umar, *Towards a Just Monetary System*, Leicester: The Islamic Foundation, 1985.

The first comprehensive study of the goals, nature and operation of the monetary system of Islam, which has elimination of *ribā* and allocation of resources to ensure justice as its most indispensable objectives. This book won the Islamic Development Bank Award and the King Faisal Award (1990) for rationally expounding the theory of Islamic Banking.

CHAPRA, M. 'Umar, *Islam and the Economic Challenge*, Leicester: The Islamic Foundation, 1992.

A clear, integrated picture of the programme that Islam has to offer to realise the kind of well-being that it envisages, and to counter the different problems now facing mankind, particularly in the economic field. A scholarly critique of socialism, capitalism and the welfare state and an authentic exposition of the Islamic Economic system and its strategy for change.

AHMAD, Khurshid (ed.), *Studies in Islamic Economics*, Leicester: The Islamic Foundation, 1981.

Presents a comprehensive and overall picture of the growth of Islamic economics, money, interest and *Qirād*, interest-free banking, fiscal policy and *Zakāt*. The book also contains a critical survey of the contemporary Islamic literature available in English, Arabic, Turkish and Urdu.

QUṬB, Syed, *Social Justice in Islam*, Washington: American Council of Learned Societies, 1953.

This is an English translation of an earlier edition of the author's *'Adl al-Ijtimā'iyyah fī al-Islām*. A competent and thought-provoking study of the Islamic approach to social problems and of the principles of social justice in Islam. The author, however, revised and enlarged the book in later editions and a new translation of the last edition is still needed.

M.S.A., *Contemporary Aspects of Economic and Social Thinking in Islam*. The Muslim Students Association of the United States and Canada, 1973.

Proceedings of a Conference organized by the M.S.A. in 1968. The book contains eight papers on different aspects of the economics of Islam.

ANṢĀRĪ, M. Fazlur Rahman, *The Quranic Foundations and Structure of Muslim Society*, Karachi: Islamic Centre, 1973 (2 volumes).

An exposition of the Qur'ānic philosophy and code of behaviour for the individual and the institutions of society.

IZETBEGOVIC, 'Alija 'Ali, *Islam Between East and West*, Indianapolis, U.S.A.: American Trust Publications, 1989.

Covering crucial and sensitive issues like creation and evolution, culture and civilization, art, morality and the prophets, this book is an inspiring and astonishingly integrated analysis of the human condition. A thoroughly modern exposition of Islam in the context of the predicament of man at the end of the twentieth century.

EATON, Gai, *Islam and the Destiny of Man*, Cambridge: Islamic Texts Society, 1985.

In this eloquent and profound study, the author examines Islam's relation to its own history, to Christianity and to the modern world.

MAWDŪDĪ, Abū'l A'lā, *Witnesses Unto Mankind: The Purpose and Duty of the Muslim Ummah*, Leicester: The Islamic Foundation, 1986.

An English version of Sayyid Mawdudi's historic address in 1946, this landmark speech calls upon the Muslim Ummah to take up witnessing, by words and deeds, before all mankind the guidance that Allah has given them. Translated and edited by Khurram Murad.

AHMAD, Khurshid, *Family Life in Islam*, Leicester: The Islamic Foundation, 1981.
This booklet explains the concept of marriage and the family in Islam.

AHMAD, Anis, *Women and Social Justice*, Islamabad: Institute of Policy Studies, 1991.

A penetrating study of the position of women in Islam in the context of the modernist critique of family and *ḥudūd* laws.

'ABD AL-'ATI, Hammudah, *The Family Structure in Islam*, Indianapolis, U.S.A.: American Trust Publications, 1977.

This book looks at major issues that are of importance while trying to understand the concept of family in Islam. It covers the foundations of the family and marriage in Islam and looks at domestic relations, marital roles, intergenerational roles. It covers the technicalities of dissolution of the family, succession and inheritance and other sensitive issues in the structure of social life.

ISLAM AND THE MODERN WORLD

ASAD, Muhammad, *The Road to Mecca*, London: Max Rheinhardt, 1954. Second edition: Tangier, Dar al-Andalus, 1974.

An absorbing story of the author's intellectual and emotional pilgrimage to Islam. The autobiographical odessy contains a thought-provoking critique of Judaism, Christianity and contemporary Western civilization and brings into focus the message of Islam in the twentieth century.

The Autobiography of Malcolm-X (Al-Haj Malik Shahbaz), with the assistance of Alex. Haley, New York: Grove Press Inc., 1965.

The story of a black man, in affluent racist America: his deprivations, his frustrations, his violent reactions, and his final discovery of Islam as the religion of human brotherhood. The last sections dealing with his experiences of the *Hajj* are not only beautiful in their own right but also present the prospects that Islam holds for afflicted humanity, black and otherwise.

BROHI, A. K., *Islam in the Modern World*, Karachi: Chirāgh e-rāh Publications, 1968.

A collection of papers and speeches of a former law minister of Pakistan dealing with Islam in the context of a number of issues and ideologies of the contemporary world: materialism, humanism, socialism and communism. Edited by Khurshid Ahmad.

NADWĪ, Abū'l Hassan 'Alī, *Western Civilization: Islam and Muslims*, Lucknow: Academy of Islamic Research and Publication, 1969.

A study of the contemporary conflict between Islam and the Western civilization and its consequences.

KHAN, Muhammad Abdur Rahman, *A Brief Survey of Muslim Contribution to Science and Culture*, Lahore: Shaikh Muhammad Ashraf.

A bird's-eye view of the illustrious career of Islam as a culture-producing factor. The Muslim contribution to different fields of learning and their impact on world civilization is essayed.

JAMEELAH, Maryam, *Islam and Modernism*, Lahore, 1968.

A collection of twenty-four essays dealing with the impact of western thought and culture on the world of Islam. A powerful critique of Muslim modernism from an American convert to Islam.

MAWDŪDĪ, Abū'l A'lā, *A Short History of the Revivalist Movement in Islam*. Translated by al-Asha'arī, Lahore: Islamic Publications, 1963.

An Islamic critique of Muslim history and an introduction to its major revivalist movements.

RAFIUDDIN, Muhammad, *Ideology of the Future*, Lahore: Shaikh Muhammad Ashraf, 1970.

A well documented refutation of the major western philosophies of life. The author presents Islam as the ideology of the future. Discussion on the theory of evolution is, however, somewhat confused.

SHARIF, M. M. (ed.), *A History of Muslim Philosophy*, Wiesbaden: Otto Harassowitz, Vol. I, 1963; Vol. II, 1966.

A major work of Muslim and western scholarship containing survey articles on the basic teachings of Islam, the life and works of leading thinkers of Islam, the Muslim contribution to different fields of learning and some aspects of the modern renaissance in Muslim lands. Although the work lacks uniformity of approach and standard it remains the best available survey of Muslim thought from a Muslim perspective.

NADWĪ, Syed Abul Hasan 'Alī, *Muslims in the West: The Message and Mission*, Leicester: The Islamic Foundation, 1983.

A collection of Nadwī's speeches in Europe and America in the 1960s and 1970s; it addresses the relationship between Islam and the West, the civilizational crises in the West and the role of Muslims living in the West. Translated and edited by Khurram Murad.

Index

272INDEX